Books by Janice Hardy

Foundations of Fiction Series
*Planning Your Novel: Ideas and Structure*

Novels
The Healing Wars Trilogy
*The Shifter*
*Blue Fire*
*Darkfall*

# Planning Your Novel:

## Ideas and Structure

### A step-by-step guide to turning your idea into a novel

## By Janice Hardy

### Fiction University's Foundations of Fiction

# Contents

## 123 Workshop Five: Developing Your Plot

## 152 Workshop Six: Determining the Type of Novel You're Writing

## 168 Workshop Seven: Determining the Size and Scope of Your Novel

## 192 Workshop Eight: Turning Your Idea Into a Summary Line

## 201 Workshop Nine: Turning Your Summary Line Into a Summary Blurb

## 232 Workshop Ten: Turning Your Summary Blurb Into a Working Synopsis

# Welcome to Planning Your Novel: Ideas and Structure

When I was first learning to write, I read every book I could on writing. Some were very helpful, others less so, but after a while I grew frustrated over a common advice element I kept running into.

I found plenty of advice on what I *ought* to be doing, but very little on how to actually *do* it.

I was inundated with writing rules that weren't helpful. Explanations of techniques that made me feel I *almost* had it, but still didn't quite get it. Some of the advice was so complicated I'd felt I never understand it enough to improve my writing.

I kept struggling and eventually figured out what everyone had been talking about. I also learned that sometimes, it's easier to tell new writers, "don't do X" than it is to explain why not, and when that rule doesn't apply—and that some new writers don't *want* to know the why, they just want to know the rules so they can get published. Most important, I learned that writing isn't so black and white and it's not about "the rules" at all.

Years later, I started teaching writing classes and swore I'd not make my students struggle as I had done. I sought to explain the hows as well as the whys, so someone could really get what those writing rules were talking about. To help my fellow writers understand the process behind those rules and guidelines.

For example, I wasn't going to tell my students "don't use adverbs;" I was going to explain why relying on them would hurt their writing and show them the difference between bad versus good adverb usage. I wanted them to understand why that rule existed in the first place—and why it's not exactly a set-in-stone rule.

Jump ahead a few more years and I started a blog, The Other Side of the Story, to share the things I'd learned in ways that made them easier to understand. The hows *and* the whys.

A few more years later, I had a wealth of information compiled. Reorganizing it into writing guides was a natural progression, but I wanted the guides to follow the same philosophy I'd always had—writing whys made simple. I wanted my guides to be instructive and helpful, with clear examples and tips writers could apply directly to their works-in-progress and see positive results.

I wholeheartedly believe a solid writing foundation allows writers to grow and improve with the confidence that they *get* it, and aren't just following a rule because a book or blog said so. Confident writers understand how the myriad of techniques and rules work together to craft a story, and how to use those tools to craft the best novel they can. That foundation, that confidence, makes the journey from idea to novel a little less scary and a lot more productive.

A lot of work goes into writing a novel, and it all starts with planning that novel. To build a strong novel, start with a strong foundation.

And that's where this book comes in.

## So, Exactly What *is* a Novel Plan?

Different writers write novels in different ways, but each novel starts with a plan. Sometimes that plan is nothing more than a vague idea or a character who won't stop whispering in your ear at night; other times it's a comprehensive summary of every scene in the book. However you do it, you decided to write a novel and then begin that process.

The goal of a novel plan is to develop enough information about that novel to be able to write it. How much information depends on the writer, because we all have a different process. That's one reason writing advice can be so frustrating. What works for one writer might not work for you and vice versa.

## What You'll Encounter in This Book

*Planning Your Novel: Ideas and Structure* is a series of self-guided workshops designed to lead you through developing a novel idea, crafting a summary line, creating a summary blurb, and finally, writing a working synopsis. Each workshop covers one step of that process, with smaller sections that focus on individual topics within that step. At the end of this book, you'll have a solid plan to craft a novel from.

For those with completed manuscripts, this book can aid you during revisions and even help you fix problem areas. The workshops and exercises are just as useful in tightening a first draft as they are in writing one.

**Workshops:** The workshops go step by step through planning and developing a novel. Each workshop offers focused topics with exercises and brainstorming sessions, tips and tricks, plus definitions of the common writing terms used in the workshop.

**Exercises:** These draw from the workshop and guide you through individual pieces of the novel-planning process. They build upon each other to take an idea and develop it into a plan (and plot) for a first draft.

**Assignments:** The assignments incorporate everything learned in the individual workshops and offer a larger step in the process. As the exercises build off the individual sections of a workshop, the assignments build off the workshops as a whole.

**"Something to Think About" Prompts:** These prompts provide additional questions or advice to consider how an idea could be developed, and opportunities to take notes while ideas are still fresh. They also offer warnings for common pitfalls about a topic.

**Brainstorming Questions:** The brainstorming questions are designed to get you thinking about aspects of that section, and help you figure out what you want from your novel as it pertains to that section.

## How to Get the Most From the Exercises, Brainstorming Questions, and "Something to Think About" Prompts

Throughout the book, you'll find exercises and writing prompts to help you develop your idea into a novel plan. I highly encourage you to do the exercises, take notes, and write down thoughts as prompted throughout the sections (as well as any ideas you might have as you read). Even when you know the answer to a posed question, the act of putting it on paper crystallizes the thought and clarifies your idea.

It's not uncommon to feel we *know* something, but then when we write it down, it's not as developed or clear as we first thought. This is one reason novels stall after a few chapters or we get stuck even though we "know" what should happen. Writing it down *really* does make the process easier.

As you do the exercises, feel free to brainstorm and pull in ideas that interest you. Sometimes you won't know what a detail will be until you answer one of the later questions. For example, you might know from one workshop that your protagonist has a dark secret, but not what that secret is until you reach an exercise that forces you to identify it. Or you might think of something in one workshop you hadn't considered before, but which really works for an exercise in an earlier workshop. Writing can be very organic, so don't be afraid to jump around if you need to. You can always go back and revise any exercise or assignment after you've done them all. Let your subconscious run free and see where it takes you.

You'll likely notice that certain information or ideas will start showing up throughout the various exercises. This repetition is good, as it means you're pinpointing what matters to the novel and adding deeper layers to those points, connecting them to other valuable elements of the story. These common elements or details are usually the core aspects of the novel—the heart and soul of the tale you want to tell. When you see these recurring ideas, try embracing them and developing them as much as possible. They're probably your subconscious telling you what's important.

## The Examples

Throughout the book you'll find examples that illustrate the various topics covered in the workshops. Unless otherwise noted, the examples are all my own creation. In the exercise examples, you'll also find three novels that are being "developed" along with you. "Bob and the Zombies" is a story I've used as an example on my blog for years, but the other two are novels I created for this book using my own advice, same as anyone else following along. They're not polished outlines for written novels, but ideas and notes right from my brain to the page, designed to show how your notes and plans might look, and the types of details you might aim for while planning your novel. No one expects your notes to be perfect or well written, or even in complete sentences. These notes are for *you*.

## What We'll Discuss in This Book

**How to:**

❏ Develop and understand your writing process

❏ Find ideas to write about

❏ Tell the difference between an idea, premise, plot, and story

❏ Develop your ideas into a workable novel concept

❏ Determine the type of novel you want to write

❏ Discover your hook

❏ Choose your characters

❏ Use theme to deepen your story

❏ Choose your setting

❏ Determine your goals and conflicts

❏ Find and develop your stakes

❏ Choose a market (or figure out what market your novel falls into)

❏ Choose a genre (or figure out what genre your novel falls into)

❏ Choose the size and scope of your novel

❏ Write a summary line that captures the essence of your novel

❏ Write a summary blurb that describe the core elements of your novel

❏ Write a working synopsis that covers the basic turning points of plot

## What You'll Get From This Book

By the end of this book, you will have: a plan to write a novel, complete with a one-sentence summary line that captures the essence of your novel; a summary blurb that hits the core elements of a novel; and a working synopsis that covers the major turning points of your plot. You'll also have a solid foundation for your character development (including your protagonist and antagonist), setting and world building, theme, and the size and scope of your novel.

Every novel starts somewhere. Let's figure out the best plan for yours.

# Workshop One: Finding Your Writer's Process

**What You Need to Start This Workshop:** An interest in exploring different writing processes and discovering what process best suits your own writing style.

**The Goal of This Workshop:** To help you determine the kind of writer you are and what (if any) changes you might want to make to your writing process.

**What We'll Discuss in This Workshop**: Different writing processes and how to examine your own process.

**Writing Terms Used in This Workshop:**

**Freestylers:** Writers who write out of chronological order and arranges the book afterward.

**Outliners:** Writers who write with a predetermined outline or guide. They know how the book will end and how the plot will unfold before they start writing it.

**Pantsers:** Writers who write "by the seat of their pants," without outlines. They often don't know how the book will end or what will happen before they start writing it.

# Welcome to Workshop One: Finding Your Writer's Process

No writer is born knowing how to write. We all have varying skills and talents, and sometimes we suffer through a lot of trial and error before we figure out what works for us. Our process can even change as we develop our writing skills and learn new techniques. This is all normal.

If you're just starting out, don't worry if you have no consistent process yet. It takes time to understand what works for you and how to put new skills and techniques into practice. It's not uncommon to feel you're doing something wrong if how you write differs from the "norm." Trust me when I say there is nothing wrong with your writing process, and there are plenty of other writers out there who write the way you do and probably feel (or felt) the same way.

On my writing site (Fiction University, formerly The Other Side of the Story), I host weekly guest authors for this very reason. They talk about their writing processes and how they create their novels, and show that everyone has his or her own way of writing. I can't tell you how often I've read in the comments: "Thank you so much, I thought I was the only one who did it that way."

No matter how you write, you are not alone.

This is important to remember, because a frequent cause of writer frustration is trying to force yourself to write in a way that's unnatural to you. That does make it tough to write a "how to write" book, since some of what I suggest might not be applicable to all writers. And you know what? That's okay. Discovering what *doesn't* work can help you figure out what *does*. We learn by trying new things and in this book I'll suggest lots of techniques to try. Take what works for you and make it your own.

I've put the workshops in an order I feel is the easiest to follow if you're new to writing, but if you develop stories in a different order, feel free to go through the exercises in the order you prefer. These exercises are designed to *help* you, not force you to abandon your natural writing process and conform to another.

If you want to know more about developing your writing process, then continue on with Workshop One. If you already know and are comfortable with your writing process, feel free to skip ahead to Workshop Two: Finding Ideas to Write About. If you have a novel idea already, then skip ahead to Workshop Three: Developing Your Idea.

## What Kind of Writer Are You?

There is no right way to write.

This is important to know because I've seen too many writers (and been one myself) who felt they *had* to write in a certain way to be successful, and that style was contrary to their own natural process.

- An outliner tries to wing it with no writing plan and feels lost, writing a book that's a huge, unfocused mess.
- A pantser tries to force her creativity into an outline and feels stymied, making her story go where it doesn't want to go just because a list of events told her to rake it there.
- A freestyler forces himself to write chronologically and feels his creativity drain out of him when the scenes he's most excited about fade away in his head .

If a process makes you miserable and hurts your creativity, there's a good chance it's not the right process for you. Don't be afraid to dump it and try something else.

However, don't reject a process idea if you've never tried it just because you don't think it suits you. I've had techniques I thought would never work be exactly what I needed to take my writing to the next level.

For example, when I first started writing I didn't outline at all, because I wanted to discover the story as I wrote it. I'd summarize my idea in a page or two, then I'd dive in and start writing. It didn't take long before the plot was going every which way and I'd lost sight of what story I was even trying to tell.

I was clearly not a pantser—someone who writes "by the seat of their pants" and discovers the story as they write it.

Then I read a ton of books on scenes and structures and I started outlining like a madwoman. Every detail, every scene, every sequel—I had a form I filled out that left nothing to chance. My scenes were so tightly controlled the life was squeezed right out of them.

I was also not a outliner—someone who plans every scene and knows exactly what will happen in the book before they write it.

So what kind of writer *was* I? It seemed like those were the only options available and I didn't fit into either one. I felt lost, frustrated, and on really bad days—like I wasn't *really* a writer.

After years of trial and error, I realized there was *lots* of room between those two points and I was somewhere in the middle. I like having a solid outline of the major events of my novel to keep me and the plot focused, but I don't plan how those events unfold. This way, I allow for spontaneity and let the characters drive the plot. I outline the framework, but let the story grow organically.

This is a perfectly acceptable process and I've met plenty of other writers who use this method as well. It felt good to learn I wasn't alone and others had felt the same frustrations I had. In fact, it's okay to pick bits and pieces of multiple processes and use them however you want. I *encourage* you to do it to find what works best for you.

If you're just starting your first novel, you might not yet know what your process is, and that's also okay. Most writers try multiple techniques before they find the ones that work best for them. Experiment with different styles (or adopt pieces from many) until you find the one that feels the most natural to you.

Let's look at a few processes and see if any fit your style:

## The Pantser

These writers write by the "seat of their pants" and enjoy sitting down at a blank screen with a general idea and letting the words take them. They don't want to know what happens before it *does* happen, and seeing how the novel ends is half the fun of writing it.

If you have no trouble finding the words when you sit down to write, but stare at the screen with a terrified look on your face when you try to plot or outline, this could be the process for you.

**Making this book work for you:** By their nature, pantsers *don't* plan, but that doesn't mean a novel plan can't help you. If you prefer to wing it first and figure it out later, then a plan can be useful after the first draft is done. Use a novel plan as the first step in your *revision* process.

## The Outliner

Writing without a plan leaves these writers with a mess of scenes and no coherent storyline. They find comfort in knowing how a novel will unfold before they type a single word. They like to list how each scene starts, how it ends, and what happens in between.

If you need to know exactly where your novel is going and how it's going to get there before you write it, this could be your process.

**Making this book work for you:** Outliners love plans, and the exercises in this book will aid you in figuring out how all the pieces of your novel fit together. The brainstorming questions will allow you to figure out plot points and character arcs before you start writing.

## The Loose Outliner

These writers like structure, but they don't want to know *every* detail before they write. They prefer to build the foundation of the novel, creating a framework in which to write that lets them control the plot without the plot controlling them.

If you like knowing enough about your novel to guide your writing without losing the mystery of the story, this might be a good process for you to try.

**Making this book work for you:** A novel plan can be especially helpful for the loose outliner, by figuring out the major points of the plot while still allowing for spontaneity. You'll get the macro ideas figured out, and the specifics can come as you write.

## The Character Writer

Characters come to these writers first, and by the time they're ready to write they know them inside and out. These writers don't always know what those characters are going to *do*, however, and they enjoy letting the characters chase after their dreams and see where they take them.

If you're the type who knows what the characters want and need, but aren't sure of the plot events to get them there, you might enjoy this process.

**Making this book work for you:** If characters drive your writing, then also let them drive your novel plan. Approach the exercises in this book from a character perspective so they reflect the characters and what they might do. Or, if you're looking for help with the plot side of things, these exercises can guide you through the plotting aspects that don't come naturally to you.

## The Plot Driver

These writers see the plot unfold long before they see the faces of the characters. They love the mechanics of plotting and figuring out how the pieces all fit together, and once that's solid, *then* they figure out who the story is about.

If structure and plot is what excites you, this could be the process for you.

**Making this book work for you:** Plotters should enjoy the structured nature of a novel plan, and how each section builds upon the last. Let the exercises enhance your natural plotting skills and provide structure to your ideas. Or, if you're looking for help in the areas you're not as strong in, use the non-plotting exercises to help you develop the more character-driven aspects of your novel.

## The Scene Sewer

Novels come to these writers in bits and pieces in random order. They prefer jumping around when the mood strikes and sewing up the plot later. They'd rather see it in their mind, get it on paper, and worry about how the puzzle pieces fit later.

If you like to let inspiration strike and then write—no matter where that scene might be in the book—you could be this type of writer.

**Making this book work for you:** The exercises can help you figure out which scenes sound like the most fun to write. A novel plan can also help you see where you might have some plot holes that need filling, or the best way to sew up the scenes you have. A plan can also be a great revision tool, helping you structure your novel after the first draft is done.

If you know your process already, adapt the exercises and writing prompts to fit that process and make the best use of them. If you don't know your process yet, don't fret, because that's what this book is designed to do—help you figure out the best way for you to plan and write your novel. Going through the exercises and trying various things will give you a better understanding of what works for you and what doesn't.

And if you fit more than one process? Take the parts that work for you and create your own style.

---

 **BRAINSTORMING QUESTIONS:**
Discover your writing process.

1. Which type of writer above do you most identify with? How does that fit with your own writing style?

2. What style would you *want* to try? What about it appeals to you? Why?

3. What style *don't* you like? Why not?

4. Is your process working for you, or do you feel like it's holding you back?

5. If it's holding you back, why? What about the process do you find frustrating?

6. Can those frustrations be eliminated by trying or incorporating any of the above styles?

# ASSIGNMENT ONE: What Kind of Writer Are You?

>>**Write down the type of writer you are and describe your writing process.**

This might seem like a strange exercise, but I've found that I've learned more about writing from examining my own process and thinking honestly about *why* I do what I do, than from actually doing it.

Writing down your process lets you clarify exactly what it is you do when you write, and sometimes seeing it written down makes you realize that you're not what you thought you were. Maybe you actually *like* to outline a little, or prefer to develop a story organically based on a list of ideas, but rejected your natural process because you never saw yourself as "that kind of writer."

Writing down your process can also reveal areas that aren't working for you, and provide direction on things to try that might improve your process and make writing easier overall.

*For example:*

▶ I like to know all about my characters before I start writing, plotting out how they're going to develop and what lessons they'll lean by the end of the book.

▶ I like a blank sheet of paper and a vague idea. Figuring out how the random details in my head all fit together makes me excited to write the book.

▶ I like planning out my scenes in detail, but don't care how they fit together until I'm almost done with the novel. I need to work out who the characters are as I write them and how the plot might work before I can see how the bigger picture looks.

In Workshop Two, we'll look at ways to come up with ideas.

# Workshop Two:
# Finding Ideas to Write About

**What You Need to Start This Workshop:** An interest in different ways to find novel ideas, and how to keep track of those ideas once you do find them.

**The Goal of This Workshop:** To help you find ways to come up with ideas.

**What We'll Discuss in This Workshop:** Different ways and places to find inspiration.

**Writing Terms Used in This Workshop:**

**Antagonist:** The person or thing in the protagonist's path of success.

**Genre:** A category or novel type, such as mystery, fantasy, or romance.

**Protagonist:** The character driving the plot. Typically the main character of the novel.

**Setting:** Where the novel takes place.

**Theme:** A recurring idea or concept explored in the novel.

# Welcome to Workshop Two: Finding Ideas to Write About

It's got to be the single most popular question a writer hears: *Where do you get your ideas?* I answer it at every event I do, often more than once for school visits. I never mind, because it's something people are interested in, and it's a great icebreaker to get other questions rolling. I know I'll get *that* question even if I get no others.

I get ideas all the time, and I'm willing to bet *you* get ideas all the time, too. Writers are creative people and ideas are our business. "That would make a great book" probably pops into your head fairly often, and probably pops out just as frequently. Ideas come from everywhere (especially the shower for some reason), but how often do we take time to actually write them down?

I didn't for the longest time and I lost more ideas than I'd like to admit. I finally started keeping them in a file called "novel ideas and hooks" and I add notes to it as they come to me.

Of course, not all of these ideas will turn into novels, and even those that do won't all be novels worth reading, but I check that file all the time, add to it, and when I'm ready to start a new novel I go there first.

And when those great novel ideas *do* hit, write down *where* you came up with the idea as well as the idea itself. Because you'll need that one day if you publish that novel. Trust me, people are going to ask.

Getting ideas probably isn't the problem—remembering them is.

**WRITING TIP: Create an Idea File.** Try starting your own idea file. It can be on the computer, your phone, a tablet, a spiral notebook, whatever you feel the most comfortable with. Keep pen and paper on hand where you most often have ideas so you can jot them down when they come to you. A small, spiral notepad and pen can fit almost anywhere, and are very handy by the bed, in a bathroom drawer, or in the car.

When you get an idea, write it down. Don't worry if the idea isn't fully formed, because it's just a spark of inspiration at this point. If you think up great titles, save them as well, as great novels can grow from great titles. Same with characters or even good lines of dialog—you never know when an idea that can use them will come to you. And if you have the ideas safely tucked away and remember them, odds are your subconscious will keep churning and will put those pieces together in an interesting way one day.

If you know you want to write, but aren't sure what to write about, then continue on with Workshop Two. If you have a novel idea already, feel free to skip ahead to Workshop Three: Developing Your Idea.

## Writing When You Don't Know What to Write About

If you want to write, but don't know what to write about, the first step is to figure out what types of stories appeal to you. The things you enjoy reading (or watching, as TV and movies also apply here) are usually the things you'd also enjoy writing.

Try looking at your bookshelf (or e-reader library). If your shelf is loaded with mysteries, you might make a good mystery writer. Full of fantasy? Maybe it's time to create your own epic world. If there's no common genre, then look for common themes. If you see mostly novels about people overcoming past traumas, then you just might enjoy writing about personal struggles to overcome a dark past.

By studying what you love to read and watch, you can gain insights into the kinds of stories you're drawn to. Pay particular attention to any story types that spark ideas or make you think you could write a novel like that—even if you feel you could write a *better* novel than that. These will most likely be the genres or story concepts you're most excited about or most familiar with.

You can also try looking for combinations of recurring plots or character types, similar themes, and common ideas. If a majority of the novels on your shelf have dark protagonists searching for redemption, that's a big clue about the type of protagonist you might enjoy writing about. If most of the novels are set in exotic lands or fantasy worlds, odds are you'll enjoy creating your own world or researching an exotic locale to use as your setting. If you have dozens of novels about kidnappings or serial killers, you just might be a crime writer.

*Write what you love* is a common writing adage for a reason. We tend to write the novels we love to read, and that's a great place to start looking for the type of novel you want to write.

 **BRAINSTORMING QUESTIONS:**
Discover what stories and novels appeal to you.

1. What kinds of novels are you drawn to? Make a list of your favorite books. Add what you love most about those books.

2. What kinds of movies or TV shows are you drawn to? Make a list of your favorite movies and TV shows. Add what you love most about them.

3. What similarities do you see? Is there a clear common genre or category?

4. What recurring story or themes do you see? Do these elements spark any ideas?

5. Is there a recurring type of character? Write down common traits in both the protagonist and the antagonist.

6. Are there recurring plots? What are they?

# ✓ EXERCISE:
# Narrow Down What Appeals to You

This is an exercise where making a list can aid you in determining what types of stories appeal to you. You might not know at first why a particular book resonates with you, but once you see several others listed beside, a pattern may emerge.

Don't think too hard on these. The first answers that pop into your head will likely be the most revealing answers.

## >>Write down:

- The three genres or novel types that most interest you
- The three types of plots you most enjoy
- The three types of characters you're most drawn to
- The three themes that appear most often in the stories you enjoy
- The three settings you'd most like to write about

# Where to Find Ideas

Although ideas may come to us at any time, creating a novel idea on demand is often difficult. No one can truly tell you where to begin—they can only offer suggestions on where to look for inspiration. I know what works for me, but if you're the type of writer who always starts with characters, giving you a plot point to brainstorm with will probably get you nowhere. If you build up from a premise, giving you ways to create cool characters might muddle your brain.

One thing is consistent though. No matter how you develop an idea, *something* triggers that first spark of inspiration.

Here are some common activities that can spark inspiration:

## Do Some Research

This might be reading newspapers, blogs, magazines, or web sites. Try looking at material that supports the type of novel simmering in your mind. If you think you might try writing science fiction, look at science magazines or science websites. Even gaming or comics sites could work.

Explore newspapers or news sites if you're considering a mystery or police procedural. Unsolved crimes could also spark ideas, or even famous crimes with well-known criminals. What might have happened if a few key details had changed?

Totally stuck on what to write? Try the weird news sites, or humor sites that collect funny or odd posts from all over. When something piques your interest, keep exploring it until either an idea forms in your mind, or you decide that's not the way you want to go.

## Do an Image Search

Look for photos of characters or places for inspiration. An unusual emotion in a portrait might make you wonder more about that person, or a beautiful or unique setting might feel like the perfect place to set a novel. Images can be powerful triggers since they can draw us in just as a novel draws in a reader.

Even cartoons or memes can spark ideas. Create a file of images that appeal to you or bookmark them online. Mix and match characters and settings, emotions and moods, until an idea forms.

## Play With Names

Naming a thing has power, and the perfect name can make a character blossom in your imagination. Search through baby name sites for names that inspire characters. Street signs can also be fun places to find names. Exit signs on highways often put two names together that could become a person or an interesting place.

## People Watch

Find a seat and watch the world go by. Malls, stores, and parks are common areas where people of all types gather, and some of them might catch your eye. What about them is intriguing? Make up stories about them, or imagine how you might turn them into characters. While you don't want to eavesdrop on private conversations, listening for dialog or snippets of conversation can also spark ideas.

## Play With Poetry

Poems can inspire ideas as well as emotions. Look for themes or imagery that you might want to explore, or even consider the type of character who might read or feel a connection to that poem. Think about what cultures or societies might be created if you used the poem or something within it as a foundation.

## Listen to Music

Music can be powerful for a lot of writers, creating moods, inspiring imagery, or even creating a character. Pick a random song and imagine the type of character who would use it as her theme song, or pretend it was the first song a couple ever danced to.

## Riff Off Favorite Books

You don't want to copy someone else's work (that's plagiarism), but a favorite book—or even a book you disliked—can be used as a jumping off point to your own original idea. There might be something about that book you find compelling and want to explore in a different way, or maybe you would write that same idea from a new angle. You might even take your three favorite books or movies and pick one element from each to create your own plot.

## Ask for Help

Ask other writers, talk with friends and family, or even ask questions on social media sites. You never know who might say something that triggers an idea. Find out what types of novels other people like to read and what stories grab them.

The struggle for ideas hits everyone at some point, at all stages of their career. If you're banging your head against the keyboard and feeling like a hopeless newbie, know that somewhere, some bestselling author is doing the same thing.

---

 **BRAINSTORMING QUESTIONS:**
Come up with some ideas.

1. Pick three news articles or blog posts that intrigue you. What about them do you find compelling?

2. What location have you always wanted to visit? What secrets might it be hiding?

3. Pick your top ten images. What about them do you find captivating? Why?

4. What are your favorite names? Why? What happens when you turn those names into names that would fit another genre, nationality, or ethnic group?

5. What are your least favorite novels, TV shows, or movies? How would you write them differently?

6. What random conversations or people caught your eye recently? What about them was memorable? Why?

# EXERCISE:
# Create Five Ideas for Possible Novels

>>**Using the list from the first exercise, and the brainstorming questions from "Where to Find Ideas," list five combinations you might want to explore further.**

Now is the time to mix and match and put together the story types you enjoy with the topics that interest you. Use as many or as few as you'd like. If you're really stuck, try picking one item from each of the first exercise bullets and seeing where that leads you. Add in anything from the brainstorming questions that might fit that type of novel. If that doesn't spark an idea, try flipping it and picking one thing from each of the brainstorming questions.

*For example:*

▶ If you'd like to write a thriller, try picking a news article that sounds intriguing, then set it in the location that most appeals to you—such as a medical thriller about stem cell research set in Taiwan.

▶ If you love heist capers, pick your favorite art piece and figure out how your character would steal it—such as an art thief tries to steal the *Mona Lisa* from the Louvre.

▶ If you love stories about redemption, try choosing a news story about a truly despicable person and come up with a way for her to redeem herself—such as a woman who killed her children tries to make amends by saving a family in trouble.

For those stuck, pick:

■ One genre or novel type that most interests you (fantasy)
■ One type of plot you most enjoy (heist)
■ One type of character you're most drawn to (the dark hero)
■ One theme that appears most often in the stories you enjoy (personal sacrifice)
■ One setting you'd most like to write about (the Arctic)

And put it all together:

▶ A fantasy heist plot, set in an arctic environment, with a dark hero who will have to make a personal sacrifice

# ASSIGNMENT TWO:
## Choose Your Idea

>>**Pick one of the ideas you came up with in Workshop Two to develop into a novel.**

These don't need to be full-fledged novel ideas, just things that pique your interest and make you want to explore them further. A spark of inspiration that makes you think, "Gee, this would make a really great book."

If you're torn, pick the ideas that most interest you and decide later which is the strongest.

*For example:*

▶ A novel about teens with secrets, where one is bent on revenge

▶ A love story set during a zombie apocalypse

▶ A retelling of *Romeo and Juliet* with a twist

In Workshop Three, we'll start developing your idea.

# Workshop Three: Developing Your Idea

**What You Need to Start This Workshop**: An idea for a novel.

**The Goal of This Workshop**: To develop the hook and general plot type of your novel.

**What We'll Discuss in This Workshop:** How to: tell the difference between an idea, plot, premise, and story; use them to develop your idea; determine if your novel is character- or plot-driven; find the hook that makes your novel unique.

**Writing Terms Used in This Workshop:**

**Antagonist:** The person or thing in the protagonist's path of success.

**Conflict:** Two sides in opposition, either externally or internally.

**Core Conflict:** The major problem or issue at the center of a novel.

**Goal:** What the point-of-view character wants.

**Hook:** An element that grabs readers and makes them want to read on.

**Premise:** The general description of the story.

**Protagonist:** The character driving the novel.

**Theme:** A recurring idea or concept explored in the novel.

**Trope:** An idea or literary device commonly employed in a particular novel type.

# Welcome to Workshop Three: Developing Your Idea

My husband and I play "what if?" a lot. One of us (usually him) will toss out a question, and we'll run with it, exploring as many scenarios as possible. It started out as a game to entertain us on long car trips, but it's evolved into an endless stream of novel ideas for me.

You'd think this would be a fabulous resource for a writer, but I end up with too *many* ideas. I can't possibly write them all, and not every idea—no matter how cool it sounds at the time—will make a good novel.

That's the sneaky thing about ideas. They're fun, they sound exciting, and they seduce us into thinking that all we need is that one, single idea to write a great novel.

It doesn't always work that way.

I've had many an idea that felt like "the one," dived right in and started writing, only to discover later that I didn't have a story, much less a plot, that would allow me to write an actual novel.

This is one reason some novels stall after fifty or a hundred pages. As great as ideas are, a novel needs a strong foundation to build upon. It needs structure to carry that great idea and give it form, and a foundation on which to grow. It needs a story worth telling.

In this workshop, we'll explore if your idea has the potential to become a novel, what about your idea is worth telling, and how to find the hook that makes your idea (and your novel) unique.

## Brainstorming Your Idea

Brainstorming is a great way to dig deeper into an idea to see if it really does have the legs to carry an entire novel. Any idea that falls flat after a few minutes of brainstorming is one that would probably have you banging your head against the keyboard by chapter three.

The goal of this brainstorming exercise is to generate enough information about your idea so the later exercises will be more effective. We'll go into more detail with targeted exercises on all of these concepts in later workshops, so for now, let your creativity flow and generate as many potential directions for this idea as you can. Don't try to confine anything at this point--write it all down even if it doesn't seem to fit or work yet. Some details you'll use, some will fall away, and others will spark even *better* ideas. This is only a jumping off point.

Look at your idea and think about:

**The conflict:** Something in the idea has to be able to cause trouble, and hopefully to a lot of people. If it can't, there won't be anything for the protagonist to strive for. No matter how cool an idea sounds, if there's no conflict, there's no novel yet. No idea is too crazy at this point, because it's all about exploring the idea's potential, and you never know where one idea might lead.

The people you can put into this idea or this conflict: Who would be affected? Who would benefit? Who would be hurt? What kinds of people would be needed for this situation? What connections might those characters have to the other people in the story? Conflict often comes from those connections, and they can help you develop the plot later.

**The goals and stakes:** Without knowing what the characters want and what they're risking to get it, the novel will be pretty boring. Goals and stakes move the plot and make readers care about what happens.

**The themes:** See if any themes have started to develop. They often do, even this early, with recurring concepts between possible character types and the conflicts discovered.

If you have several ideas that interest you, ask the same questions of all of them to see which one has the strongest potential for a novel. If they all feel strong, start thinking about which one grabs *your* attention . Your excitement for the idea will translate to the novel itself, which will help make the novel better in the end.

**BRAINSTORMING QUESTIONS:**
Consider how the following question might apply to your idea.

1. Who wants what and why?

2. Who would be against these goals and why?

3. Is there one major conflict or problem that needs solving?

4. Who is the most likely person to be involved in this problem on a personal level?

5. Where can huge failures occur (because that might just turn out to be what your protagonist is after)?

6. What situations would lend themselves well to the growth of a character?

# EXERCISE:
# Write Down Your Idea

If you've already done this in Assignment Two, you can skip this exercise.

## >>Write down your idea.

Don't worry if it's vague or unformed at this stage, or if the idea is "bad writing." The goal is to get it on paper so you can study it and determine if it has what it needs to become a novel. It's for you to keep track of that original spark of inspiration so you can refer to it later. It's not uncommon to lose track of where you want the novel to go or what inspired you about your novel in the first place. Having it written down can remind you if you go off track later.

This is also to give you some direction so later exercises can be more focused and more productive.

*For example:*

- ▶ Three teens with dark secrets meet at a diner in the middle of the night and change each other's lives
- ▶ A story set during a zombie apocalypse, where a guy was about to ask for a divorce when the world just fell apart, and now he wants to find his true love and not get eaten
- ▶ A *Romeo and Juliet*-type romance between old friends, set in a small town

If your idea is longer than these examples, that's okay. Write down as much or as little as you want. The first step in planning a novel is knowing what you want to write about.

## The Difference Between Idea, Premise, Plot, and Story

An idea is something that sparks the imagination, but very few of them contain enough information to drive a character through four hundred or so pages. Novels have a lot of parts that work together to tell a compelling tale to readers. Miss any one of those parts and the novel stumbles. Miss more than one, and it stops working altogether.

Ideas are just the first part.

One of the many frustrating aspects of writing is how the same terms are often used interchangeably. Idea, premise, plot, and story can all describe what a novel is about, but each word also serves a different function and has a different meaning. This can sometimes cause problems in the planning or drafting stage.

Thinking you have a plot when you really have an idea can make it difficult to write a novel. It *feels* like there's enough to work with, but you get stuck a few chapters after the initial setup of the novel is done, because all the idea gave you was the basic setup. You have nothing beyond that to work with.

*For example:*

▶ Four siblings go into a wardrobe and discover a door to a magical world (The Chronicles of Narnia)

**Why this isn't a plot:** There's no conflict and nothing for the characters to do. If someone sat down to write this novel with only this one line, they'd likely get as far as entering the magical world, describing it, and then staring at the page with no idea what happens next. Nothing about this idea suggests where the plot goes.

Let's look at those subtle differences between idea, premise, plot, and story:

## The Idea

Ideas are those moments of inspiration that first excite or interest you. They can be broad or specific, but something about them sets the creative wheels in motion.

*For example:*
- ▶ A novel set in ancient China
- ▶ A novel about a girl named Lila who can heal by touch
- ▶ A novel about an estranged couple in a zombie apocalypse

**Why ideas are important:** Without ideas, there's nothing to write about. It's okay if an idea is vague or unformed when it first hits you, as few novel ideas appear with all the pieces figured out. The goal of studying an idea is to find something that piques your interest and then explore it until the larger story emerges.

**What's great about ideas:** Ideas are liberating. Anything can happen and there are no restrictions to an idea. You can riff off a favorite book or movie, invent something new, or mash together elements of genres you like. That freedom allows you to be as creative as you want to be.

## The Premise

The premise is a general description of the novel's set up. It's what the novel is about and the next step to developing an idea. While an idea can be anything, a premise typically narrows that idea down to something that can be contained in a novel. For example, "a novel set in ancient China" can be anything at all. It's an idea, but it's unformed. A premise would take that idea and focus on what aspect of ancient China the novel will be about.

The premise is the larger framework for the idea to exist in—the first traces of what kind of novel this idea could turn into. A key factor in a good premise is a hint of the conflict that will drive the plot. This is the problem the characters will explore over the course of the novel.

*For example:*
- ▶ A lower caste member in ancient China fights for freedom against his tyrannical masters.
- ▶ A girl who can heal by touch is forced to use her gift to help the people who murdered her family.
- ▶ A man considering divorce is thrown into a zombie apocalypse with his estranged wife and the woman he wants to leave her for.

**Why the premise is important:** A premise forces you to shape an idea into a workable novel. It helps narrow the focus down to a problem (a conflict) you can work with within the standard parameters of a novel. It also provides the first layer of structure to build on. The conflict guides you to the larger story problem the protagonist will have to overcome to resolve the plot. In essence, it says what the protagonist is going to do for four hundred or so pages.

**What's great about a premise:** The narrower focus can help you quickly test if the idea is big enough to write a whole novel. If you can't flesh out that idea into a premise, that's a big red flag that it's still missing the conflict needed to develop a solid plot.

⚠ **SOMETHING TO THINK ABOUT:** *Take a look at the idea you wrote down. Is there a premise building there or is it still vague? Take a moment and add any new elements that might have come to you while thinking about the premise.*

## The Plot

Plots are all about the specific conflicts and actions that illustrate the novel's premise (that focused idea). The plot provides external problems to be resolved that give the characters something to do over the course of the novel. The plot is the skeleton that the individual scenes are built upon. Plots are external, because they cover the things the characters have to do in the novel—the actual physical actions they take to make the novel happen in a step-by-step fashion.

Plots have the classic story structure elements that drive every scene: goals, conflicts, and stakes. A plot tells readers what the protagonist has to do to win, who or what she's up against, and what will happen if she loses.

*For example:*

- ▶ A lower caste member in ancient China fights to overthrow his tyrannical masters to save his wife from an unjust execution.
- ▶ A girl who can heal by touch is forced to use her gift to help the clan who murdered her family seize control in a civil war, but she works from within to bring about the demise of that clan.

▶ A man in an unhappy marriage tries to get rid of his wife during a zombie apocalypse so he can be with the woman he loves, unaware that one of the women is secretly plotting against him.

**Why the plot is important:** It gives the novel direction and clearly states what constitutes a win for the protagonist. It tells you how the novel will be resolved. It shows the specific elements and problems of the novel. If you listed out "what happens" in the novel, these are the moments you'd list.

**What's great about a plot:** It's the skeleton that holds the story together and becomes the foundation on which the novel is built. Because the novel has structure, it's easier for you to find the best way to tell that story.

⚠ **SOMETHING TO THINK ABOUT:** *Take a second look at your idea. Is there enough conflict to enable you to craft a plot? Are there clear things for your characters to do and problems for them to resolve? Go ahead and add any additional thoughts to your original idea.*

## The Story

Story is the reason for the novel. It's the journey the characters take and the core conflict driving them. It reveals the theme and creates the emotional connection to the readers. Stories show the motivations and why someone is doing all these exciting things we, as writers, have asked them to do. Story is the internal struggle the character goes through to resolve a personal issue (the character arc). The plot is how they accomplish that struggle.

*For example:*

▶ A lower caste member in ancient China must overcome his fear of authority to overthrow his tyrannical masters and save his wife from an unjust execution.

▶ A girl who can heal by touch is forced to use her gift to help the clan who murdered her family seize control in a civil war, and must learn to trust those she fears in order to work from within to bring about the demise of that clan.

▶ A gullible man in an unhappy marriage must learn the value of his own happiness when he tries to get rid of his wife during a zombie apocalypse so he can be with the woman he loves, unaware that the one of the women is secretly plotting against him.

**Why the story is important:** Story encompasses the theme and the larger, relatable elements of a novel. A story is about the lessons learned, the growth achieved. It turns a series of actions into actions with meaning.

**What's great about a story:** A good story will resonate with readers long after they've put the book down, because it explores the universal themes of the human spirit. It lets you be lofty and artistic, while at the same time tell a story that's an action-packed thrill ride (or a softer, emotional journey if you prefer). Stories *connect*.

⚠ **SOMETHING TO THINK ABOUT:** *Take one last look at your idea. Do you see the story there? Write down any larger story ideas that may have come to you after reading through these descriptions.*

Idea. Premise. Plot. Story.

All four play valuable roles in developing a novel, but skipping a step in the process can lead to frustration. So next time inspiration hits you, take a moment to consider if it's just an idea, a premise, or if you have a fully formed plot with a story behind it.

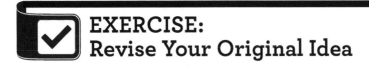

# EXERCISE:
# Revise Your Original Idea

## >>Go back to your idea and include any additional notes and thoughts.

How did your idea change? What do you know now that you didn't then?

Don't worry if you still have generalities in the idea. You might know that something brings your characters together, but not the specific details about it yet. It's okay at this stage to just know conceptually what you want to have happen. If you know specific details, that's great, too.

*For example:*

▶ Three teens with dark secrets meet at a diner in the middle of the night, each with a reason for being there that isn't what they claim.

▶ A love story set during a zombie apocalypse, where a guy wants a divorce but can't have it because the world just fell apart, and he needs his wife's survival skills to stay alive and help him find the woman he really wants to be with.

▶ Two childhood friends from feuding families reunite when the death of a favorite teacher causes them to return home.

# Discovering Your Hook

Hook is a term used in a variety of ways. It might be the hook of a query letter (the one-page summary used when we submit a manuscript to an agent or editor), a hook to make a reader keep reading, a hook line in the text that stands out and makes a reader smile and think, "Great line." No matter how it's used though, a hook is anything that makes the reader want to read more. It "hooks" the reader, captures attention, and piques interest in the novel.

In the brainstorming stage, the hook is the gotcha—the twist that will make the novel compelling and fresh. It's the "ooooh" factor that probably got you excited about the idea in the first place. It might be a plot point, a character goal, or a conflict. It could even be the theme.

**Why the hook is important:** The hook is what sets the novel apart from other books, and makes the novel different. The stronger the hook, the better the chance of selling the novel. (No pressure, right?)

In harsh terms, the hook is why a reader (or agent) should care about *your* book and not pick up someone else's. It's also how readers choose the novels they read, because one book will stand out and be more appealing than another—one "hooks" more than the other. If you're just writing for fun, a hook isn't vital, but if your hope is to one day publish a novel, a good hook is a necessity.

However, it's important to remember that a hook doesn't mean an original or unique idea. It's easy for writers to get caught up in thinking that they have to be unique to be published, and throw out great ideas for not being different enough. Just being different doesn't mean you'll have a good hook.

What makes a hook strong is the type of reaction it gets from a potential reader. A novel about sentient snails might be unique, but it probably doesn't make you want to read it. *The Wizard of Oz* told from the Wicked Witch's point of view gives you a new perspective on something you already love—and probably something you've always wanted to know yourself.

Strong hooks *can* be unique, but they can also be fresh takes on a much-loved idea. Look at how many times *Romeo and Juliet* has been done. Same story, new hook, by changing something and approaching it in a fresh way. So while hooks are important to a novel, don't feel pressured into feeling you must be unique *and* compelling. That's a lot to ask from a writer. When in doubt, go for the most compelling concept.

Hooks are most often found within the protagonist, the core conflict, the theme, the setting, or the concept, but they can be anything that piques interest and shows off the compelling aspect of your novel. They might be phrased as a question, or just a statement about a situation or a character.

*For example:*

- ▶ What if a killer shark attacked a beach during a major holiday? (*Jaws*)
- ▶ A world where everyone over thirty is killed. (*Logan's Run*)
- ▶ A healer who can use other people's pain as a weapon. (*The Shifter*)

There's no formula for a good hook, but it typically presents an unexpected combination of things or a surprising question or image.

## The Protagonist Hook

There's something different about the protagonist. She has a power, she's someone unexpected, she has a compelling occupation. Often the protagonist has decided to do something unexpected with that ability or skill. The protagonist is what hooks readers to want to read more about this person.

*For example:*

- ▶ A serial killer becomes a cop to put his homicidal urges to good use by killing only people who beat the legal system and get away with murder. (Dexter)
- ▶ A boy who is a strategic genius helps the military win a battle against an alien foe. (Ender Wiggins)
- ▶ A brilliant, yet abrasive, detective solves crimes no one else can. (Sherlock Holmes)

## The Core Conflict Hook

The core conflict of the novel revolves around a special or unexpected event or situation. The problem itself draws readers in, and they want to see how this issue is resolved and what happens.

*For example:*

▸ Children are chosen at random to fight to the death in a televised event. (*The Hunger Games*)

▸ An American civil war between the red and blue states. (*Empire*)

▸ A town cuts itself off from the rest of the world during an epidemic. (*The Last Town on Earth*)

## The Theme Hook

The theme explores an idea in a compelling way. Often these novels are more literary in nature, but a solid theme hook can also drive a more commercial novel. The hook poses a philosophical question the reader finds intriguing and then explores it.

*For example:*

▸ Two guys with the same name have a chance encounter that profoundly changes both their lives. (*Will Grayson, Will Grayson*)

▸ A girl who longs to run away from home discovers there's no place like home after all. (*The Wizard of Oz*)

▸ In a world where humanity is falling apart, what does it mean to be human? (*The Road*)

## The Setting Hook

A setting hook offers readers a world (in the most general terms) that intrigues them and makes them want to explore it. It's unusual and a place readers might want to visit regardless of what kind of novel is set there. It usually triggers a sense of adventure or what kinds of adventures might occur there.

*For example:*

- A wizard school hidden within the normal world. (*Harry Potter and the Sorcerer's Stone*)
- A boarding school for teen spies. (*I'd Tell You I Love You, But Then I'd Have to Kill You*)
- The moor surrounding a mysterious estate. (*Wuthering Heights*)

## The Concept Hook

The basic idea is unusual and poses a question that begs an answer. The concept is so intriguing readers want to see how the novel unfolds. These are often posed as "what if" questions.

*For example:*

- What if Peter Pan grew up? (*Hook*)
- What if Napoleon had had dragons? (*His Majesty's Dragon*)
- What if you could clone dinosaurs? (*Jurassic Park*)

Wherever the hook comes from, it's the thing that makes people's eyes light up when you mention it.

---

 **BRAINSTORMING QUESTIONS:**
Explore what's compelling and different about your novel.

1. List three critical things about your protagonist.

2. List three critical elements of your conflict.

3. List three critical things about your theme.

4. List three critical things about your setting.

5. List three critical things about your novel concept.

Does anything on your lists jump out as a strong hook? What feels compelling or offers a new twist to an old idea? What best shows the strength of your novel?

---

## Adding a New Twist to an Old Idea

There are more contradictions than words in publishing, and one of them is the old, "I want something fresh, but the same as what's selling" conundrum. As writers, how do we know what's fresh and what's the same old, same old? And harder still, how do we put that fresh face on *our* "been-there-written-that" novels?

Any plot can be made fresh with a new twist. It's our jobs as writers to put the brain cells to work and think up those twists. It also helps to remember that many well-loved genres or story types are fun *because* readers can see the end coming a mile away. My love of underdog sports movies is a classic example. I *know* the underdogs are going to win, but I'm on the edge of my seat anyway, and I cheer when they do win. The journey with new characters I can root for is what makes this type of story fun for me.

### Try a New Perspective

A different character can add a new dimension to a well-known story. Gregory McGuire took the world by storm by writing *The Wizard of Oz* from the Wicked Witch's perspective in *Wicked*. Jackson Pierce's *Sisters Red* is a retelling of *Little Red Riding Hood* with a twist.

Look at the idea, but also look at the genre. What's typical in that genre? Is there a character or character type that hasn't been heard from? Is there a different take on what everyone assumes? Can a sidekick or minor character take center stage with a new perspective on things?

### Try a New Location

A different setting can also add depth and dimension. *Forbidden Planet* is just Shakespeare's *The Tempest* on another planet. Meg Cabot moved Camelot to high school for her Avalon High series.

Can you explore a fresh angle if you move your idea to new location? A different city or even a different world? What if you expanded it to epic scale? How about narrowing it to a small area like a small town, or even a single house?

## Try a New Time

*Clueless* is just Jane Austen for the modern day, but giving it a teen setting made a classic story fresh again. Agatha Christie's *The Mousetrap* riffs off *Hamlet*.

Perhaps your idea could benefit from a shift in time. Modernize it if it's a classic, or go classic if it's modern. Could it be set during a particular historical period that would work thematically with the conflict? Would adding or eliminating a common piece of technology or knowledge shake things up?

## Try Doing the Opposite

*Villains By Necessity* by Eve L. Forward takes the classic fantasy quest novel and flips it by showing what happens *after* the good guys win, where the villains now have to save the day.

If everyone will expect your novel to unfold one way, what happens if it goes the opposite way? What does everyone think it *won't* do? What would happen if the protagonist *lost* instead of won?

**BRAINSTORMING QUESTIONS:**
If your idea has already been done, explore ways to add a new twist to it.

1. Is there a character type who can be involved in this idea that's totally different from what's come before?

2. Can the setting make it different? Shift it into the future or the past? (This has worked for many modern retellings of fairy tales.)

3. Can you change it culturally?

4. Can you play with the narrator's perspective?

5. Is there an aspect of it that hasn't been explored?

6. Could you add something from another genre to it?

7. Could you do it in a totally different genre than expected?

8. Are there any common tropes you could turn upside down?

9. Are there any genre rules you could play with? A "never do..." or an "always do..." you could ignore?

10. If you didn't do *anything* on the common tropes list, what might you come up with?

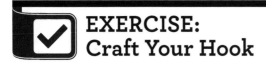

# EXERCISE:
# Craft Your Hook

## >>Write down your novel's hook.

While you want to find the "ooooh" factor, this hook doesn't need to be agent-ready quality. Focus on what makes your idea fresh and compelling. You'll also have time to develop this further as you learn more about your novel and characters.

*For example:*

▶ What if your worst enemy knew your darkest secret?

▶ A soap opera love story set in the zombie apocalypse

▶ *Romeo and Juliet* meets the Hatfields and McCoys in a small, southern town

# Determining if Your Novel is Character-Driven or Plot-Driven

Now that you know a little more about your idea and where it might be heading, let's take a moment to see how you might get there. This is something I like to determine early on, because it will affect how you approach the rest of the exercises. It's helpful to know what will drive your novel—the character actions and decisions that make the story happen and advance it toward the end of the novel—so you can tailor the plot and story to that.

Writers (and novels) typically fall into one of two camps: character driven or plot driven If you're the kind of writer who comes up with characters first and figures out the plot as you write, then you might find it frustrating to try to work out a plot first. Just like a plot-driven writer might find it difficult to develop the characters first. Knowing which you are makes going forward much easier.

If your idea (or writing style) leans more toward one side than the other, don't worry. Writing is a process, not a fill-in-the-blanks, one-size-fits-all template.

⚠ **SOMETHING TO THINK ABOUT:** *Take a look at your revised idea. Do you have a character-driven or a plot-driven idea?*

Unsure? Then let's find out.

## Character-Driven Ideas and Plots

Character driven means the focus is more on the character and her internal journey than the external issues of the plot. This doesn't mean plot isn't important, but the issues the character deals with are personal and often affect only that person or the people closest to her.

The main point of the novel is to show character growth and have the protagonist learn a valuable lesson about herself that allows her to be a better person (or points out a fatal flaw that causes her doom in a darker tale. Not every novel has to have a happy ending.)

Character-driven ideas typically manifest as a character with a problem first. This person has an issue that is central to the story and the journey to understand that issue is at the heart of the conflict. What that character is going to do isn't always clear at first, because the journey and the emotional story arc is what matters more.

*For example:*

▶ A woman with a fear of commitment must learn to let others in.

▶ A selfish boy must learn to think about others.

▶ A workaholic must learn to take time for family.

**How this works with a plot:** These problems are all internal, even though they likely have external problems due to these issues. A fear of commitment might translate to being alone and unhappy, selfishness could lead to having no friends, and working all the time often ends in divorce.

But the end goal isn't as simple as "find someone to marry" or "make a friend" or "quit a job." Those goals won't solve the underlying problem until the character goes through her emotional journey. There will be goals and problems that allow the protagonist to grow and learn what she needs to learn to achieve a specific goal, and that's where the focus lies.

## Key Elements of a Character-Driven Novel

■ The protagonist is responsible for what happens to her and acts to make the novel happen.

■ Internal forces affect the protagonist.

■ Personal growth and emotional change of the protagonist are major parts of the resolution of the novel.

⚠ **SOMETHING TO THINK ABOUT:** *Does your idea have the elements of a character-driven novel? If so, write them down.*

## Plot-Driven Ideas and Plots

Plot-driven means the focus is more on the external elements forcing the characters to act than on the personal journey. The stakes are frequently higher and matter more on a larger scale. This doesn't mean the characters are unimportant, but solving the problem is more important than character growth or lessons learned, though characters can grow and learn even in plot-driven novels.

Plot-driven ideas typically manifest as a situation or problem first. An interesting situation has occurred and someone is going to have to deal with it. Who that someone is might not matter at first, because resolving the problem is what matters more.

*For example:*

▶ Terrorists are planning to blow up the Golden Gate Bridge

▶ A plane goes down in the wilderness and a survivor has to make it to safety

▶ A protest at a factory turns into a riot

**How this works with characters:** These problems are all external, even though each will focus around a character who will likely have personal issues to deal with as she resolves her problem. Stopping terrorists entails personal risk, survival in the wilderness draws on untapped strength or knowledge, dealing with a riot requires commitment and diplomacy.

But the end goal isn't "face your fears to stop a terrorist" or "find your inner strength" or "redeem yourself for a terrible mistake." The novel won't be about the growth or lessons learned, even though the protagonist will likely change a little over the course of the novel as she resolves the external problem.

## Key Elements of a Plot-Driven Novel

■ External forces trigger the plot and cause the protagonist to act by reacting to that event.

■ Resolving the external problem matters more than a personal change in the character.

⚠ **SOMETHING TO THINK ABOUT:** *Does your idea have the elements of a plot-driven novel? If so, write them down.*

## Mixing the Two

It *is* possible to have both—a strong protagonist with a compelling emotional journey who is put into an interesting situation that needs to be resolved. Through resolving the plot problem, the emotional journey of the protagonist is experienced and achieved.

This is a powerful combination and it's not a bad thing to aim for with every novel. But don't worry if your idea leans more to one side than the other at this stage. You'll have plenty of time to develop both sides—character *and* plot—if you want to do both.

*For example:*

- ▶ An FBI agent faces his own seditious past while trying to prevent a terrorist attack.
- ▶ A timid girl discovers her own inner strengths when her plane crashes in the wilderness.
- ▶ A workaholic realizes the value of family when a protest at work turns into a riot.

**How this works with both:** These all have external problems that are made more difficult by internal issues. Stopping a terrorist exposes a dark secret, survival in the wilderness triggers a realization of personal strength, a protest turns deadly and reveals what matters most. The external end goal is the catalyst that forces the protagonist to change internally. The novel is about the growth and lessons learned as the protagonist resolves the external problem. The two sides work in tandem to craft a plot arc and a character arc that depend on each other.

## Key Elements of a Plot- and Character-Driven Novel

- ■ External forces trigger the plot and affect the protagonist in a personal way that forces her to act.
- ■ The protagonist can't avoid the external problem because it would have serious repercussions on an internal issue.
- ■ Resolving the external problem is what will allow the protagonist to resolve her internal issue.

⚠ **SOMETHING TO THINK ABOUT:** *Does your idea have the elements of both a character-driven and a plot-driven novel? If so, write them down.*

Books don't have to be fully plot driven or fully character driven. These are just terms for common writing styles that can help you figure out how to approach writing a novel. Don't feel you *have* to be one or the other or your novel won't work, but if you *do* know you think a certain way (plots first or characters first), that can be an asset in the planning process.

 **BRAINSTORMING QUESTIONS:**
Explore if you have a character-driven or plot-driven novel.

1. What internal forces are causing your characters to act?

2. What external forces are causing your characters to act?

3. Does resolving the external problem resolve the internal?

4. Where does your idea fall on the character-driven vs. plot-driven scale?

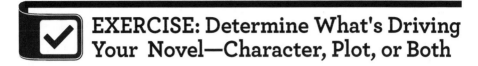

# EXERCISE: Determine What's Driving Your Novel—Character, Plot, or Both

## >>Describe how your novel is plot- or character-driven (or both).

Use any notes taken during the workshop to help you. Add in any new information that might have come to you. Also, don't worry if your novel changes as you work on it. A plot-driven novel could develop a strong character arc in later workshops and that's okay. Understanding what drives the novel now is just a guide to help you develop it.

*For example:*

▶ **Character driven:** The dark secrets are the internal forces causing the three teens to act. They each came to the diner of their own free will to do something about their secrets. Their personal reasons will drive the plot and force internal, emotional changes over the course of the novel. The book is more about who they are and what their secrets are than what they're doing.

▶ **Plot driven:** The zombie apocalypse is the external force that triggers the plot to survive. It also makes the protagonist realize he wants to be with the woman he loves, not his wife. Survival and being with the woman he loves matter more than how the protagonist changes. The bulk of the plot will focus on these elements.

▶ **Both plot and character driven:** The death and funeral of the favorite teacher is the external force that causes the protagonists to return to their hometown. Their reasons for being there are the internal forces, as the teacher affected each of them in some profound way. Fulfilling a promise to the teacher causes them to interact and eventually fall in love. The book is about the internal journey to fall in love, but the external actions in fulfilling the promise will drive much of the plot.

Be honest about the type of writer you are or the type of novel you want to write. Don't force it into a type because you feel one is better than the other, but also feel free to push yourself a little to think of ways you can deepen your idea using each of these types. If it doesn't work or feel right, then just scrap it. Nothing is wasted, because you never know where a thought might lead.

**Moving Forward:** If you're a plot-driven writer, you might be more comfortable skipping ahead and doing the plot sections before the character sections. If so, go ahead and jump to Workshop Five: Developing Your Plot. If you're a character-driven writer, you might be more comfortable continuing on to Workshop Four: Developing Your Characters, Point of View, Theme, and Setting.

# ASSIGNMENT THREE:
## Flesh Out Your Idea

>>**Summarize your idea, focusing on what makes the novel compelling and what aspect (plot or character) it will focus on.**

This assignment is about clarifying all the brainstorming and note taking you've done so far. Try pinpointing the elements of your idea that most excite you, and the direction you feel the novel will take moving forward.

Feel free to add questions *you* find intriguing or want to explore with this novel. The things that excite you about a story are the same ones that will likely excite a reader. These questions can also guide you later when thinking about the themes or important story arcs.

*For example:*

▶ A contemporary novel about teens with secrets, where one is bent on revenge and the intended victim is someone with secrets worth keeping. Ideas of secrets and truth will be explored, and how keeping dangerous secrets might affect someone. What *would* happen if your enemy threatened to reveal or even revealed your darkest secret?

▶ A love story set during a zombie apocalypse with a meek husband and an overbearing wife. Ideas of gender roles and marriage will be explored, contrasted against the backdrop of the zombie apocalypse. How might a guy bossed around by his wife handle the end of the world?

▶ A mash-up of *Romeo and Juliet* meets the Hatfields and McCoys. Ideas of how much your family should influence and affect your life will be explored. How far are two lovers willing to go when their families don't want them to be together for long-forgotten (or even stupid) reasons?

In Workshop Four, we'll look at developing your characters, discovering your theme, and choosing your setting.

# Workshop Four: Developing Your Characters, Point of View, Theme, and Setting

**What You Need to Start This Workshop:** An idea for a novel.

**The Goal of This Workshop:** To help you develop your characters, choose a point of view, find your novel's theme, and determine the novel's setting.

**What We'll Discuss in This Workshop:** How to: create characters, including the protagonist and antagonist; choose a point of view for the novel; determine your novel's theme; choose where your novel takes place.

**Writing Terms Used in This Workshop:**

**Antagonist:** The person or thing in the protagonist's path of success.

**Backstory:** The history and past of a character that affects his or her actions in a novel.

**Conflict:** Two sides in opposition, either externally or internally.

**Core Conflict:** The major problem or issue at the center of the novel.

**Filter Words:** The specific words used to create narrative distance in the point-of-view character.

**Goal:** What the point–of–view character wants.

**Hook:** An element that grabs readers and makes them want to read on.

**Point of View:** The perspective used to tell the story.

Protagonist: The character driving the novel.

**Narrative Distance:** The distance between the reader and the point-of-view character.

**Stakes:** What consequence will befall the protagonist if she fails to get her goal.

**Theme:** A recurring idea or concept explored in the novel.

# Welcome to Workshop Four: Developing Your Characters, Point of View, Theme, and Setting

Character versus plot are the external and internal aspects of a novel. One side (character) explores the internal emotional and personal journey, while the other (plot) explores the external action and decision-making journey. They're deeply interconnected, but they do focus on slightly different things, which makes it a little easier to develop each side.

Characters convey the aspects of writing that pertain to the more emotional side—the people, the points of view, the themes, and even the setting. These elements help shape who the characters are and how they became that way. They also set up where the characters are as the novel opens and shows the direction they need to go to reach the end of that emotional journey.

So it makes sense to look at these aspects as one unit, and see how they build off each other to create a well-rounded emotional layer for the novel.

Novels are about characters with problems, and no matter which side of the character/plot-driven style you prefer, your novel will have characters in it. They might be non-human characters if you're writing science fiction or fantasy, or even animals if you're writing for children, but the novel will be about someone doing something. The better the characters, the better the overall novel.

Someone will also narrate the novel, allowing readers to see the story events unfold and giving them a point of view (or several) to follow and connect with. Characters show readers the things that are important to the book, acting like story guides. That point of view might be a literal perspective in the novel itself, or an opinion about what's happening in that novel (or both for point-of-view characters).

Since these characters have opinions about the world they live in, they also search for meaning in their lives—which translates to the theme of the novel. What's it all *about*. They'll struggle to understand concepts or issues that have a larger ramification on their world. You'll find theme even in a plot-driven novel, because theme will make all those action-packed scenes have greater meaning.

All of this takes place in the character's world, whether it's a small town in the Midwest or a planet on the other side of the universe. Setting is where the characters' lives happen, and it's just as important to character development as point of view or theme. Where someone grows up or lives helps determine who that person is and how they got that way.

The emotional side of the story is all connected, and the tighter the weave, the more interesting the story can be.

In this workshop, we'll create characters for your novel, focusing on the protagonist and antagonist, determine what point of view you'd like to write the novel in, find and develop your theme, and choose and create the right setting.

## Discovering Your Characters

For a lot of writers, character is what comes first—a story idea is born from the glimmer of a character.

- A girl who can fly
- A boy who lost his parents in a war
- A man who is obsessed with the color blue

Something about that vague person sparks interest and an entire novel (or series) develops from that. Odds are, some secondary characters, like the antagonist, will appear soon after the protagonist comes to mind. Sidekicks or best friends are usually easy to add. But the rest? It's not always clear who will be needed or why.

There are some archetypes though—character types that frequently populate novels because they're useful, like the sidekick/best friend type. The protagonist will need someone to talk to to help move the plot along. A love interest is also typical, as is an enemy who isn't the antagonist just to keep the pressure on. Family members, both good and bad, frequently make appearances, and it's not uncommon to meet a mentor type.

As you consider your potential characters, think about the people who are going to provide information to the protagonist. These could be wise mentors, a chatty gal at the records office, even a double agent. Look at the broad scope of the novel and its world and see where information might come to the protagonist. Maybe one of those areas can spawn a great character.

Some of these people are going to get in the protagonist's way. The antagonist is the obvious one, but other people are going to deny the protagonist things over the course of the novel, and it won't always be due to a menacing plot. A rival mom at school or someone up for the same promotion could cause trouble. That on-the-edge-of-evil magic student might be pushed over the edge and turn against the protagonist.

There will likely be specific types of people commonly found in the world, situation, city, job, or environment the novel is set in. If the novel revolves around a police detective in a city, you'll know right away the types of people she'll likely come into contact with. Same if she's a rancher in Montana. People with roles in the world or setting can make great secondary characters as well as bring valuable information and insight to the protagonist. Think about the people the protagonist will come into contact with and if any of them are worth keeping around.

Some people are going to be in charge, and those people will be able to affect the protagonist's goals and life in all kinds of ways, even if they're not actively trying. There's a good chance the antagonist is going to come from this pool of characters.

Somebody is getting a raw deal somewhere. There's a good chance the protagonist falls into this category, or maybe someone she knows or cares about. Even if she's not part of this group, she might have strong feelings about them and their situation. A lot of plot can come from people being victimized.

There are always those people who are capable of anything—good and bad. You might even have some inkling of who these folks are, as they often have some ability the protagonist needs in the novel. A power, a secret, access to something or someone. Plot events will likely hinge on these people.

If you don't know who any of your characters are at the start, don't fret. Maybe you prefer to develop the plot first and worry about the characters later.

If you prefer to develop the people first and then see how the world develops around them, that's okay, too. Both are viable ways to plan a novel.

 **BRAINSTORMING QUESTIONS:**
When deciding who is going to be part of your novel, try thinking about the types of roles you might need.

1. Who are the people that are going to provide information to the protagonist?

2. Who are the people who are going to get in the protagonist's way?

3. What types of people are commonly found in the world/situation/city/job/environment your novel is set in?

4. Who has the power?

5. Who are the victims?

6. Who are the wild cards?

## Character Interviews

Many writers interview their characters to learn more about them. This can be a great way to get to know the characters without having a plot color the answers (This might not work for plot-driven writers, and that's okay.)

When interviewing or asking questions about the characters, try to look beyond the physical traits. While it's good to know eye and hair color, birthplace, or occupation, just knowing the "what" doesn't reveal how that character will react in a situation—unless those traits have *reasons* behind them, like:

▶ The brown-haired girl who dyes her hair red because she loves to be the center of attention

▶ The redhead who dyes her hair brown because she hates being the center of attention

Questions that shape personality also help shape plot. The two girls in the above example will do different things in the same situation based on their personalities—they'll have different points of view about how their world works and their role in that world.

Here are some sample questions to ask or consider about a character:

▶ What events affected the way the character feels about something important to the novel?

▶ What were her past relationships like?

▶ What's the worst thing to ever happen to her and how did that change her?

▶ What's the best thing to happen and how did that change her?

▶ What is her biggest fear? Why?

▶ What's the worst thing she ever did? How did that affect her?

▶ What does she hope no one finds out about her?

## Choosing Your Main Characters

Whether you have a character-driven or a plot-driven idea, you'll have to choose a main character. This is the person (or people) readers will follow over the course of the novel, and who they will care about enough to want to read that novel.

Some books have multiple main characters—romance is a good example here, with the hero and the heroine both moving the plot forward toward a clear goal—but having too many main characters can be an indication that the conflict isn't defined yet.

If no one is a clear protagonist, the plot can lack drive, and you might find yourself halfway through the novel and wondering what happens next.

If every character is trying to have their say, you might find yourself with multiple plot lines that leave readers wondering if they're reading three books in one.

When thinking about who the main characters are going to be and who will be driving the story, also consider who will make the best protagonist and antagonist.

 **BRAINSTORMING QUESTIONS:**
Consider characters for your novel.

1. What kinds of characters might be in this novel?

2. Who are the good guys?

3. Who are the bad guys?

4. What characters are already forming?

5. What characters do you know have to be there?

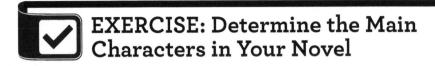

# EXERCISE: Determine the Main Characters in Your Novel

**>>List the main characters in your novel, and any information you know about them so far.**

These are the characters the novel is going to revolve around. The ones with the most to gain and lose, and who will play a strong role in the novel's conflict. At this stage it isn't necessary to know protagonist and antagonist, but if you do know that, go ahead and write it down. It's also okay to write down any additional smaller characters that you think you might need or want.

*For example:*

▶ Lana (protagonist), Miguel, and Zachary (antagonist). A waitress at the diner. An unexpected diner who causes trouble.

▶ Bob (protagonist); his wife Sally (antagonist); Jane, the woman Bob is in love with.

▶ Adam and Hannah (protagonist). Adam's parents, Hannah's parents (the antagonists will come from these two families), the dead teacher, siblings or friends that are close to Adam and Hannah.

Sometimes you know you want a certain type of character even if you don't know who they are yet. For example, you might know you need a best friend, but you haven't created that character yet. Or a love interest, or a rival. It's okay if the details of that character are still vague at this stage.

## Identifying Your Protagonist

The protagonist is the person driving the plot. In most cases she's the main character, and the plot will focus on her resolving the novel's core conflict (the problem at the center of the novel).

There are plenty of things that make a great protagonist a great character, but in the idea and planning stage, it's helpful to look at the traits that also help develop a plot or character arc. Tailor your notes and brainstorming to the side you prefer, or do both if you want to develop both sides simultaneously.

**Why the protagonist is important:** She's the character readers will have to connect with, relate to, or empathize with in some way that makes them want to see how she resolves the problems placed in her path. She's the reader's guide to the novel.

### Elements of a Strong Protagonist

**A strong protagonist has a problem that needs solving.** The protagonist is the one with the problem that has to be solved. No one else can solve this problem (or solve it as well as she can) and she's central to the entire issue. This holds true for both character-driven and plot-driven novels.

**A strong protagonist has the ability to act.** Protagonists who do nothing but react to the situation are boring. A good protagonist makes things happen by making conscious decisions that move the plot and character arc through actions and choices. If the protagonist isn't in a position to effect change, consider how to adjust it so she is. For character-driven novels, it might appear more as an opportunity to act provided by an outside source, such as a judge sentencing the protagonist to rehab due to her own destructive behavior.

**A strong protagonist has reasons to act.** Plenty of characters might be *able* to do something, but unless they have a good reason, it starts to stretch credibility why they would get involved in something that clearly doesn't matter to them. Imagine how weak *Die Hard* would have felt if John McClane hadn't been a cop and hadn't had a wife being held hostage by the bad guys. What if he'd been some random guy who happened to get locked in a building with terrorists? Why on earth would he have risked his life to stop the antagonist? The motivations for acting (plot driven) or changing (character driven) should be clear and believable.

**A strong protagonist has something to lose.** Just having a reason to act isn't always enough. Losing something that matters is a powerful motivating tool and will force the characters to do what they normally wouldn't do. Even better, having something to lose helps create the stakes that will keep a reader reading. Stakes are the consequences that will befall the protagonist no matter what type of novel it is. Creating stakes for *both* the character-driven and plot-driven problems is even better, as there's more to lose.

**A strong protagonist has something to gain.** This is an important aspect of the stakes. Watching someone *not* lose has its merits, but to really root for a character, it's important to see her rewarded for all her hard work and sacrifice. She needs a reason to keep going when everything tells her to give up, and a reason to risk everything that's positive. This is especially important in a character-driven novel where growth and change results in a happy ending.

**A strong protagonist has the capacity to change.** Character growth adds the soul to the novel. It's what turns it from a series of plot events into a tale worth telling. A great protagonist has the ability to learn from her experiences and become a better person. Allowing the protagonist to change in a plot-driven novel makes it feel more personal and often more satisfying for readers. The external events mean *more* in the end. Having a capacity to change in a character-driven novel is crucial, since that change is what it's likely about.

**A strong protagonist has a compelling quality.** Something about the character is interesting. Maybe she's funny and likable. Maybe she's twisted and fascinating. She might have an unusual talent or skill, or a unique manner about her. Whatever it is, there's a quality that makes readers curious to know more about her. In plot-driven novels this is often what makes the protagonist the person who needs to solve the problem. In character-driven novels, that quality is often her greatest flaw, strength, or both, and will be central to the character arc.

**A strong protagonist has an interesting flaw.** Perfect people are boring—it's the flaws that make them interesting. Flaws also provide an opportunity to show character growth and give the protagonist a way to improve. Maybe she knows about this flaw and is actively trying to fix it, or she has no clue and change is being forced upon her. Maybe this flaw is the very thing that will allow her to survive and overcome her problems, or the cause of the entire mess. In plot-driven novels, this flaw is often at the root of the internal conflict and what the protagonist has to face to succeed in the climax. In character-driven novels, this is often what's keeping the protagonist from growing and becoming who she really wants to be.

**A strong protagonist has a secret.** Open-book characters are too predictable, and predictability usually leads to readers putting down the book. If the protagonist is hiding something, readers will wonder what that secret is and how it affects the novel. Secrets work well for both types of novels, as learning more about the characters is one way to hook readers and keep them reading.

**A strong protagonist has someone or something interesting trying to stop her.** A protagonist is only as good as the antagonist standing against her. Where would Sherlock Holmes be without Professor Moriarty? Officer Brody without Jaws? Neo without Agent Smith? A great protagonist needs someone (or something) worth fighting or her victory is meaningless. For plot-driven novels this is vital as the stakes tend to be larger and the focus is on the external problem. For character-driven novels, the obstacle is often symbolic or represented by an outside force that mirrors the internal problem.

⚠ **SOMETHING TO THINK ABOUT:** *Go back to your notes about your main characters. Which one would make the best protagonist?*

The protagonist is the character we, as writers, should love (even if she's not the nicest person) and hope that readers also love. If we aren't excited about our protagonist, odds are readers won't be either.

**For plot-driven writers:** It's not uncommon for plot-focused writers to have underdeveloped characters during a first draft. Discovering how those characters handle the problems in the book is how we get to know them. There's time during revisions to flesh out the characters and turn them into three-dimensional people.

**BRAINSTORMING QUESTIONS:**
If you're not sure who your protagonist is yet, answer the following questions with whoever is the best character for that role. If you do know who your protagonist is, think about how these questions apply.

1. Who has a problem that needs solving? What is that problem?

2. Who has the ability to act? How?

3. Who has reasons to act? What are they?

4. Who has something to lose? What is it?

5. Who has something to gain? What is it?

6. Who has the capacity to change? How so?

7. Who has a compelling quality? What is it?

8. Who has an interesting flaw? What is it?

9. Who has a secret? What is it?

10. Who has someone or something interesting in the way? Who or what is it?

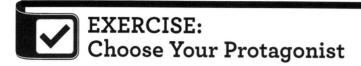

# EXERCISE: Choose Your Protagonist

## >>Describe your protagonist in a few paragraphs or less.

Not just the physical look (that's okay if you know it already), but the type of person he or she is and any history you might know at this stage. Try to get a sense of who this character is and how the novel might unfold with a protagonist like this.

*For example:*

▶ Lana is a cautious girl because she doesn't want anyone to know the truth about her. She deflects questions with humor, directing conversations back onto others. If anyone gets too pushy, she finds a way to start an argument and distract them, allowing her to storm out and escape. Because of this, she doesn't have a lot of friends.

▶ Bob is an average guy who's in an unhappy marriage with an aggressive woman. He never feels like he's good enough or man enough for her, which has created a major inferiority complex in him. The only bright spot in his life is Jane, a sweet, sensitive woman at his office. He's fallen in love with her but is too scared to ask for a divorce or even tell Jane how he feels. His situation is made a lot worse when zombies attack, because now he clearly isn't strong enough to defend himself let alone take care of Jane. But he thinks maybe he can turn this disaster into a way to be the man he thinks is worthy of Jane.

▶ Adam is a headstrong entrepreneur who enjoys risks and pushing the edge. His favorite childhood teacher encouraged this, and he credits her for giving him the drive to escape his hometown and do something exciting and worthwhile with his life. Hannah is a shy introvert who wishes she were more daring, and she takes risks in quiet, unassuming ways. She also was influenced by this teacher, but never fully embraced the lessons to be the person she really wanted to be. The teacher's death comes at a time when both Adam and Hannah have just undergone traumatic events that make them question their lives.

## Identifying Your Antagonist

The shadowy mirror of the protagonist is the antagonist. The type of conflict used in the novel often determines who or what this is (and vice versa). If the conflict is against another person, then the protagonist will need a worthy adversary. If the antagonist is nature or society, then the protagonist will be fighting against obstacles larger than herself. If the protagonist is her own worst enemy, then the antagonist will be someone who represents all that the protagonist is fighting. (More on these conflict types in the next section.)

Villains (even villainous societies) can easily become cardboard clichés if we focus only on the bad and what the antagonist wants to do to the protagonist. The antagonist becomes a plot device to cause the protagonist trouble, not a fully developed character in her own right. But villains have feelings too, and even antagonists have some redeeming qualities.

**Why the antagonist is important:** The antagonist provides the necessary conflict by giving the protagonist someone or something to struggle against. The fire in which the hero is forged. The better the antagonist, the stronger the protagonist will look.

Marvel Comics has one of the best villains ever, and a perfect example of a great antagonist. Erik Lehnsherr, otherwise known as Magneto. This is a villain that is so human (ironically enough, considering he's a mutant), so relatable, so sympathetic that we almost want to take his side. He survived the Nazis, watched his family killed, his people tagged, labeled, and gassed for being "different" and "less than human" (Jewish). He was used and abused for his powers.

Jump ahead in his life and we can clearly see how a man with this background would react to folks trying to identify, label, and control mutants for being "different" and "not human." When he lays out his argument for why the mutants need to band together and protect themselves against humanity, it's hard to argue with him. History has taught us that humans do pretty horrific things to those who are different and those they can't control.

This is an antagonist readers *understand*. And that makes him all the more compelling.

Take this a step further and look at the society Magneto lives in—a world where humans are mutating and developing superpowers. Not everyone who has these powers uses them for noble purposes. Imagine if the Mafia suddenly had superpowers. How far would *you* want the FBI to go to stop them? What laws might you be willing to support if it meant stopping super-powered criminals?

Now we have understandable motivations on *both* sides, and both arguments make sense from a certain perspective. It becomes a gray area where there is no clear right or wrong.

The gray area is where great antagonists live, be they people, societies, or situations.

⚠ **SOMETHING TO THINK ABOUT:** *A great antagonist can take a novel to a new level. Think about your favorite stories (books, movies, or TV). Which antagonists stick out in your mind as the great villains who were the perfect foil to the heroes you love? What about them do you love?*

No matter who the antagonist is, she had reasons to become who she is. Like Magneto and the Nazis, there's a defining event or series of events that crafted why she's the person she is or the way things are. Events shaped this person or this society. Maybe good intentions went horribly wrong, or it was a bad idea founded in evil or cruelty.

People do the wrong thing for the right reasons all the time, and society is no different (being made up of, well, *people*). Maybe the antagonist is trying to do something noble on the grand scale, but she's choosing to get there in a less than honorable fashion. Think about how fear of something worse might cause otherwise good folks to do the wrong thing.

Odds are your antagonist didn't win every battle, thwart every foe, or have a life on easy street before she met your protagonist. Tough choices had to be made and these choices helped create this person. Think about the key moments where a choice shaped that person or society into who and what they are. And better still, consider the places in the novel where you might exploit that.

Villains who want to destroy the world and kill everyone in it never made sense to me because, um, don't they need those things to survive as well? (Unless you're one of Doctor Who's Daleks. Their desire to destroy the world makes sense for them.) An antagonist with a plan that has *some* element worthy of all the nasty things she's doing is a lot more compelling. Readers *get* why she's acting as she is, and why those good intentions have gone wrong. Think about what's worthy in the antagonist's evil plan.

Antagonists can be anything that gets in the protagonist's way, but I don't think it gets any better than an antagonist readers can understand and even agree with a little. It's those human qualities that make them more than just villains. They become people, heroes in their own minds and their own stories, trying to do what they think is best—even if that goes against what the protagonist may want and think is best.

Not every antagonist in every novel needs to be like Magneto, however. Sometimes we *want* the crazed killer or unrelenting force of nature, and that's okay. But it's worth a few minutes to consider how rounding out the antagonist might make the overall novel better and richer.

---

 **BRAINSTORMING QUESTIONS:**
Here are some things to consider when choosing and developing your antagonist.

1. How did she/he/it get this way?

2. Is there honor or nobility to the antagonist's actions?

3. What tough choices have been made?

4. What about the "evil plan" is actually *worth* pursuing?

## The Four Classic Conflict Types

Conflict is vital to any novel, but it isn't always between people. Some novels pit the protagonist against society or a natural disaster. Others have the traditional protagonist vs. antagonist setup, or protagonist vs. protagonist. Let's look at the four classic conflict types, how they define the basic conflict structure, and how they affect the antagonist.

### Person vs. Person

This is a character against another character, people vs. people, even if those people are non-human. They're still a character like any other. The person standing in the protagonist's way is another person. A person is the antagonist.

*For example:*

▶ An alien bounty hunter wants to capture the protagonist and sell her to the highest bidder.

▶ A scientist needs to find the cure to stop a madman with a virus.

▶ An orphan girl needs to save her sister from bad men.

⚠ **SOMETHING TO THINK ABOUT:** *Could your antagonist come from a Person vs. Person conflict? How?*

### Person vs. Self

This is when the protagonist is at odds with herself and fighting something personal and internal. The person standing in the way of the protagonist is the protagonist. The antagonist is often represented by another character or a place or object that carries great emotional meaning.

*For example:*

▶ A drug addict who refuses to stay in rehab

▶ A man who ignores all the signs that he's seriously ill

▶ A girl who alienates all her friends to hang out with the cool crowd

⚠ **SOMETHING TO THINK ABOUT:** *Could your antagonist come from a Person vs. Self conflict? How?*

If the conflict doesn't involve one person against another, then it might be a Person vs. Society or Person vs. Nature novel. In these types of novels, the antagonist is something to overcome or survive. A blizzard must be endured, a law must be changed (or a person unfairly condemned by that law must be freed). Something is keeping the protagonist from winning, and that something plays the role of antagonist.

## Person vs. Society

This is when the protagonist has a problem with something that is status quo in the world. It's not any one person who is causing trouble, it's how things are being done. Everyone is standing in the protagonist's way, but not everyone is at fault. The antagonist is often represented by another character that shares or symbolizes the society and its problems.

*For example:*

- ▶ A man tries to change an unfair law.
- ▶ A girl rebels against a tyrannical society that forces kids into slavery.
- ▶ A woman questions why she can't go to school like her brother.

⚠ **SOMETHING TO THINK ABOUT:** *Could your antagonist come from a Person vs. Society conflict? What aspects of the society is your protagonist fighting? Who might represent that aspect?*

## Person vs. Nature

This is when the protagonist is up against nature, and that is what's keeping her from her goal. There is no person standing in the protagonist's way, it's the world itself. The antagonist is something that must be endured.

*For example:*

- ▶ A woman is trapped in a blizzard and has to survive.
- ▶ Kids lost in the forest need to find their way home.
- ▶ A group of fishermen battle a raging storm.

⚠ **SOMETHING TO THINK ABOUT:** *Could your antagonist come from a Person vs. Nature conflict? What aspect of nature is preventing your protagonist from achieving her goal?*

When choosing an antagonist, it's helpful to remember that no matter who or what is the conflict, he, she, or it makes it harder for the protagonist to resolve the problem. Take out that antagonist and the protagonist can just waltz in and win with no struggle. No blizzard, nothing to survive. No unfair law, no reason to protest. The antagonist provides the conflict to drive the plot.

## BRAINSTORMING QUESTIONS:
Here are some things to consider when choosing and developing your antagonist.

1. What type of conflict might prevent your protagonist from succeeding?

2. What type of conflict might produce the best antagonist?

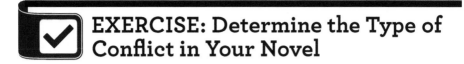

# EXERCISE: Determine the Type of Conflict in Your Novel

## >>Write down the conflict type you feel would work best for your novel. Explain why.

It's okay if the details of that conflict are still unformed, but try to pinpoint the *type* of conflict if you can. Not only will this force you to consider the potential obstacles in your protagonist's way, it will make it easier later to determine what your core conflicts are, and how the antagonist fits into that conflict.

If you're not sure or think it could be a combination of conflicts, go ahead and write both down. You can pick a specific antagonist later in the workshop, and that choice should clarify which type of conflict you have. Sometimes it's not always clear, or you decide to change it as the novel develops.

*For example:*

▶ **Conflict Type:** Person vs. Person. The three teens will be against each other to resolve their issues. The other teens are the ones in the way of whatever each wants, and keeping them from being happy.

▶ **Conflict Type:** Person vs. Nature. The zombie apocalypse is an unstoppable force the protagonist can't stop. He has to survive it to get what he wants. It could also be a Person vs. Person since he wants a divorce and his wife is keeping him from being with the woman he really loves.

▶ **Conflict Type:** Person vs. Person. Other people will be in the way of the two characters trying to keep their promise. Also, they could be in each other's way if they're trying not to fall for each other or get involved and make their families mad.

The conflict could change as you develop your novel, so don't worry if you have a few possibilities at this stage. If there are multiple types of conflict, you might decide to use all of them for different characters or plot arcs. What matters most is to think about the conflict and the areas where your characters are going to hit obstacles. One common reason novels get rejected is due to a lack of conflict, so it's important to build strong conflicts into your characters.

## If the Antagonist is a Person

When I was working on my first ever novel, I had a writing instructor who said the reason she enjoyed my antagonist so much was that he was practical, and that made her understand why he did what he did. Being inside his mind was scarier because he was rational and logical about the things he was doing. He was also funny, and had a dry wit and an interesting take on his situation. She said this was a guy who, if he wasn't trying to destroy the world, she'd probably hang out with after work.

That's the kind of antagonist readers remember.

An antagonist that's likable on some level is unpredictable. She already defies stereotypes by not being pure evil, so readers aren't sure what she'll do.

To help determine which main character should take the antagonist role, look at traits that elevate the antagonist to more than just the villain.

### Elements of a Strong Person vs. Person Antagonist

**A strong antagonist is trying to accomplish something.** The antagonist has a plan, an *evil* plan in most cases. She's acting because something is driving her to act and she wants to accomplish something in particular. In plot-driven novels, this is often the event that triggers the protagonist to act. The big bad thing that will occur if someone doesn't step up and do something to stop it.

**A strong antagonist is acting on personal desires.** Even if the antagonist is a mercenary hired to kill the protagonist, she's still motivated by *something*. Greed, an enjoyment of violence, a personal demon. The antagonist doesn't just wake up one morning and decide to be evil for the heck of it. She wants something and has determined her plan is the best course of action to get it.

**A strong antagonist is highly motivated to act.** Strong and understandable motivations will make the antagonist feel like a real person and make the novel that much better. The more plausible the motivations, the more understandable the antagonist will be, and the easier it will be to plot later. For character-driven novels, this motivation might be similar to the one that's driving the protagonist to personal destruction.

**A strong antagonist is trying to avoid something.** The antagonist has things at stake as well, just like the protagonist. Failure should mean more than just not succeeding in the plan. There will be consequences if she doesn't succeed—nasty ones. She might even be the cautionary tale if the protagonist took a darker path or gave in to temptation.

**A strong antagonist is trying to gain something.** No one goes to as much trouble as a good antagonist does without a prize in the end. If she wants to take over the world, *why*? What about that action makes her happy? Being evil for the sake of evil risks having a cardboard villain that isn't scary or interesting.

**A strong antagonist is willing to adapt.** Don't make the antagonist dumb, trying the same things and falling for the same old traps over and over. A strong antagonist adapts and learns from what the protagonist is doing. She forces the protagonist to grow and change by always being one step ahead.

**A strong antagonist is compelling in some way.** To keep her from being a two-dimensional cliché, give the antagonist good traits as well as bad. Things that make her interesting and even give her a little redemption. This will help make her unpredictable if once in a while she acts not like a villain, but as a complex and understandable person. She doesn't always do the bad thing.

**A strong antagonist is flawed in relatable ways.** Human weakness is something every reader can relate to. If your antagonist has flaws that tap into the human side of her (even if she's not human) then she becomes more real and readers can see her side of the argument.

**A strong antagonist is hiding things.** The antagonist has secrets. She fears people finding out certain things, usually because she's up to no good. Sometimes those secrets expose weaknesses or flaws she doesn't want anyone else to see, but sometimes they're the vulnerable parts of her.

**A strong antagonist is in the path of the protagonist's goal.** An antagonist who never crosses paths with the protagonist isn't much of an obstacle. Let her cause the protagonist hardship and trouble over the course of the novel, even if she's not doing it deliberately. Her plan and actions can create trouble even if she's not yet aware the protagonist is fighting her. But at some point, these two will come face to face and only one will win.

Fleshing out the antagonist doesn't mean adding her point of view in the novel—though if the antagonist is a point-of-view character, develop her as much as the protagonist. It's more about creating a well-rounded and believable character that will enrich the novel overall.

---

 **BRAINSTORMING QUESTIONS:**
Answer the following questions as they pertain to your novel. If you're not sure who your antagonist is yet, answer with whoever is the best character for that role. If you do know who your antagonist is, think about how these questions apply to him or her.

1. What is this person trying to accomplish? Why?

2. What is this person's personal desire? Why?

3. How is this person motivated to act? Why?

4. What is this person trying to avoid? What happens if she doesn't?

5. What is this person trying to gain? What happens if she doesn't?

6. How might this person adapt?

7. How is this person compelling?

8. What are this person's flaws?

9. What are this person's strengths?

10. What is this person hiding?

11. How does this person stand in your protagonist's way?

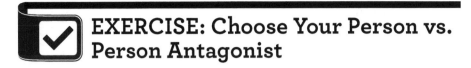

# EXERCISE: Choose Your Person vs. Person Antagonist

## >>Describe your antagonist.

Not just the physical look (that's okay if you know it already), but the type of person he or she is and any history you might know at this stage. Try to get a sense of who this character is and how the novel might unfold with an antagonist like this.

*For example:*

▶ Zachary is the mastermind behind the plan, tricking the others into coming to the diner and pretending to be just as clueless as them about why they're there. He's cunning, manipulative, and consumed with revealing the secrets of the other two for his own nefarious purpose. This obsession is his weakness and causes him to push things farther than he should and risk revealing his own secrets.

▶ 1. The zombies are the villains, because they want to eat people. 2. On a more personal level, Sally is an antagonist because she's keeping Bob from Jane, the love of his life. Sally is tired of Bob's failure to live up to the potential she first saw in him when they were dating, and she thinks that if she pushes him hard he'll step up. When he doesn't, she gets angry and takes it out on him. The more he depends on her for survival, the less respect she has for him and the more she feels he can't possibly survive on his own. 3. A government guy, who came up with the zombification virus and is up to no good.

▶ The feuding families don't want Adam or Hannah to be together, because they've hated each other for generations. Adam and Hannah carry that prejudice, and this makes their feelings for each other very confusing for them. They resist for dumb, outdated reasons and a sense of family loyalty, even though being with each other is what will make them both happy.

## If the Antagonist is Self

In a lot of novels (especially genre novels) the antagonist is a physical being that can be fought against. But sometimes the antagonist isn't someone to overcome, it's something the protagonist is dealing with personally, like depression or a self-destructive streak. She's her own worst enemy, so technically, there's nothing plotting against your protagonist for her to fight.

In these cases, look for representatives of the problem the protagonist is dealing with. The problem might be the depression, but *people* are involved in how the protagonist deals (or doesn't deal) with that depression. One of those people is probably a good candidate to symbolize what your protagonist is fighting in her own nature.

Even when the protagonist is dealing with something difficult, she'll still have an external force to reckon with. She'll still have a goal to work toward. She isn't sitting in a room trying to will herself *not* to be depressed/grief-stricken/addicted/a workaholic/closed off emotionally.

Someone in the novel will symbolize what the protagonist is fighting for. If she *wants* to get well/find love/slow down, then the party friend/local booty call/boss who supports her destructive behavior could be the person leading her back to the dark path. This person is everything she doesn't want to be, but she can't help herself and keeps going back or listening to him—the devil on her shoulder leading her astray.

If she *doesn't* want to get well/find love/slow down, then the person who wants her to change might be a good antagonist. They want her to change but she's happy just as she is, unaware of the danger her behavior is putting her in. They're the angel on her shoulder that she's ignoring.

Maybe it's a painful memory that's keeping the protagonist from being happy, and returning to the scene of the memory is exactly what she needs to move past it. Something about that place will require her to return, and that's what she's externally fighting as she battles her inner demons.

It could even be something that reminds her of her flaw or weakness, driving her to act in destructive ways. A trophy she knows she didn't earn that forces her to win at all costs, a trinket from her past that belonged to the person she let down or was never good enough for.

Crafting an antagonist for a Person vs. Self novel can be a little tougher, but if you look at what the antagonist is supposed to represent, it makes it a lot easier to find the right foil for your protagonist.

**BRAINSTORMING QUESTIONS:**
Here are some things to consider when choosing an antagonist for a Person vs. Self novel.

1. Who or what in the novel represents what the protagonist is fighting?

2. Who or what in the novel represents what the protagonist is struggling toward?

3. What place represents what the protagonist is fighting?

4. What item represents what she's fighting?

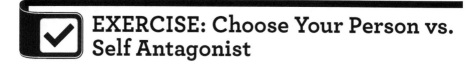

# EXERCISE: Choose Your Person vs. Self Antagonist

>>**Describe how your protagonist is also the antagonist.**

>>**Describe the person who represents the antagonist.**

Don't just describe the physical look (that's okay if you know it already), but the type of person he or she is and any history you might know at this stage. Try to get a sense of who this character is and how the novel might unfold with an antagonist like this.

**BONUS TIP:** Even if you have a Person vs. Person antagonist, it can be helpful to think about how your protagonist might be messing up her own life. Try doing this exercise to also find the flaw in your protagonist and how that hurts her in her quest to reach her goal.

*For example:*

▶ Lana is letting her secret control her and ruin her life, because she can't see how it's pushing everyone away and driving her toward destructive behavior. Miguel represents the antagonist for her personal struggle, because he's trying to reach her and knows she's in trouble, but she won't let him help her. Allowing Miguel to help her will let her shed the pain of her secret and escape the torment it's caused her for years.

▶ Bob is letting his insecurity rule his life and keep him from what he wants. If he stood up for himself he'd be able to divorce Sally and be happy. He might even become the man Sally married again and work things out with her. The zombies represent the dangerous aspect of Bob's flaw because they're slaves to mindless actions that will never satisfy them. They also represent the overwhelming feeling of helplessness in the face of adversity, because Bob can't defend himself against them, same as he can't stand up to Sally. Bob needs to stand up and defeat the zombies, defend the women in his life, and take care of himself before he can see he does have value as a man and a husband.

▶ Adam and Hannah are letting childhood prejudices keep them apart. There's no reason for either of them to dislike the other, but they do because of their loyalty to their families. Individual family members on both sides represent the self antagonist by keeping them apart (the voices of their upbringing telling them what to do). The family symbolizes all sides of the long-term conflict, and each time Adam or Hannah come to terms or deal with a member, they get one step closer to working out their problems.

## If the Antagonist is Society

Sometimes the antagonist isn't a specific person but the society at large. There's no one person trying to stop the protagonist from getting what she wants, it's just how society works.

A great example of a Person vs. Society antagonist is Harlan Ellison's short story "Repent Harlequin! Said the Ticktockman." Society has become a place where every moment is accounted for, and every tardiness is taken off the end of your life. Use up too much time and you're turned off. The protagonist is the Harlequin, who sets out to disrupt society and make people late. He's trying to change a society bent on adherence to a schedule by affecting that schedule.

Just like Person vs. Self, a Person vs. Society antagonist will be a representative of what the society stands for. In the Harlequin's case, it's the Master Timekeeper (the Ticktock Man) who's just doing his job and trying to keep the system running efficiently. The protagonist is trying to break that system and elicit change, even if it's for a brief time.

This is a key element to a Person vs. Society conflict—changing the status quo. Whether or not it happens doesn't matter, it's the fight to do so that provides the goals for the novel. Sometimes the protagonist seemingly loses, but her actions do indeed bring change and readers can see that this is the ripple that will change the pond.

A Person vs. Society antagonist will have many of the same elements as a Person vs. Person antagonist.

### Elements of a Strong Person vs. Society Antagonist

**A strong antagonist is trying to accomplish something society feels is vital.** In a Person vs. Society conflict, this is often the job that society has asked the antagonist to do, and that puts her in conflict with the protagonist (who is breaking the rules of that society). She represents the status quo of the society.

**A strong antagonist is acting on societal desires.** She may or may not believe in what society does, but she's carrying out what they want because that's more important to her than her own needs.

**A strong antagonist is highly motivated to act.** She feels bringing down the protagonist saves the society, or her leaders or superiors are putting pressure on her to succeed.

**A strong antagonist is trying to avoid the consequences of the protagonist winning.** The societal leaders fear changing the society will lead to disaster, and the antagonist often views the protagonist as the true villain trying to cause chaos and anarchy.

**A strong antagonist is trying to keep the peace.** Maintaining the society and the rules is part of her orders, or part of her evil plan. Wanting to keep things as they are could be for noble reasons or selfish desires.

**A strong antagonist is willing to bend the rules.** This doesn't hold true for all Person vs. Society antagonists, but it's not uncommon to find an antagonist who starts to sympathize with the protagonist or is so incensed by her that she breaks the rules she swore to uphold just to catch her.

**A strong antagonist is compelling in some way.** An antagonist who represents the evils of a society is often an unlikable character. But with a twist, she can become more than just a symbol.

**A strong antagonist is flawed in relatable ways.** Perhaps the flaw also represents society, and the antagonist is a symbol of what is wrong about the society, and hints at what needs to be done to change it.

**A strong antagonist is hiding things.** Societies have even more secrets than people do. Maybe the antagonist knows more about what's really going on, or she actually supports the protagonist's position, or she's working for a much darker section of the leadership.

**A strong antagonist is in the path of the protagonist's goal.** If the protagonist is fighting society, the antagonist is typically a very active foil in trying to stop her. Often she's tasked with doing just that, but those in power or those who run society are the ones the protagonist is really fighting.

It's common for the protagonist to run afoul of someone who symbolizes what's wrong and what she hates about her society. Often it's a member of the government, though not always. The antagonist is there to create obstacles and keep the protagonist from what she wants. Sometimes the antagonist is just doing her job, but she might truly believe society is in the right. Or, it might just be a job, and deep down this person agrees with some or all of what the protagonist is trying to do.

A Person vs. Society antagonist can be a lot of fun to create because she often comes with a history to work with. She's part of the world and the society that's hurting the protagonist. She gets to be everything the protagonist is working against, or the person who is stuck in the same system the protagonist is trying to change.

 **BRAINSTORMING QUESTIONS:**
Here are some additional things to consider when picking a Person vs. Society antagonist.

1. Who represents what the society stands for?

2. Who is in the way of what the protagonist is trying to do?

3. Why does the antagonist believe in stopping the protagonist?

4. Does the antagonist sympathize with the protagonist's argument?

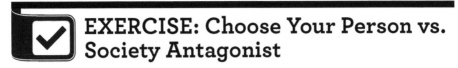

# ✔ EXERCISE: Choose Your Person vs. Society Antagonist

## >>Describe the society and how it works as the antagonist.

It's okay if you don't know every detail at this stage. Just try to get down the basic conflict that will help develop your antagonist.

*For example:*

▶ The government established a law in order to prevent a greater problem, but the people who are trying to uphold a "greater good" are sacrificing innocents to an unjust law. People have given up their rights to due process in order to punish those trying to tear apart their society. At first it worked, and allowed police to arrest criminals with far less evidence, but before long the "laws" became more and more strict and unfair. The slightest infraction can land someone in jail for decades. Society is the antagonist because the law is what caused the man's wife to be imprisoned, even though she didn't really do anything. He has to fight those who uphold the law to free her. He has to change society to get what he wants.

▶ A town rich in diamonds has made a deal with the inhabitants. They're cared for and protected as long as they send every child to the mines to work for four years. Children are eligible at age fourteen, and given a "starter kit" upon completion of their service—a place to live, a little money, and a job. The children have no say in where they go or what they'll do after. The society is the antagonist because no one wants to change things, and the law is about to send the protagonist into the mines. She doesn't want that and fights against the law to be free.

▶ A woman questions why she can't go to school like her brother in a world where women aren't allowed an education. They're given basic classes through elementary school, then sent to learn womanly trades to serve them in a marriage or household capacity. Any attempt to speak out is severely punished. Society is the antagonist because the cultural norm of not educating women has created an oppressed class who have no say over their lives. The protagonist fights this oppression by trying to change the tradition and be allowed to attend school.

## If the Antagonist is Nature

One of the hardest antagonists to write has got to be Person vs. Nature. Nature is impersonal, abstract, and unpredictable. It's the unstoppable force that the protagonist has to survive more than defeat.

That unstoppable force is key to this type of antagonist.

If the protagonist is actually going to defeat the forces of nature, there's a decent chance it's really a Person vs. Person (represented by a beast or supernatural force instead of a human) or a Person vs. Self (represented by something that brings out the worst in the protagonist). It's hard to *defeat* nature.

Person vs. Nature antagonists are often more about the character arc than the plot, because the protagonist has to survive. In that survival, she learns something critical about herself that enables her to either come through alive, or die in peace (or die realizing that her life was meaningless if that's the tale you want to tell).

Also consider the role or purpose of nature in the novel. Why a hurricane or a snowstorm? Something about this outside, unstoppable force should allow you to do what you can't achieve with any other antagonist. It's the reason you choose *this* force to stop your protagonist and not a person.

Just like a Person vs. Self or Society novel, there's a metaphoric element to what nature means. It's more than just a storm; it's there to show the protagonist something she couldn't see otherwise, or to be a symbol for a theme in the novel.

A good antagonist ups her game and makes things tougher on the protagonist, and nature is no exception to this. Look for ways to escalate the stakes and push the protagonist to her limits.

A Person vs. Nature conflict might be tough to write, but when done well, it can add a wonderful layer of theme and metaphor to a novel.

**BRAINSTORMING QUESTIONS:**
Here are some things to consider when picking a Person vs. Nature antagonist.

1. What's the purpose of nature in the novel?

2. What does nature represent?

3. How does nature get worse over the course of the novel?

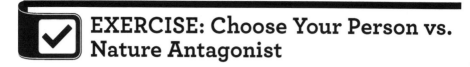

# EXERCISE: Choose Your Person vs. Nature Antagonist

## >>Describe how nature is the antagonist.

It's okay if you don't know every detail at this stage. Just try to get down the basic conflict that will help develop your antagonist.

*For example:*

▶ The blizzard is the antagonist because the protagonist has to survive it in order to get home. It creates obstacles to everything the hero tries to do, and his only recourse is to find a way to ride out the storm.

▶ The forest is the antagonist because it stands between the kids and getting home. It doesn't care if they do or not, but all their obstacles come from dealing with the forest and what lives there.

▶ The storm is the antagonist because it's keeping the fishermen from getting back to port, and it might sink them and kill them all. They have to battle it to stay afloat and make it home.

## Finding Your Character Arcs

A character arc is the internal struggle and progress a character goes through over the course of a novel that changes her in some way. It's usually connected to the internal conflict so that what she does (plot) forces changes in who she is (character arc). It can sometimes be confused with character motivations (a character worries over something so she acts to prevent that something) but *why* a character acts is different from how she changes *because* of her actions. Motivation drives the actions. Growth is the result of the actions.

Character arcs in general can take many forms. Some writers plot them out just like, well, plot, and know every step a character needs to take to reach her end state. Others let characters run and see where they go. Both are acceptable.

Most novels end with the protagonist undergoing some kind of growth, but not every protagonist needs to. Long series often keep the protagonist as is, since part of the reader's enjoyment is coming back to an old friend. But if the whole point of the book is to undergo some kind of personal change, then knowing that change will help get you there. And even in a series I still think it's a good idea to have *some* growth. Watching a character who makes the same mistakes all the time gets old fast and is hard to take seriously.

Nobody changes just for the fun of it, though. Something made this person reevaluate her behavior and realize she needed to make a change or else. She probably suffered a bit. Sometimes the suffering is minor if the change is small, like realizing she could be a bit more polite when dealing with co-workers, but for real change you need real incentives. If the protagonist is going to evolve in a major way, the events that force that change are likely to be equally major.

Character arcs often involve showing the protagonist engaging in the behavior that needs to change and having it turn out badly for her. Eventually, she'll do the right thing and be rewarded. She also doesn't do this on her own—someone or something acts as a catalyst of some type that forces the character to take a hard look at herself and her life.

Change also works both ways. Negative reinforcement might gain positive results, but bad things can also push the protagonist *away* from the change she needs to make. It's a dark moment event, where she backslides and wonders if it's all worth it. There might be some bad times ahead before that change occurs.

If she backslides, she might rebel or do something that does indeed grow her character but not the way she probably should go. She might lash out, do something just *because* she knows she shouldn't. She might do the opposite of what she knows is right to show she doesn't *have* to do things someone else's way.

It's very likely the character arc is going to connect to the novel's theme or premise in some way as well, as character growth is a great vehicle for illustrating theme.

**Secondary Characters**

Main characters aren't the only ones who can have character arcs. While they won't be as strong or as plot-driving, giving a secondary character a small arc that mirrors or thematically links to the protagonist or antagonist can be a great way to deepen a novel. It can also help develop subplots later.

 **BRAINSTORMING QUESTIONS:**
Things to think about when creating character arcs:

1. Where do you want the character to end up?

2. How much does the character need to suffer to achieve this change?

3. Who or what brings about that change?

4. How might the changes be for the worse?

5. How might the character grow in the opposite direction?

6. How does the change reflect the premise or theme?

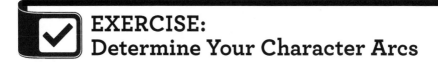

# EXERCISE:
# Determine Your Character Arcs

## >>Describe how your main characters might grow or change over the course of the novel.

Be as detailed or as vague as you need to at this stage. You might know the protagonist needs to "learn to accept her limits" but not specifically how she'll do that. The arc is coming to terms with personal limits.

Feel free to create arcs for as many characters as you wish, and write as much or as little as you need to.

*For example:*

- ▶ Lana learns to trust others (through trusting Miguel) and realizes her past doesn't define her. A mistake can be just a mistake. She's able to redeem herself for letting someone get hurt by stopping Zachary from hurting others. Zachary doesn't learn this lesson, playing the dark side of Lana's arc, a look at what she could become if she doesn't change her ways. Miguel is caught in the middle, and he discovers his own inner strengths by standing up to the others.

- ▶ Bob starts out as a hopeless and helpless mess, but as he's forced to fight to survive, he gains confidence. His constant battles for life and death make him realize that life is indeed short and he could lose so much in an instant. He has to be strong and tell Jane he loves her, and make peace with Sally and their failed marriage. Overcoming the zombies is like cutting out the rot and decay in his own life and soul.

- ▶ Adam and Hannah are both wounded by events in their past caused by the family feud. Their teacher helped both of them break out of the destructive patterns of behavior and escape the town, but now that they're back they're being sucked into it again. By accepting each other they can help end the feud, but first they have to accept themselves and stand up to the families that caused the original traumas. As they deal with individual family members, they realize the truth behind the feud and find the solution to ending it. Ending it and making peace with their families heals the wounds and allows them to move on. Their relationship is the symbol of a new beginning for them and the families, healed and able to move forward again.

# Choosing Your Point of View

Point of view (POV) is one of the strongest tools in a writer's toolbox. A novel can drastically change just by who's telling it and how those characters feel about those events. Point of view also allows you to look at a variety of opinions or views about a topic through the various characters, comparing and contrasting ideas. Point of view lets you control how information is conveyed to the reader.

Who you choose as your point-of-view character will influence how you tell your story to readers. The character with the most to lose is the protagonist, so most times the protagonist is the point-of-view character. It's her story, and she's the one telling it. If you have a novel with multiple main characters, then you might have multiple points of view, each one bringing something different to the novel. Sometimes a genre has a common point-of-view type, like multiple third person for epic fantasy or first person for cozy mysteries.

If you have a clear point-of-view preference, write in that style. Whatever you enjoy writing in will be the stronger novel. If you want that "totally there in the moment" perspective, then consider a close point of view—such as first person or a tight, limited third person (single or multiple). First person is great if you want zero narrative distance (the distance between the narrator and the reader); third person limited is great if you want a small step between the reader and character. If you want more separation, a medium or far narrative distance might be a good choice (more on narrative distance next section). Maybe being an observer suits the type of tale you're telling, and being too close in the point-of-view character's head will feel overwhelming. An omniscient narrator can be a great choice if you want an outside narrator who knows all the details and can convey information that can't be known otherwise.

Don't write a point-of-view style just because that's how the genre usually does it, but if it makes no difference to you, and most books in that genre are written in a particular pointof-view style, it could be a good choice to use. Readers are used to it, you know it works and sells, and you'll have tons of examples to study.

Different points of view have different benefits and disadvantages. Choosing a point of view that lends itself to the type of novel you're writing can allow you to do things another point of view can't.

Personal stories often do well with a tight point of view so readers really understand the nuances of that personal struggle. Epic tales that tell a bigger picture story often use multiple people to show all sides. If the novel is about a person and her journey, close and single points of view (third or first) can be a great choice, because they allow you to get into the head of that character and focus on the problem. A novel about a situation, be it a quest, a war, or a terrorist attack, might be better told through the eyes of characters who can see all sides of it.

Even if the tale is personal, you might choose to look at the bigger picture to convey a theme or ideal, or a massive situation might be seen from the eyes of one single character. Think about what aspect of the story you want to focus on. Big tales don't *have* to be told by a big cast, same as personal tales can involve more than one person.

Multiple points of view can work well when each point-of-view character brings something unique to the story—a fresh perspective, goals, a subplot that connects to a larger theme that encompasses the entire novel. However, if the *only* reason a point-of-view character is there is because you can't show that part of the story any other way, then you might want to reconsider using it. If there's no goal driving that character, she'll feel flat and her sections will feel pointless—or the reader will sense that she's just there to explain exposition or backstory.

## Types of Point of View

Along with choosing a point-of-view character, you also need to pick a point-of-view style. Let's do a quick review of the most common fiction points of view: first person, third person limited, and third person omniscient.

### First Person

First person is the "I" point of view. It's told from one person's perspective, and it's the closest of the points of view. First person only shows what that one person can see, feel, think, know, etc. It gives a sense of closeness and immediacy to a novel, because readers are right there inside the head of the point of view character. Tense also plays a role, and you often seen past tense as well as present tense in first person.

**First Person Past Tense:** Readers are inside the narrator's head seeing and experiencing what she did. It has a sense of things happening in the now, and the narrator has no prior knowledge of the events.

*For example:*

▶ I hid behind the tree, holding back a giggle. Chuck and his new dog were almost to the skunk's den. Three more steps and that boy would *so* get what he deserved for embarrassing me in front of the whole class.

**Retrospective First Person:** Readers are inside the narrator's head experiencing what she has experienced, but the narrator is reflecting on something that's already happened. She has prior knowledge of the events.

*For example:*

▶ If I'd known how hard it was to wash skunk off a golden retriever, I'd never have played that prank on Chuck and his new dog.

**First Person Present Tense:** Present tense shows events happening as the novel unfolds. Present tense is almost a running commentary, and the narrator has no prior knowledge of the events.

*For example:*

▶ I hide behind the tree, holding back giggles. Chuck and his new dog are almost to the skunk's den. Three more steps and he'll *so* get what he deserves for embarrassing me in front of the whole class.

**Pitfalls of First Person:** Probably the most common pitfall in first person is describing everything the narrator is doing, with "I did this, I did that" type phrases. We end up telling the story instead of showing it. There's also very little internalization, which is odd since first person is all about the internal view. This happens even more frequently in first person present tense, since events are happening as the novel unfolds.

*For example:*

▶ I ran down to the forest to set up the trap for Chuck. I was so mad at him for embarrassing me in class the other day, and I was determined to make him pay.

Words like *to* and *for* in this example are telling the motive of the narrator. She's heading to the forest to set a trap, but we don't actually see her running there or setting the trap. It's an explanation of what she plans to do, not what she does. Same with *for*. It's explaining why she's mad, not showing her being mad. A more solid point of view would be something like...

*For example:*

▶ I jumped over the log at the edge of the forest, the bag of payback tight under my arm. Chuck wouldn't know what hit him. He deserved it, though, after what he'd done. Did he really think he could embarrass me like that and get away with it? He was *so* gonna pay.

## Third Person

Third person is the "he/she" point of view and can either be very close in the narrator's head or very detached, depending on the narrative distance. Like first person, it can use either past or present tense, though past tense is the standard and what readers are used to.

The two types of third person are limited and omniscient.

**Third Person Limited:** Readers are inside the narrator's head and see only what she can see, feel, know (like first person with different pronouns). They can see what she sees, and get to hear what she's thinking.

*For example:*

▶ Maria jumped over the log at the edge of the forest, the bag of payback tight under her arm. Chuck wouldn't know what hit him. He deserved it, though, after what he'd done. Did he really think he could embarrass her like that and get away with it? He was *so* gonna pay. (A close narrative distance).

▶ Maria jumped over the log at the edge of the forest, the bag of payback tight under her arm. *Chuck won't know what hit him*, she thought. He deserved it, though, after what he did. Did he really think he could embarrass her like that and get away with it? He was *so* gonna pay. (A medium narrative distance).

**Third Person Omniscient:** An outside narrator sees and knows all and can describe things the characters aren't aware of. Readers can either be in one character's perspective, or jump from head to head and cover everyone.

*For example:*

▶ Maria hurdled the log at the edge of the forest, her lean legs carrying her over the terrain with the easy grace of a three-time district champion. But competition wasn't on the to-do list today. Her mind churned with thoughts of revenge, as would any girl who'd been wronged as she had been. Maria clutched the bag of payback tight under her arm. *Chuck won't know what hit him*, she thought. *He deserves it, though. Embarrassing me in front of the whole class like that.* She'd make him pay, and pay big. She picked up speed, her anger pushing her harder through the brush.

**What makes this omniscient and not limited:** There are things here that Maria wouldn't know or wouldn't think about the same way, such as how she looks jumping over a log. Readers also get a sense that someone else is telling Maria's story, and interjecting his or her own judgment and opinions into this. "The easy grace of a three-time district champion" is how an *outsider* would describe Maria, not something she'd think about herself. Same with "but competition wasn't on the to-do list today. Her mind churned with thoughts of revenge, as would any girl who'd been wronged as she had been." This is what someone besides Maria is thinking. An omniscient narrator can be very subtle, such as "She picked up speed, her anger pushing her harder through the brush." Would Maria really be aware of what was making her run harder or would she just run? If we're in her point of view, she'll just run and experience the sensations of running hard.

**Pitfalls of Third Person:** The most common third person pitfall is showing what the point-of-view character wouldn't know. It's a halfway point between omniscient and limited, and it feels okay because we're describing the scene, but instead of staying in the point-of-view character's head in the scene, we're in this weird state where readers aren't sure who the narrator is.

*For example:*

▶ Maria jumped over the log at the edge of the forest, her lean legs carrying her easily over the terrain. Chipmunks scurried away as she landed, their tiny squeaks alerting a hunting rat snake that lunch was nearby. Maria clutched the bag of payback tight under her arm. *Chuck won't know what hit him,* she thought. He deserved it, though, after what he'd done. Embarrassing her like that in front of the whole class. She'd make him pay, her anger pushing her well past her usual common sense.

Who is describing Maria's legs as lean—Maria or someone else? Same with the chipmunks and the snake. Maria won't know what's going on in the forest as she runs through it, or know what's going through the head of a nearby snake (That's something only an omniscient narrator would know.) The last line is something she probably wouldn't be self-aware enough to notice. If she realized her anger was affecting her, she might stop and think about it.

The same lines can also spell trouble in omniscient, because there's no solid sense of someone else telling this story. It's distant like omniscient, but the judgment is gone. Why mention the chipmunks and the snake? How do they affect the story? There are omniscient details, but because there's nothing motivating the details, they feel flat or unnecessary. It's not bad writing, but it does lack the soul of a good story.

## Multiple Point of View

All of these points of view can be used either singularly, or in multiples. Typically, a novel changes scenes or chapters whenever it changes the point of view so readers have no confusion over whose scene it is. It's also a good idea to make it clear in the first paragraph (or line) of that new scene whose head readers are in to ground them so they don't feel lost.

## Pitfalls of Multiple Point of View

**Too Many, Too Fast:** It's hard for readers to keep track of a lot of points of view, so be wary of how often the perspectives change and how many heads readers are in.

**Unnecessary Heads:** Sometimes a point-of-view scene is added because the protagonist can't know certain information and we want to convey it to readers. But throwing in someone out of the blue or switching to a character who doesn't have a storyline can be confusing.

Picking the right point of view for your novel can aid you in both planning and writing it, because you'll have characters to see the story through. You'll know who is telling the tale, and how their views will color the novel as a whole. A solid point of view will also help you figure out what matters to the novel and what doesn't.

 **BRAINSTORMING QUESTIONS:**
Determine which point of view would work best for your novel.

1. Which point-of-view style do you prefer?

2. How close do you want the reader to get to the characters?

3. What's common for the genre?

4. Is this a personal story or an epic tale?

5. What scope do *you* want to show? An epic tale, a personal struggle, or somewhere in between?

6. Who has the freedom to act?

7. Multiple or single point of view?

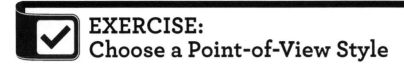

# EXERCISE:
## Choose a Point-of-View Style

### >>Write down which point-of-view style appeals to you and why.

Sometimes a novel demands to be written in a style you don't normally write, so don't worry if your favorite or natural style isn't right for a certain idea. You can decide if you want to try something new, or find a way to make the idea better fit the point-of-view style you want to write in.

*For example:*

▶ Third person omniscient, because it allows seeing inside the heads of all three teens and will enable the book to show things the characters might not know

▶ First person, because it's Bob's story and he doesn't know what's going on, so seeing things from his perspective will make it feel more personal and scary

▶ Third person limited, because it allows the reader to be inside the heads of the two major characters

## Narrative Distance

Narrative distance is another tool to help determine which point of view to use. Do you want readers to feel in the character's head and in the moment, or more like an observer? There is no wrong answer here. Just like in choosing point of view, personal preference goes a long way to deciding which narrative distance to use. If your strengths fall with a certain point of view, then use it. Don't do first person because "everyone says first-person young adult novels sell better." Great novels sell better, and if writing in first person makes you feel stifled and causes you to tell everything, then you won't write a great novel.

Narrative distance is how far from the point-of-view character readers feel while reading the novel. The more distance we put between readers and narrator, the more detached they'll feel from the character. "Distance" is how close inside the head of the character readers feel. A close narrative distance feels like readers *are* the character (such as a first-person narrator) while a far narrative distance feels like readers are standing on the side having the events told to them (such as an omniscient third-person narrator). Certain words (filter words) can affect how close or far the narrative distance feels.

## Filter Words

No matter who your narrator is, this is the person readers see the novel through. Whether it's a tight first person or an omniscient third, everything is filtered through that person's eyes. Sometimes this filter is invisible and readers don't feel any distance between them and the point-of-view character. Other times the filters are obvious and readers feel the wall between them and the characters. One style looks *through* the eyes of the point-of-view character, the other looks *at* the point-of-view character.

Filter words can also remind readers they're reading, explain things that are obvious, and lead a writer into telling or crafting passive sentences. Filter words include: saw, heard, felt, knew, watched, decided, noticed, realized, wondered, thought, and looked.

A point-of-view character by definition is relaying everything she sees, hears, feels, touches, smells, and thinks. If it's described, readers know she experienced it in some way.

*For example (with filter words):*

▶ Bob saw three zombies shambling toward him.

▶ Jane heard a scream from the hotel bathroom.

▶ Sally knew she had to get out of there.

▶ I felt the cold metal of the shotgun against my back.

Look at these same sentences without those filter words:

▶ Three zombies shambled toward Bob.

▶ A scream echoed from the hotel bathroom.

▶ She had to get out of there.

▶ Cold metal pressed against my back.

Some filter words are a little more ambiguous. Words like wondered, realized, decided, and noticed.

▶ Bob realized he'd have to make a run for it.

▶ Jane wondered if they'd make it out of there alive.

▶ Sally decided they'd just have to jump and see what happened.

▶ I noticed the shotgun was missing.

In most cases, eliminating the filter words makes it feel more inside the point-of-view character's head.

▶ He'd have to make a run for it.

▶ Would they'd make it out of there alive?

▶ They'd just have to jump and see what happened.

▶ Oh crap, where's the shotgun?

However, sometimes you want that filter word if it's important to draw attention to that act (the feeling, hearing, watching), or it just sounds more dramatic with that filter, such as a chapter or scene enders. You might also want more filters if you're doing a far narrative distance or a omniscient narrator.

► Bob watched the perimeter, eyes and ears alert for zombies.

► Jane closed her eyes and wondered if any of them would survive til dawn.

Filter words can help determine the narrative distance, but narrative distance is more of a sliding scale than predetermined levels. You can use filter words and still feel close to the point-of-view character, same as you can be in first person and still feel detached and far away. Narrative distance is achieved by how information is conveyed to the reader from the narrative.

Here are some general guidelines:

### Far Narrative Distance

► Bob frowned and decided he just didn't have time to wash the car.

This has a far narrative distance. We can tell by the word "decided" because that's the author telling readers what Bob is doing. We don't see Bob make that decision. Far distances put readers in the observation seat, often getting information the point-of-view character doesn't know from an unknown narrator.

**Benefits of a Far Narrative Distance:** A far narrative distance can provide a larger view of the story and allow you to share information the point-of-view character might not know. It can also add a sense of retrospection and a feeling that the events have already occurred and are being related after the fact.

**Pitfalls of a Far Narrative Distance:** A far narrative distance runs the risk of sounding flat, having more told sections and less showing. The farther away you get from the character's head, the easier it is to make her do what *you* want, not what *she* wants, because the narrator often becomes the author at that point. The author knows all, and starts telling readers everything so they can keep up.

### Medium Narrative Distance

► Bob glanced at his watch and frowned. *No time to wash the car,* he thought.

This is a medium narrative distance. We can tell by the "he thought," which is the author telling readers what Bob is thinking. Readers can observe Bob glancing and frowning, but they need the author to tell them what's in Bob's head. Medium distances use phrases that remind readers they're reading a story. We're told what Bob thought, what he realized, etc. We can "see" the action, but the mental aspects have to be pointed out because we're not fully in the head of that character. We're told the thoughts only when the author feels we should know them.

**Benefits of a Medium Narrative Distance:** A medium narrative distance can be the middle ground for those who want a small step between reader and character. It can be useful for multiple-point-of-view novels where characters could get confused without a little extra information about who is thinking or saying what.

**Pitfalls of a Medium Narrative Distance:** A medium narrative distance can easily slip into telling, because some of it is told and there are more filter words used. Sometimes it can feel like a wall is between reader and character, and readers never *quite* get to know the protagonist. The occasional filter word can also jump out and pull readers from the novel, reminding them that they're reading when that reminder wasn't necessary.

## Close Narrative Distance

▶ Bob glanced at his watch and frowned. No time to wash the car.

This is a close narrative distance. We can tell because there are no explanations from the author to tell us what Bob is doing. Readers can observe his actions and "hear" his thoughts just as Bob does and thinks them. Close distances let readers see, hear, and think everything as the point-of-view character does. If things aren't how the point-of-view character thinks they are, readers have to figure that out on their own.

**Benefits of a Close Narrative Distance:** A close narrative distance can put readers inside the head of the point-of-view character and immerse them in the story. It can create a more emotional connection to the characters.

**Pitfalls of a Close Narrative Distance:** First person or a tight third can sometimes make you feel that you have to explain *everything*, and you can get an "I did this, I felt that" thing going. So instead of having a tight point of view, you have a narrator who's not actually *in* the novel, just observing it and relaying it to readers. These types of characters can often be yanked from the novel and the events won't change all that much. A bad thing, especially if the point of view happens to be first person.

# EXERCISE:
## Determine Your Narrative Distance

## >>Write down which narrative distance appeals to you and why.

Knowing how close or how far away you want to feel can help you decide which point-of-view style would best suit your novel.

*For example:*

- ▶ Far narrative distance, because the observer feeling will add to the mystery and suspense of what's really going on

- ▶ Close narrative distance, because being inside Bob's head and having limited information will add to the personal nature and help raise the tension and stakes

- ▶ Close narrative distance, because being inside the heads of the romantic leads will let the reader see why these two belong together

## Choosing Your Point-of-View Characters

Odds are, the point-of-view character is going to be the protagonist, which makes choosing a point-of-view character fairly easy. If there's no doubt about who your point-of-view character is, feel free to skip this exercise. If the point-of-view character isn't obvious, continue on.

Not every novel is told from a single point of view. In mysteries or thrillers, it's common for readers to see both sides of a tale with the protagonist and antagonist. Romances are often told from both the male and female leads. More epic tales--such as fantasy, science fiction, and historical fiction-- might use several characters to show various parts of the story.

### Things to Consider When Choosing a Point-of-View Character

**Is more than one point-of-view character needed?** Giving a character a point of view is asking readers to invest time in her, so this character should be worthy of that. Seeing the story from her perspective should bring something valuable to the novel. If the only reason a character is a point-of-view character is because parts of the book can't be told any other way, or because the protagonist wouldn't be able to be there, that's a red flag that the character is only there to dump information.

**What do multiple points of view allow you to accomplish?** Look at the specific benefits each possible character brings to the story. How might seeing this other perspective enhance the plot? Deepen the theme? Illustrate some aspect of the world?

**If you don't see that character's point of view, what is lost?** Sometimes it's easier to identify what points of view are needed by what disappears if the story *isn't* told from that perspective.

**Does every potential point-of-view character have her own plot or story goal?** If there are too many plots unfolding at once, the novel can feel disjointed and have too many things going on. Each plotline should connect to the core conflict in some way and work with the other plots and subplots to tell a complete story.

**How do the points of view work together to tell a larger story?** Think about how these different perspectives work to advance the overall story. Does every character have moments that raise the stakes? Do they create conflict for the other points of view?

 **BRAINSTORMING QUESTIONS:**
Answer the following questions with each of your potential point-of-view characters in mind.

1. If you don't see that character's point of view, what is lost?

2. Does every potential point-of-view character have her own plot or story goal?

3. How do the points of view work together to tell a larger story?

4. Which characters have the most to gain or lose?

5. Is more than one of these points of view needed?

6. If so, what do the multiple points of view allow you to accomplish?

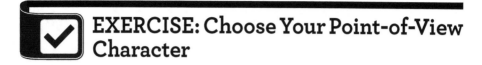

# EXERCISE: Choose Your Point-of-View Character

## >>Write down your point-of-view character(s) and explain why they make the best point of view for the novel.

Don't forget to consider what the point-of-view character brings to the story. If the character is important enough to have part of the novel in her perspective, then she'll directly affect plot and not be there solely to convey information to readers.

*For example:*

- ▶ Lana, Miguel, and Zachary. The story is about these three and what secrets they're keeping, so seeing what's in their heads will help create mystery.

- ▶ Bob, because it's his story and seeing the plot unfold through his eyes will allow the reader to connect with him and want to see him win.

- ▶ Adam and Hannah, because they're the love interests and readers need to get to know them and see who they are from their perspectives in order to want to see them live happily ever after together.

## Writing From the Antagonist's Point of View

Writing from the antagonist's perspective can be a tricky point of view to do, because often the tension in a novel is created by readers wondering what's going to happen next and what bad things are going to occur. Being inside the head of the antagonist can steal some of that tension because the mystery is all gone. Readers know what's going to happen because the antagonist told them.

The challenge is finding ways to keep the wonder and mystery alive even though readers know both sides. To reveal information that will change the outcome, but in a way that readers can't predict—or hint at things that have been building in the background, but readers haven't yet picked up on--that will shock them and they'll smack themselves for not seeing it coming.

**If the antagonist will be a point-of-view character, then develop her as fully as the protagonist.** She'll have goals and motives driving her. She'll be in it for reasons that frequently have nothing to do with the protagonist—the protagonist just happens to be in the wrong place at the wrong time—or if it *is* personal and directed, then crafting a solid antagonist becomes even more important.

**Make the antagonist the hero of her own story.** Few people actually consider themselves evil or bad, so even if there's a bit of conscience bugging her, she'll rationalize it same as the protagonist would. To *her*, the protagonist is the one getting in the way and messing things up. The protagonist is *her* villain.

**Let the narrative and internalization reflect this attitude while in the antagonist's point of view.** It's easy to let our views on the antagonist color her scenes, because *she's the villain*, but this will have the opposite effect of what we want to accomplish by being in her head. We might accidentally treat her as being evil, maybe put the protagonist's attitude on her even though she'd never think of herself or her actions in that way.

When point-of-view antagonists become real people with real problems, readers are much more likely to find them fascinating. And there's a bonus: Since both sides (protagonist and antagonist) are fully developed characters, we usually craft better plots because both are being driven by real motives.

**BRAINSTORMING QUESTIONS:**
Explore why you might show your novel from the antagonist's perspective.

1. What does the antagonist bring to the plot that can't be seen otherwise?

2. Does the antagonist have a story arc or is she just there to tell the reader information?

3. Will the plot be spoiled if the reader sees what the antagonist is doing?

4. Can tensions be raised if readers see the antagonist in action?

5. How much of the book would appear in the antagonist's point of view?

6. Are you considering this point of view to make it easier or because it would make the book better?

# EXERCISE: Determine if You Want to Use the Antagonist's Point of View

>>Decide if the antagonist's point of view is needed or not.

>>If yes, describe why the antagonist's point of view is needed and how it will benefit the novel.

*For example:*

▶ Yes. Knowing what's going on in Zachary's head will help create mystery because he'll know things the others don't, and they'll be making assumptions and decisions based on wrong information. Readers will see things are not what Lana and Miguel think, but not know the whole story because Zachary has things he won't admit even to himself.

▶ No, because seeing that Sally actually does care for Bob and is trying to do what she thinks is best for him will reveal that too early and make Bob's struggles less meaningful. Sally also doesn't have a different enough plot arc to sustain her own point of view and make it feel different from Bob's.

▶ No, because the antagonist role is played by multiple family members and none of them have their own storyline to warrant a point of view.

# Finding Your Theme

We often think of theme as this big literary thing lurking at the edges of our work—the stuff of English classes and literary novels, not something that applies to commercial fiction. But theme is really just the underlying element that connects all the pieces of a novel together. Like romance is about love, horror is about fear, mysteries are about justice.

Theme is the soul of the novel.

Theme deepens the story and makes it resonate with readers. A great book is *about* something, and that's never just the plot mechanics.

**Why theme is important:** Themes are universal, which helps readers connect to the novel on an intimate or profound level. Readers might not even consciously pick up on it, but by the end of the novel, they'll feel like the book was about more than just the plot. From a technical standpoint, theme is another way of adding structure to our writing so when we have to decide between the protagonist doing A or B, we can see which one illustrates the theme better. That can connect to previous scenes, and lay the groundwork for future scenes. When we describe settings, details, or actions, we can consider words and imagery that reflect the theme in some way. While we don't have to connect *everything* to the theme, it can be a useful tool in weeding out what's unnecessary and what's worth keeping.

**For pantsers:** If you're the type of writer who doesn't want to know how a novel will turn out before you start writing it, theme might be the guiding light you'll love—a structure without outlines, and a guide that lets you be as spontaneous as you want.

Take a look at some of your favorite novels—especially the best sellers. These are the types of novels often criticized for not being "literary" enough, despite the millions of readers who love them. And a book millions of readers love is doing *something* right, even if it's not your type of book.

*Jurassic Park* is just a novel about dinosaurs that get loose and eat people, right? But look closer and you'll see the themes all throughout the novel: Should humans play God with science? Are there lines we shouldn't cross just because we can? Should the past remain in the past? Serious, meaty topics explored using something most people loved as a child—dinosaurs. The plot makes the themes accessible.

*Twilight* has been criticized as strongly as it's been praised, and one of its themes is something our parents have told us since we were little: everyone is special. This universal theme is so relatable it helped millions of readers fall in love with the book. Mix in the other strong themes of love conquers all and forbidden love, and it's no wonder it was a success. These are themes everyone understands. Who doesn't want to feel special and believe that love will find them and lead to an extraordinary life? This is the power of theme.

If you're unsure what the theme of your novel is, try thinking about what the novel is about on a larger, emotional scale. Not the details of the plot, or the character with the problem, but the general emotion the plot will help illustrate. Determine what *about* that concept (love, fear, etc.) is being explored. That's probably the theme.

⚠ **SOMETHING TO THINK ABOUT:** *If you had to pick three words to describe the emotions of your novel, what would they be? What would it be if you had to pick just one word?*

Crazy as it sounds, theme can often be found by looking at the adages we stitch on pillows or the clichés we put on posters. Love conquers all, pride goes before the fall, don't count your chickens before they hatch. These can all be themes that tie the novel together. Love gets the protagonist through difficult times, a proud protagonist fails until she learns humility, a dreamer must learn to plan for her future instead of assuming everything will work out as she hopes without effort on her part.

How often have you seen, "There's no place like home" stitched or stamped on something hanging on a wall or sitting on a shelf? It's a classic theme and you can't hear it without thinking about Dorothy and *The Wizard of Oz*. The theme is so ingrained in that story it's become its own cliché.

A catch phrase can also help show theme, as in the movie *Galaxy Quest*. "Never give up, never surrender," is portrayed as a cheesy line in the movie, yet it's exactly what the protagonist lives by. No matter how bad (or how strange) things get, he refuses to give up or surrender, knowing he can count on his friends to help him get through it.

⚠ **SOMETHING TO THINK ABOUT:** *What cliché or adage best describes your novel? What might your protagonist's favorite saying or catch phrase be?*

We can also look at characters to see if a theme is developing there. It's not uncommon to find every character in the book sharing a thematic problem, or similar problems recurring throughout the novel.

In my own fantasy novel, *The Shifter*, every character is trapped in some way. Some characters are trapped financially, others emotionally, and some literally through imprisonment. Finding a way to free yourself from what traps you (the desire for freedom) is one of the themes of the novel, and it's a driving force behind the plot and character arcs.

⚠ **SOMETHING TO THINK ABOUT:** *What are the flaws and dreams of your characters? Is the world a metaphor or symbol of a larger idea? Are there recurring actions or problems that point to a larger concept?*

Take a look at your brewing novel and see if there are any recurring ideas. These could be possible themes to explore.

*For example:*

- ▶ If everyone in the story is hiding who they really are, then identity or knowing yourself could be a theme.
- ▶ If everyone is being held back or oppressed, standing up for what's right could tie the novel together thematically.
- ▶ If the world is representing an idea, like power corrupts, then the theme might be how people handle power.

## Multiple Themes

Novels can have more than one theme, and often do. You might have a story theme that supports the character arcs (such as "love conquers all" for a romance), a personal theme for a character (such as "never give up, never surrender," to show her determination and even stubbornness that must be overcome), and a general theme for the entire novel (such as "love is about compromise," to show that the stubborn heroine can learn to compromise and find that love can indeed conquer all). Multiple themes that support each other and a larger concept can work quite well together.

Be wary of themes that contradict each other or pull the story in different directions, however. A "love conquers all" theme mixed with a theme of "trust no one but yourself" is likely to create a novel at odds with itself. You don't want to send mixed messages to the reader and weaken your novel.

---

 **BRAINSTORMING QUESTIONS:**
Explore possible themes for your novel.

1. What larger concepts do you want to explore with your novel?

2. If you had to pick one cliché or adage to describe your novel, what would it be? How might you adapt that as your theme?

3. What are common problems in the novel? Do they point to a theme?

4. What are common character flaws or dreams?

---

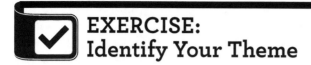

# EXERCISE:
## Identify Your Theme

### >>State your theme.

Write down the theme of your novel. If there are any character themes, write those down as well. Be as specific or as vague as you need to at this stage. If you have only a general idea so far, that's okay. You can always refine it later.

*For example:*

▶ **Novel theme:** Secrets can ruin lives. **Story theme:** Things are never what they seem. Character theme: The truth can set you free.

▶ Courage through adversity, standing up for yourself to get what you want

▶ Love shall prevail

# Choosing Your Setting

Where a novel takes place is just as important as who's in it, because the setting can help determine what inherent problems (conflicts) the characters will face. Challenges in Manhattan are different from those in Montana, and neither come close to the challenges of living on a small moon off Jupiter. So even if we're writing about a gal from Ipanema, setting plays a big role.

A novel about isolation might work best in the middle of nowhere, or it might play off contrasts and be set it in the biggest city in the world. A novel about a character with a troubled past could work well somewhere where that past can do the most damage if revealed, or a location that also has a troubled past to layer the theme and character arcs and tie it all together.

**Why the setting is important:** Setting not only gives readers a world to lose themselves in, it allows us to craft elements that can enhance the novel. Where something occurs can strengthen mood or atmosphere and trigger the emotions we want readers to feel.

A great example of how setting can influence a story is the movie *District 9*. An alien ship is space-wrecked on Earth and the crew has spent the last twenty years living in a controlled area called District 9. As any oppressed people do, the aliens begin to rebel and cause problems.

The alien ship could have settled over any city on Earth, but the screenwriters made the inspired choice of Johannesburg, South Africa. Since South Africa has a history with racial strife and apartheid, attitudes toward the aliens were strongly affected by that past.

In this case, it wasn't an issue of race, but of species. The events depicted in the film would not have happened the same way had this been set in, say, Los Angeles, Tucson, or London. What happened in the movie fits very well with the history of the setting, and the setting brought a cultural history to the problem that made it very believable for plot events to have unfolded as they did.

Where someone lives influences how she thinks and how she'll act. Setting is an invaluable tool in creating characters and character arcs.

Think about the places *you* love. If you set your novel in a favorite location, that passion will spill over into your novel's setting. A favorite city could be the perfect place for your characters to live. If there's no specific place, you might look at someplace general like the beach or the mountains. Even somewhere as specific as a carnival midway could work if that's what you truly love.

Maybe it's not a favorite location, but a mood or tone that inspires you. If you want a dark and creepy novel, odds are you won't set it on a bright and sunny beach (or maybe you will, because you want the contrast). The atmosphere of a place bleeds into the novel and will either enhance the mood, or give all the wrong signals if it's conflicting with what you envision.

What's common for the genre also can play a role. If most novels in your genre are set in small towns, that's a pretty good indication that readers expect and look forward to this setting. But that doesn't mean you *have* to go with the norm. Maybe a compromise with a slight twist to what's common for the genre is more appealing.

Themes can influence the setting as well. If your novel is about the effects of war, setting it in the middle of a war gives you a lot to work with. If the theme is love, setting it in the most romantic city in the world might be a great idea. You might even want to flip it and use the setting to show what's lacking in that conflict or theme, by having a love story set in a land of war and hatred.

Also consider the scope of your setting and how it relates to your novel. Maybe you want a small town, or just a small room. You might want a novel that spreads across continents or galaxies. Big cities offer things rural towns don't and vice versa. Even if your setting is your own creation, you have options on how metropolitan it will be.

A setting feels differently to someone who's lived there her whole life versus a newcomer. You might want the protagonist and the reader to feel like a newcomer, or you might choose to set the novel in your hometown. Familiarity could bring unexpected details, while a new locale could capture your attention as well as your reader's.

Wherever you set your novel, try to pick a place that will enhance the story and add depth to your characters and theme. The more real a setting feels, the more immersive it can be for the reader.

**BRAINSTORMING QUESTIONS:**
Here are some things to consider when choosing a setting.

1.  Where are *your* favorite places? List five locations you love.

2.  What mood or atmosphere do you want the novel to have? Write down the dominant mood of your novel.

3.  What settings are common to your genre? List five favorite settings common to your genre.

4.  What location would enhance the novel's conflict and/or theme? List five locations that enhance your novel's conflict. Do the same for the theme. Are any of them the same location?

5.  Do you want a real or fictional location? Write down which type of location you prefer.

6.  Is it a small or large scale location? Write down the scale of your setting.

7.  Do you want an urban or rural area? Write down which type of area you prefer.

8.  Does the protagonist know this place or is she new to it? Write down how well the protagonist knows your setting.

9.  Do you want a setting you're familiar with or something you'd need to research? List five familiar settings you think might work for your novel. List five more that you've always wanted to visit.

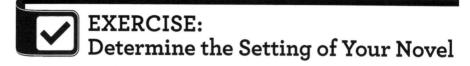

# EXERCISE:
## Determine the Setting of Your Novel

## >>Describe your setting.

If you have more than one, describe all the important locations you might need. Don't worry if you're not sure, as more locations will no doubt occur as the novel unfolds. Focus on the general sense of the place or world as well. As a fun extra, try to explain why you chose this setting and what you feel it can add to the novel.

*For example:*

▶ Modern day, a rundown roadside diner just off a highway. It's dark, spooky and a little foreboding to set the tone of the darkness of secrets and the danger ahead for the characters. School, in the areas where outcasts and the unpopular kids hang out. The scene of the original accident. Settings will all be "secretive" in some way to reinforce the theme of secrets. As the secrets slowly come out and become less important, the locations will become more and more public (the truth revealed). **Why I chose these settings:** These are all places where people hide things or hide the truth, which helps reinforce the theme of secrets.

▶ Cleveland, OH, not far from the Rock & Roll Hall of Fame, a favorite spot for Bob, who goes there to dream and escape his life. Locations change as the characters head south to a rural town rumored to be well fortified against the zombies. The government lab where the cure can be found. An abandoned mall with zombies that look like mannequins at first and surprise them. Settings start out normal, then turn disastrous as the zombies take over and hope fades. But as Bob gains confidence, he starts seeing things in more hopeful and defensible ways. **Why I chose these settings:** These are places that show Bob's desire to be more than he is, and places where he's less than he wants to be (like home and on the road where he fails and is saved by his wife). They're also places to explore the horror factor and create cool situations with the zombies.

▶ Henderson, a small town with a southern feel like something out of an old movie. On the surface it looks picture perfect, but underneath you see the signs of age and decay, or someone trying too hard to keep a smile on a sad face. It's the end of summer, just before autumn and leaves are beginning to fall. Details start out in decline, symbolizing the slow fade and growing despair of the characters, then brightens as their relationship grows. Small details in the background like fresh flowers or babies, signaling new life and starting over. **Why I chose these settings:** Small towns are typically thought of as peaceful and friendly, so a town at war keeping two people apart contradicts the reader's expectations. It's also small enough to be plausibly changed by the actions of two people.

# ASSIGNMENT FOUR: Flesh Out Your Characters, Theme, and Setting

>>**Summarize the characters in your novel, focusing on their character arcs and how they grow over the course of the novel. Also summarize how theme affects their character arcs and how the setting influences their views.**

This assignment is designed to get you thinking about the connections among your characters, theme, and setting. You've developed them individually, but summarizing them as they relate to each other helps to establish and clarify how they work together. In some summaries, you might include the conflicts and plot aspects of the novel if they directly affect these elements, while others might focus solely on the character arc and emotional growth side.

Feel free to do this exercise with as many or as few characters as you'd like. You might find just doing the protagonist is enough, or you might want to do each major character. If you're not sure, consider which characters will have character arcs and use those, or use the character with the most story-driving arc. You can even combine characters if their arcs are closely linked to the novel.

Try this if you're still stuck on what to write:

1. List three critical details about the character—one that shows who she is, one that shows how she illustrates the theme, and one that shows how she illustrates the setting.

2. List the kind of person the character is at the start of the novel and at the end of the novel. Add a general description of how she gets from one to the other.

3. Create one to three sentences that contain all three traits and one to three sentences that summarize that journey, and then craft one connected paragraph that covers everything. Flesh out this paragraph with any additional details you'd like to add.

*For example:*

▶ **Details:** She's guilt-ridden over a mistake. She wasn't watching her brother and he got hurt, and no one knows she actually caused the accident. She hides her guilt by trying to look like a normal girl to fit in with her normal school and town. **Arc:** She starts off guilt-ridden and withdrawn and ends up redeemed and forgiven. She gets there by having her secret forced out of her, facing her past, and taking responsibility for her actions.

**Summary:** Lana is a girl who made a terrible mistake that caused her brother to wind up in a wheelchair. She struggles to look like a normal, carefree girl to fit into her normal school and town, but her guilt is tearing her apart and she knows someone will find out what she did and ruin her. When someone threatens to expose her secret, she's forced to face her past and come to terms with what really happened. She discovers the truth of her brother's accident and that she wasn't the one at fault, and that she has nothing to hide after all.

▶ Bob is a man in an unhappy marriage who dreams of bigger and better things. He spends his days at the Rock & Roll Museum, fantasizing that he's a rock star who overcame great personal challenges to succeed and now everyone looks up to him, then goes home and is belittled and looked down upon. He wishes he could tell his wife he wants a divorce so he can be with the woman he's fallen in love with, but he's too scared to stand up to her. His wish is answered when zombies crash through the front window and an apocalypse forces him to become the "rock star" he always wanted to be. In order to win the love of his life and survive being eaten, he'll have to find the strength of his heroes and stand up for himself once and for all.

▶ Adam and Hannah were both encouraged by the same teacher to take risks, live life, and see the world—a contradictory view for everyone else in the small town of Henderson. Adam took the advice to heart, leaving home and living life to the fullest, yet that life is empty and he finds himself with no friends or family to support his "full steam ahead" lifestyle. Hannah made it as far as leaving home, but has never been able to gather enough courage to take risks or live life as her teacher encouraged them to do. She feels that something is missing, but doesn't want to risk her almost-happy life for a chance at something better. When the teacher dies, both Adam and Hannah are forced to face a broken promise—that they never visited to tell their adventurous tales to their teacher. They each decide to return home and share what they've done, even if those stories are told over a grave. Being home again makes them both realize that they never truly lived the way their teacher encouraged, and they find themselves reminiscing about her. Hannah is encouraged by Adam's risk-taking nature to do and say things she'd only dreamed about, while her joy in the smallest aspects of life make him realize how much of life he's been missing. Their families, however, have other ideas, and they do everything in their power to keep Adam and Hannah apart, home, and safe from all risks. But if they listen to their hearts, Adam and Hannah they can fulfill their individual promises to live life, take risks, and see the world together.

In Workshop Five, we'll look at developing your plot by determining goals, conflicts, and stakes, as well as a look at basic story structure.

# Workshop Five: Developing Your Plot

**What You Need to Start This Workshop:** An idea for a novel.

**The Goal of This Workshop:** To identify and develop the goals, conflicts, and stakes of your story so you can develop a plot from them.

**What We'll Discuss in This Workshop:** How to: create goals and decide how they affect your novel; determine the core conflict of your novel; determine what your stakes are.

**Writing Terms Used in This Workshop:**

**Antagonist:** The person or thing in the protagonist's path of success.

**Backstory:** The history and past of a character that affects his or her actions in a novel.

**Conflict:** Two sides in opposition, either externally or internally.

**Core Conflict:** The major problem or issue at the center of your novel.

**Goal:** What the point-of-view character wants.

**Hook:** An element that grabs readers and makes them want to read on.

**Point of View:** The perspective used to tell the story.

**Premise:** The general description of the story you plan to tell.

**Protagonist:** The character driving the novel.

**Narrative Distance:** The distance between the reader and the point-of-view character.

**Narrative Drive:** The sense that the plot is moving forward.

**Stakes:** What consequence will befall the protagonist if she fails.

# Welcome to Workshop Five: Developing Your Plot

Great characters don't have much to do without a plot. They need goals and obstacles to help them grow and teach them the lessons you want them to learn, as well as resolve whatever problem you've created for them. The plot is just the series of events that allow you to illustrate that character's story—the physical things she does—just as the character arc is *why* she does it.

What the protagonist wants is key to any good plot, since that's what's going to be driving the entire novel—the goals. It's like a complicated connect-the-dots puzzle, with each dot leading the protagonist to the next step of the plot. But if the novel is nothing more than reading about a character methodically getting what she wants, readers will get bored and go looking for the remote.

That's where the conflict comes in—the obstacle to the protagonist's goal, and whatever is making it harder for her to succeed. Without conflict, there *is* no story, because there's nothing to overcome. One of the most common reasons manuscripts get rejected is due to lack of conflict.

Of course, just reading about someone struggling to overcome obstacles isn't enough either—the protagonist needs stakes to make it all worthwhile and motivate them to keep going. A consequence for failure that will give those goals and conflicts meaning.

Goals. Conflicts. Stakes. The building blocks of plot that will drive every scene in your novel.

In this workshop, we'll look at basic story structure, how to develop goals for your characters, determine the conflicts and obstacles to those goals, and create the stakes that make achieving the goals so important.

## The Three-Act Structure

Even though this book is about planning a novel, understanding some basic story structure will make both the planning and the final plotting a lot easier. Novel structure formats offer plot turning points to aim for and provide a framework for your plot. Even if you're a pantser, structure can help during revisions when you have a first draft done and want to make sure all your plot points are working.

**How story structures work:** A structure is like a rough map or the line drawings in a coloring book. How you overlay your story (color in the line drawings) is up to you, but the structure provides guides and boundaries to help keep you focused. Turning points like, "leave the ordinary world" are just a way of saying, "the protagonist does something new that starts the plot." This can be a literal "enter a magic wardrobe and discover Narnia," or "decide to wear a dress to school for the first time ever to catch the eye of the boy you like."

Some writers worry that structure will create a formulaic novel. If you follow it exactly and take it literally, then yes, that *could* happen, but the strength of story structure is to let it guide you and remind you of the important plot elements of a novel. The moments are metaphorical or symbolic, and they suggest types of situations to aim for. And even when a novel does follow them exactly, if it's done well, readers don't even notice. The novel feels tightly plotted, not predictable.

## Common Structure Formats

**The Three-Act Structure:** The basic beginning, middle, and ending format we're most familiar with in storytelling. Setup, rising action and stakes, resolution.

**The Hero's Journey:** Joseph Campbell's seventeen-step myth structure that outlines the journey a mythic figure (hero) undergoes on an adventure.

**Michael Hauge's Six-Stage Plot Structure:** A variation of the Three-Act Structure that focuses on six critical elements of a plot. This one is also connected to the internal character arc structure.

**Blake Snyder's *Save the Cat* Beat Sheets:** A screenwriting format for crafting great screenplays using fifteen beats (or turning points). It's been adopted by novelists everywhere because the same basic rules apply to novels.

I'm going to focus on the Three-Act Structure, because it's the most common story structure out there, and it's easy to use for both beginning and experienced writers. The other formats also generally follow this structure, so it's a good foundation to have.

People have broken the Three-Act Structure down in a myriad of ways, but it unfolds basically like this:

## Act One: The Beginning (The Setup)

Act one is roughly the first 25 percent of the novel. It focuses on the protagonist living in her world and being introduced to the problems she needs to resolve. Something about her life is making her unhappy, but she's not yet ready to do anything about it. She might not even be aware of the problem, but she feels unsatisfied in some way. She's presented with an opportunity to change her life, and she either accepts the challenge or tries to avoid it and gets dragged into it anyway. By the end of the first act, she's on the plot path that leads to the climax of the novel.

Everything in this first act familiarizes readers with the world and characters and sets up the problem the novel is going to spend the next 75 percent trying to resolve.

Act one is all about showing the protagonist's world (her life, dreams, issues, etc, as well as the literal setting) and letting readers see the problems and flaws she'll need to overcome to get what she ultimately wants. In essence, it's where you say, "See how messed up this gal's life is? This is what she has to fix before she can win."

Act one typically contains three key plot moments:

### Opening Scene

This is the introduction of the protagonist, the opening scene problem, the setting, the rules of the world, any critical traits or details readers need to know, etc. Something is happening that will draw readers in and allow them to get to know (and like) the protagonist.

## Inciting Event

This is when the opportunity to change or fix what's wrong in the protagonist's life presents itself. The protagonist is uncertain whether to take advantage of this opportunity, but eventually she does, either through her choice or from outside forces acting upon her.

The inciting event focuses the narrative (and plot) toward the core conflict of the novel. This is the moment when you say to your readers, "Here's what the plot is going to be about." Even if the problem is going to get bigger later, the seed of the conflict the plot needs to resolve will be right here. The protagonist might not even be able to see the bigger picture yet, but you know this is the point when things change for her. Had she not experienced this, the plot would not have unfolded the same way.

## Act One Problem

This problem transitions to the middle of the novel and gives the protagonist something to do (a goal), and a choice to make. It's the first major step once the protagonist is on the path to the core conflict. It's also where the stakes are significantly raised for the first time.

The choice is the big moment here and the protagonist must *choose* to act. Greater forces could have gotten her here, but she must decide to move forward on her own. Agreeing to act will force her out of her comfort zone (her normal life) and into an unfamiliar (and often emotionally scary) situation. This step into the unknown is vital for her goals, both the external plot goal and her internal character arc goal. This choice is what officially launches the middle of the novel.

## Act Two: The Middle (Figuring Things Out)

Middles make up roughly 50 percent of a novel. The protagonist leaves what's familiar to her and undergoes a series of challenges that will allow her to get what she wants. She struggles and fails repeatedly, learning the valuable lessons she'll need in act three to defeat the antagonist.

Good middles show this struggle and growth, and braid together the plot and subplots, crashing the conflicts against each other Each clue, discovery, and action brings her closer to the act two disaster that sends her hurtling toward the climax and resolution of the novel. She'll start off with some level of confidence, sure of her plans, but as things spiral out of control she'll become more and more uncertain and filled with self-doubt until she's forced to consider giving up entirely.

Act two typically contains three key plot moments:

## Act Two Choice

The act two choice is a transitional moment, linking the beginning and the middle. The protagonist embraces whatever problem she's confronted with, and accepts the opportunity it offers to resolve that problem. How she decides to deal with that problem establishes how the plot is going to unfold until the next step on the plot path.

This problem is going to be a big one, because it's going to drive the plot for the next 25 percent of the novel until the midpoint (at roughly the 50 percent mark). It'll be the first major piece of the core conflict puzzle. In most cases, it ends in failure, because the protagonist hasn't yet learned the things she needs to learn to be victorious.

The act two choice usually launches the protagonist's character arc as well, because her flaw will be her weakness during the middle of the novel. She'll struggle and fail, not seeing what she needs to do to become the person she wants to be.

## Midpoint Reversal

The midpoint reversal occurs in the middle of the novel. Something unexpected happens and changes the worldview the protagonist has had all along. Her plan no longer works or is no longer viable, and things have to change. This choice and the creation of a new plan is what sends the plot into the second half of the middle (the 50 to 75 percent marks).

A good midpoint reversal will also raise the stakes, even if they were high to begin with. It often adds a level of personal consequence that wasn't there before, or reveals a secret (or problem) that was hidden. Sometimes it requires a sacrifice, be it a personal belief or an ally. Sometimes it's all of these things at the same time.

This moment also will be large enough that it can carry the plot from the middle to the 75 percent mark (the next 25 percent of the book) and the beginning of the climax.

## Act Two Disaster

The act two disaster hits around the 75 percent mark of the novel. It's the moment when it all goes wrong for the protagonist, and is often the result of trying to fix whatever went wrong at the midpoint. The big plan to save the day fails miserably and she's worse off now than she's been the entire novel. The stakes are raised yet again, and it all becomes too much to handle.

Usually, whatever lie the protagonist has been telling herself is stripped away, forcing her to see the truth, however harsh. If the antagonist has been a secret or a mystery, this is often when that identity is discovered (often with devastating effect). Even if the antagonist has been known all along, new information is revealed about him to make the task seem insurmountable now.

In cliché speak, it's the darkness before the dawn. It all becomes too much and the protagonist feels like giving up, but finds the strength to carry on. She realizes the only way to succeed is to face the problem head on and do what she's been scared to do all along.

## Act Three: The End (Facing the Antagonist)

The ending is the last 25 percent of the novel. The protagonist decides to take the problem to the antagonist. She'll use all the things she's learned over the course of the novel to outwit and defeat that antagonist. They battle it out, and she'll win (usually), then the plot wraps up and readers see the new world the protagonist lives in, and the new person she's become after undergoing these experiences.

The final battle with the antagonist doesn't have to be an *actual* battle, just two conflicted sides trying to win. The protagonist gathers herself and any allies and challenges the antagonist. There is often a journey involved, either metaphorical or literal, as a final test.

Act three typically contains three key plot moments:

## Act Three Plan

After digging deep down and finding the emotional strength to continue, the protagonist puts a new plan into action, using everything she's learned over the course of the novel. She finally knows who she is and what she's supposed to do, and she sets off to accomplish that.

The plan is usually ambitious, clever, and unexpected, even though it also feels inevitable. This is what the protagonist and the supporting characters were meant to do all along. The plan may or may not be revealed to readers at this point. Often the actual details are kept secret, even though the general idea is mentioned to help drive the plot forward. The plan doesn't *have* to be something that will actually work if you want to surprise the protagonist in the climax and force her to think on the run. What's important is that the protagonist thinks it will work. Once the climax starts, plans can fail and the protagonist can have to revise in a hurry to win.

## Climax

The climax is the final showdown with the antagonist. The protagonist faces whomever or whatever has been making her life miserable for four hundred or so pages, and because she's learned XYZ over the course of the novel, she wins (or loses spectacularly if that's the type of novel you're writing). This realization is also what was missing in her life all along. Whatever happens, the core conflict problem is resolved.

The climax often has one last increase in stakes, making this final battle matter on a bigger scale. It's usually something the protagonist has at stake on a personal level, and it ties into the story from a thematic aspect so the ending has more poignancy. It's not uncommon for this rise in stakes to happen after a twist or surprise.

## Wrap Up

The wrap up is the happily ever after, or the burning apocalypse if that's how you prefer it. What the protagonist is going to do now that she's resolved her problem. In essence, the final scene says, "Yes, there was a point to this novel and here it is." It gives readers a sense of closure and reassurance that the novel was worth their time.

What makes any plotting structure so valuable as a tool is that these elements can be anything you want them to be. The structure is just a frame to hang the story on, and knowing solid, proven turning points can help you decide what events need to happen to get the most out of your own plot.

They also help you find holes in your plot and places where the stakes might need to be raised. If you notice the protagonist never fails, that's a red flag that you might not have enough at stake or enough conflict driving the plot. Or you might not have a solid character arc that allows your protagonist to grow. It's a map, a guide, but the scenes and problems encountered are all up to you.

## Determining Your Goals

Goals are the driving force of the novel. The protagonist (or protagonists in multiple-point-of-view novels) *wants* something. Probably a lot of somethings. Some of them will be small, like finding something to eat; others will be huge, like stopping a terrorist attack on the White House. Whatever they are, these goals will determine how the protagonist acts, and that will determine how the novel unfolds.

Goals are at the center of every scene in the novel, and there are a variety of goal levels. Individual scene goals, larger chapter goals, personal character goals, story goals, and plot goals. For now, let's focus on the broader novel-developing type of goals. Story and plot goals.

What makes plotting tough is that vague thematic statements like, "find love again" or "learn to trust others," are great *story* goals (and good for internal character arcs), but unhelpful *plot* goals. Think of it like this: Go out right now and find love again. Um, you can't, not really. It's not like "love again" is something you can go get at the store. But you can *act* in a way that will help you find love again, like go to a museum and talk to cute guys.

The external physical goal (plot) is "go to the museum and talk to cute guys." That's something a protagonist can do to move the plot forward. Internally (character arc), she hopes one of those cute guys will be the love of her life.

That's why trying to plot with only story goals can leave us hitting a plot wall at page one hundred. We know conceptually what we want our protagonist to do, but there's no concrete, actionable plan to follow. No plot goals to get her there.

## Story Goals

Story goals are the larger thematic goals that describe the character growth or the idea behind the novel. They're more conceptual and work as guides to determine the types of plot goals the protagonist will encounter. Knowing that the protagonist wants to find love helps figure out the types of things to do to achieve that goal. You need to know what your protagonist wants before you develop the steps she'll take to get it, and then you can figure out the internal story goal to give her reasons to strive for that external plot goal.

**Why story goals are important:** They represent the internal conflicts and the emotional needs of the characters.

*For example:*

▶ To find love again after a bad breakup (this is what the story is about, and the plot will focus on the external steps needed to achieve this)

## Plot Goals

Plot goals are the physical things the protagonist does to achieve those more lofty story goals. They're the choices she makes and the things she does to help her achieve her dreams. "Being hungry" is an internal want (a story goal) but "getting up and making a sandwich" is an external goal (a plot goal), though granted, not a very exciting one. But there's no reason for the protagonist to get up and make a sandwich if she's never hungry in the first place.

**Why plot goals are important:** Plot goals give the protagonist something to do and help drive the novel to the climax. They make readers feel like the novel is progressing and moving toward a resolution.

*For example:*

▶ Go to the museum and talk to cute guys (this is part of the plot, one step that will allow the protagonist to find love, which is her story goal and motivation for acting).

The story goal is an end desire, and the plot goals are the steps that will get the protagonist to that end desire.

 **BRAINSTORMING QUESTIONS:**
Explore possible character goals.

1. What does your protagonist want?

2. What is your protagonist willing to do to get that want?

3. What are some possible goals (and steps) the protagonist might take to get that want?

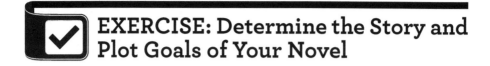

# EXERCISE: Determine the Story and Plot Goals of Your Novel

## >>What are the story and plot goals of your protagonist and antagonist?

*For example:*

▶ **Protagonist: Story goal:** Lana wants to redeem herself for a past mistake that put her older brother in a wheelchair. Everyone thinks it was an accident, but she knows she caused it and it's all her fault, even if he doesn't remember. She wants to make it up to her brother but has no idea how. **Plot goal:** To keep her secret when she's summoned to a diner in the middle of the night by someone threatening to expose her secret and ruin her.

**Antagonist: Story goal:** Zachary blames Lana and Miguel for something that happened to him and wants to destroy their lives as he thinks they destroyed his. **Plot goal:** To force Lana and Miguel to publicly confess what they did, which will exonerate him for a past deed he was wrongly accused of.

▶ **Protagonist: Story goal:** Bob wants to find happiness with Jane and escape his difficult marriage, regaining his freedom and his manhood. **Plot goal:** To survive the zombie apocalypse and divorce (or get rid of) his wife.

**Antagonist: Story goal:** Sally is trying to keep Bob and herself alive, hoping the zombie threat will force Bob to step up and not be a wuss all the time. **Plot goal:** To survive, and intentionally put Bob in dangerous situations to trigger his own survival instincts.

▶ **Protagonist: Story goal:** Adam realizes his life is all about work and not family, a side effect of his overbearing family growing up. He needs someone to share his life with or he will become the soulless person his business reputation claims he is, and this terrifies him. Hannah feels her life is passing her by, yet she's too timid to get out there and be adventurous. She needs someone to encourage her to take risks and be the person she's scared to be. **Plot goal:** Adam and Hannah want to work together to fulfill the promise they made to their childhood teacher after they attend her funeral. They also need to fall in love.

**Antagonist: Story goal:** The families want to beat the other side and keep the lovebirds apart, but what they really need to do is make peace. **Plot goal:** To do everything they can to ruin the growing relationship between Adam and Hannah, culminating in disaster when they try to prevent them from going to the teacher's funeral.

## Discovering Your Conflict

Conflict is at the heart of every novel. More than that really, it's at the heart of *every* scene. It's not uncommon for people to hear the word conflict and immediately assume fighting, but it's not always violent, nor should it be. Conflict is just two things in opposition.

"I can't make that meeting, I have a conflict."

Sure, it's not life threatening, though it could be in the right circumstance. But what it *does* do is force the person with the conflict to make a choice. That's what's so great (and helpful in the plotting stage) about conflicts.

Conflicts force characters to choose. And choosing forces them to act.

Conflicts are the things standing in the way of the protagonist's goal. The obstacles that must be overcome for her to get what she wants. A conflict can be a person, a situation, or a personal struggle—pretty much anything that prevents the protagonist from getting her goal or doing what needs to be done.

*For example:*

▶ Mom wants to take a nap after a long day; the kids want to play monopoly with her.

What she wants is in conflict with what they what. This isn't going to turn into a literal fight, and there's no bad guy here; just two sides that both want something different and are willing to act to get what they want.

And that's key to non-violent trouble. Different wants. Because wanting something isn't the same as doing something violent to get it.

Conflicts don't have to be aggressive or even dangerous. Quiet conflicts are especially good for character-driven novels where the focus is more internal than external, but they also work well for internal goals and character arcs.

There are two different kinds of conflicts every protagonist will deal with over the course of a novel—external and internal. These two conflicts will work together (usually by working *against* each other, ironically enough) to create the novel.

## External Conflicts

External conflicts are the external obstacles in the protagonist's way that require choices and actions to resolve or overcome. They're external problems that are standing in the way of what the protagonist needs or wants. The external conflicts help create the plot.

*For example:*

▶ Sneaking past Dad to attend a forbidden party

▶ Defeating the guard holding the girl captive

▶ Finding enough money to pay the ransom

**Why external conflicts are important:** External conflicts give the protagonist something to do. They provide the obstacles and goals the protagonist has to resolve to get what she wants and save the day. They get her moving, make her proactive, and force her into situations where she has to make those reader-hooking choices that drive the plot forward.

## Internal Conflicts

Internal conflicts are the issues the protagonist faces on a mental or emotional level. They're internal battles that require emotional sacrifices and tough choices that challenge a personal belief. The internal conflicts help create the character arc.

*For example:*

▶ She wants a new dress she can't afford, but stealing is wrong

▶ He wants to date the girl, but he'll have to break a promise to his best friend to do it

▶ He can save the king, if he agrees to become everything he despises

**Why internal conflicts are important:** Internal conflicts drive the character growth and character arc by giving the protagonist something personal to overcome. They also help create unpredictability in the protagonist. If she always does the right thing (as heroes often do), then there's no doubt how she might act when faced with a tough situation. But if her beliefs conflict with "the right thing," then her actions become uncertain. Will a protagonist who's been oppressed her whole life risk her life to save the son of her oppressor?

What makes these two conflict types work so well together is how they can pull the protagonist in different directions. The internal conflict drives the character growth, while the external conflict drives the plot. In other words, the external conflict decides the plot and creates the goals, while the internal conflict makes those goals harder to accomplish and teaches the protagonist a lesson in the process.

⚠ **SOMETHING TO THINK ABOUT:** *What conflicts do you see in your idea? Write down anything that might be a problem to your protagonist, internally or externally.*

 **BRAINSTORMING QUESTIONS:**
Explore possible conflicts.

1.  What are some possible conflicts in your idea?

2.  What characters might be in conflict with each other?

3.  What larger conflicts might occur in your world or setting?

## Finding Your Core Conflicts

Even at the idea stage, the core conflict is at the center of the novel. It's the problem the novel has to solve and the whole reason the characters are acting at all. It drives the plot (externally) and the character arc (internally).

### External Core Conflict

The external core conflict is the problem the protagonist is facing on the outside. This conflict triggers the series of obstacles the protagonist will have to deal with in order to resolve whatever the novel is about. Discovering this problem is the beginning of the novel, and resolving this conflict is the end of the novel. In plot-driven novels, this is where the main focus of the book lies.

*For example:*

- ▸ A girl must survive a battle-to-the-death televised combat (*The Hunger Games*)
- ▸ A hobbit must destroy a magic ring to keep it out of the hands of an evil warlord (*The Lord of the Rings*)
- ▸ A girl must find and save her missing sister (*The Shifter*)

**Why the external core conflict is important:** This conflict holds the novel together. It's the issue the protagonist must resolve at the climax and what is driving the overall plot.

### Internal Core Conflict

The internal core conflict is the problem the protagonist is facing on the inside. It's most often a personal struggle that deals with the protagonist's self-worth or beliefs in some way. This is the conflict that will create the character arc and allow the protagonist to grow however she needs to in the novel. In character-driven stories, this is where the main focus of the novel lies.

*For example:*

- ▸ A girl must take advantage of a smitten boy to survive in a battle-to-the-death televised combat (*The Hunger Games*)

▶ A terrified hobbit must leave his home and find his inner hero to destroy a magic ring (*The Lord of the Rings*)

▶ A girl with a power she must keep secret has to use it to find and save her missing sister (*The Shifter*)

**Why the internal core conflict is important:** This conflict holds the character arc together. It's the flaw or weakness holding the protagonist back, the personal issue that needs resolving, or the belief system that's being tested. This is often where the theme is explored and where the growth of the protagonist comes from.

The core conflicts are the heart of the novel. These are the foundations the novel is built on.

It's not a bad idea to keep these handy while both planning and writing the novel.

## Conflicts Beyond the Core Conflicts

These two conflicts aren't the only conflicts in the novel, however. They're the most important ones, but conflict will exist all throughout the novel. Every scene will have its own conflict that will help move the plot to the next step, and those strings of conflicts will lead to the core conflict.

The individual conflicts will also put the protagonist in difficult situations so she's forced to make tough choices, both moving the plot forward and causing her to learn valuable lessons for her character growth. Tough choices are key to strong conflicts. It's through these tough choices that the plot advances and the novel unfolds.

**BRAINSTORMING QUESTIONS:**
Explore the major conflicts driving your characters and your novel.

1. What are the external conflicts in the book? List five possible conflicts.

2. How might these conflicts keep the protagonist from getting what she wants? List how and why.

3. What are the internal conflicts in the book? List five possible ways your characters can be conflicted.

4. How might the protagonist's personal beliefs hinder her in achieving her goal? List five possible ways her personal goals might conflict with her plot goals.

5. What are the most critical conflicts, both externally and internally? List them and state why.

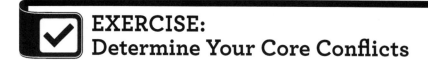

# EXERCISE:
# Determine Your Core Conflicts

## >>Summarize your external and internal core conflicts.

It's okay if some things are still uncertain, especially if you like to discover your novel as you write it, but try to pinpoint the goal your protagonist is trying to accomplish that will drive your novel.

*For example:*

▶ **External Core Conflict:** Three teens are trying to figure out why they're all at the diner and who summoned them there. **Internal Core Conflict:** Trying to keep their secrets a secret.

▶ **External Core Conflict:** Bob is trying to survive the zombie apocalypse and win the woman he loves. **Internal Core Conflict:** Bob can't survive unless he stays with his wife, and he's struggling to feel worthy of surviving and being with Jane.

▶ **External Core Conflict:** Feuding families are trying hard to keep Adam and Hannah apart. **Internal Core Conflict:** Wanting to be together even though it would cause trouble with their families.

# Finding Your Stakes

Now that we have the conflict, protagonist and antagonist, and goals figured out (even if it's on a general level), it's time to consider the stakes.

The stakes are the motivating factors for the protagonist's goals, and why she has to overcome those conflicts *right now* as opposed to whenever she gets around to it. The stakes are what happens if she doesn't succeed. Stakes are bad. Stakes are killer. The higher the stakes, the more tension is created and the more compelling the plot. They're the "or else" in every threat.

There are different levels of stakes, however, and what will grab readers and keep them on the edges of their seats isn't always what we'd expect. The end of the world feels like the highest stake of all, but readers know the world isn't *really* going to end, so it's not a credible threat. Death of the protagonist is another seemingly high stake, but again, very few protagonists actually die.

Personal stakes are personal and specific to the protagonist and make readers care if she succeeds or not.

Plot stakes are the larger, more abstract stakes that can happen to people besides just the protagonist.

## Personal Stakes

Personal stakes are what the protagonist doesn't want to have happen because it will hurt her personally. She'll lose her job, the serial killer will murder her child, or the action will go against everything she believes in. They drive the story and make readers care about the outcome as much as the protagonist does. They're consequences that can (and do) happen to make the protagonist's life harder or her job tougher, and force her to sacrifice and make some difficult personal choices.

They're also what keeps the protagonist from running away when it gets tough. The consequence that stops her from saying, "Yes, I don't really want the evil sorcerer to take over and enslave the city, but if I take off right now, I can be far away when it happens and I won't have to die or deal with this mess." It's better if she *can't* run because a loved one is being held captive by that evil sorcerer and if she runs, that person dies.

Personal risks are also things that can and likely *will* happen. They move the novel forward and are real consequences for readers to worry about. Readers know the protagonist is going to stop the serial killer in the end, though that killer *might* kill the protagonist's wife or child before he's caught.

*For example:*

▶ Save your child from the serial killer or save your wife (the consequences of both choices will matter personally to the protagonist)

**Why personal stakes are important:** Personal risk is *much* more compelling than faceless tragedy. That's why one family dying in a car crash on Christmas Eve hits us harder than millions of people dying of a terrible disease every year. Find a solid answer to that all-important question: Why should the reader care about *this* person and *this* problem?

⚠ **SOMETHING TO THINK ABOUT**: *What are some possible personal stakes for your protagonist? Add those to your list.*

At some point in the novel (typically during the second half of the second act) the protagonist often has to sacrifice something to get what she wants. It's not uncommon to see the personal stakes shift and become those larger "save the world" stakes *because* of this sacrifice (so you can have those big stakes *and* still have the personal ones). A personal sacrifice serves the greater good, and the greater good issue allows the protagonist to get something she values more than anything else.

## Plot Stakes

Plot stakes are those consequences that matter to the world at large. The bigger, plot-driving consequences that will happen if the protagonist fails to do whatever the core conflict requires her to do. If the princess doesn't stop the evil wizard, the land will be enslaved. Plot stakes are the bigger, more horrible outcomes, and while they're something the protagonist is trying to stop, odds are it won't *actually* come true.

*For example:*

▶ Stop the serial killer before he kills again (a terrible consequence, but it doesn't affect the protagonist on a personal level)

**Why plot stakes are important:** The plot stakes provide a larger scope in which to develop a novel. They can give those smaller, personal stakes greater meaning by showing how a protagonist's sacrifice might benefit others. It allows characters to be noble (or selfish), rise above their personal struggles (or collapse under the weight), and become a force for good (or evil) in their society. Plot stakes often resonate with readers on multiple levels because they work with the big picture.

⚠ **SOMETHING TO THINK ABOUT:** *What are some possible plot stakes for your novel? Add those to your list.*

## What Stakes Are Not

A common pitfall when developing stakes is choosing those that might *feel* important, but when we look at them up close, there's nothing actually at stake.

*For example:*

▶ Trying to decide between two different things when either choice gives basically the same reward (though having to choose between things where *both* sides have a sacrifice is good). Where's the sacrifice for a man torn between two women who are both great women, and the only consequence is one woman is going to get hurt if he chooses the other? The protagonist feeling bad because he hurt someone's feelings isn't going to be a strong enough stake to carry an entire novel.

▶ It's also *not* having to decide between two things where the answer is obvious. Pull the lever and save the world, vs. don't pull it and everyone dies. Well, duh, who's *not* going to pull the lever? Good stakes force the protagonist to make a decision where both choices have a bad consequence.

If the stakes only work from a cold, flat, plot perspective, and even *the writer* doesn't care if the problem is solved or not beyond an "ooooh that's cool" interest, odds are the personal stakes are still missing. Without those, we risk ending up with a novel that's all mechanics and no soul (and if you have a completed manuscript and readers just aren't connecting to it, this could be why).

Don't look at just the plot side of things when creating character stakes. Think about how those stakes affect the protagonist personally. Do *you* care about this character and what happens to her, or are you just running her through a gauntlet of problems to illustrate a plot idea? If it doesn't affect you to put her in danger and cause her trouble (either hurt you or make you giggle in glee), then why should readers feel any more emotion?

If the protagonist has nothing personal at risk, and can stop at any time with no personal repercussions, there's a good chance the stakes are low, even if they're high from a plot standpoint (such as high plot stakes but low personal stakes). "They could die" feels high, but if she walks away she'll live. Problem solved. Sure, others might die, but do readers *really* care about a faceless mass of unnamed people? Nah.

A great test to see if the stakes are personal is to put the second-most important character in the protagonist's slot and see what would change. If the novel would unfold pretty much the same way, odds are the stakes still aren't personal enough. "The bad guys invade the kingdom" is a good start, but again, so what? Anyone who lives in that kingdom has that same thing at stake.

If we feel it, then the characters will feel it. If the characters feel it, the readers will feel it. Once they care, they'll read on, which is exactly what we want for our novels.

---

 **BRAINSTORMING QUESTIONS:**
Explore possible stakes and determine if they're high enough, or personal enough to your protagonist to carry a novel.

1. If the protagonist walked away, what would change?

2. If you put the second-most important character in the protagonist's slot, what would change?

3. What does the protagonist lose if she walks away from this problem?

4. What sacrifice does the protagonist have to make for everything to turn out the way she wants?

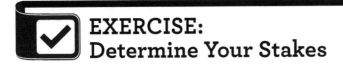

# EXERCISE:
# Determine Your Stakes

## >>Describe your stakes.

What does the protagonist have to gain, what does she have to lose, and what are the consequences if she fails at her task?

*For example:*

▶ Lana's reputation and relationship with her family will be ruined if they find out the role she played in her brother's accident. The few friends she has left will shun her and she'll be an outcast at school. She fears she might even wind up in jail. But if she comes clean and redeems herself, she can shed the guilt that's making her sick and ruining her life anyway. She even has a chance of stopping Zachary, who played a role in the accident himself, though she's not aware of that. Uncovering his secrets will allow her to finally let go of hers.

▶ Bob's life and happiness. Zombies could eat him at any time. His wife could leave him behind to fend for himself, or he could lose Jane to zombies. She might reject him if she doesn't feel the same way. He might learn that he really is as pathetic as he fears and ought to be left behind as zombie food. But if he stands up and tries to be the man he wants to be, he'll find the strength to face the zombies and be able to tell Jane he loves her, and Sally he doesn't. He'll learn how to fend for himself on both a physical and emotional level.

▶ Adam could wind up alone and throwing himself into a job that's slowly eating his soul. He'll resent his family and cut off all ties with them. Hannah could listen to her family and give up her dream of adventure and love, returning to her hometown and living the life her family always pushed on her. But if they both listen to their hearts and stand up to their families, they can be together and fill the void each has in their lives. They'll find happiness and give each other the strength and support they need to overcome their weaknesses and be happy.

# ASSIGNMENT FIVE: Flesh Out Your Plot

>>**Summarize the main goals, conflicts, and stakes of your novel and how they might create your plot.**

This assignment is designed to get you thinking about the plot and how the novel will unfold on a larger scale. It'll help you determine what the driving forces are behind your characters—what they want, what's in their way of getting it, what's at stake if they fail, and how those stakes might escalate over the course of the novel. It's an opportunity to summarize the plot side of the novel and determine which aspects most excite you as a writer.

Feel free to do this exercise from a pure plot perspective or an individual character perspective. If you have multiple characters, you might show each character's plot arc or even how those plots interconnect. Don't worry if things are still vague in some areas. This exercise can also help you discover where you might need to flesh out the plot and where any holes might be.

Don't worry if you discover the beginning of the novel is more developed than the middle or end at this stage. That's normal, since we've been doing a lot of setup development so far. Use what's developed and brainstorm where the story or plot might go using what you know so far. You can always revise it later.

There's also no set way to do this exercise. The goal is to brainstorm what you've developed so far and find connections and possible plot paths for your ideas to take. Some novels will have clear plot paths; others will take a little more development before that path is clear.

Sometimes, great ideas will strike us when we start thinking about how stakes might escalate, so if you see how the stakes might be raised, even though you haven't figured out that aspect of the plot yet, write it down anyway. This type of exercise is where moments of inspiration come from. You know you need to raise the stakes, but nothing in your planning so far will let you do that—so it's time to get creative and *then* figure out how to make it work. Think about ways to make the stakes higher each time, and that will lead you to think of bigger and tougher goals and conflicts.If you're stuck, try phrasing each goal-conflict-stakes piece as one statement. Character wants X, but Y is holding her back, and Z will happen if she doesn't get X. Or, start with the ending and work backward, figuring out the steps needed to get from the opening of the novel to the end of the novel.

If you're really stuck on what to write try this:

1. List possible goals in your beginning, middle, and ending. Use story goals, personal goals, or both.

2. List possible conflicts in your beginning, middle, and ending. Use external conflicts, internal conflicts, or both.

3. List possible stakes in your beginning, middle, and ending. Use the personal stakes, story stakes, or both.

4. Combine everything and summarize where the plot might come from. Add in any details that help flesh out the goals, conflicts, and stakes listed.

*For example:*

▶ **Goals: Beginning**–to pretend everything is okay, to find out who summoned her to the diner. **Middle**–to keep her secret, to find out who is threatening to expose it. **Ending**–to find out what really happened to her brother, to stop Zachary and save Miguel.

**Conflicts: Beginning**–guilt makes her want to confess, but fear of reprisal keeps her quiet. **Middle**–fear of getting caught makes her want to run, but fear of exposure makes her want to stay and figure out who's behind this. **Ending**–she wants to expose the truth and Zachary, but he wants to ruin her through lies.

**Stakes: Beginning**–her family will disown her if they find out she caused her brother's accident. She'll be humiliated in front of everyone she knows. She might even wind up in jail. **Middle**–she'll never find out the truth about her brother and won't be able to redeem herself. **Ending**–she'll be blamed for the terrible things Zachary has planned, won't be able to find peace, and will lose her life and maybe even Miguel's life.

**Summary:** Lana is struggling to keep her life together and not let her family know she caused her brother's accident, when she finds a note in her locker at school. It says "I know what you did" and summons her to a roadside diner in the middle of nowhere. If she doesn't show, they'll expose her secret. She has no choice but to go, and finds two other boys who got the same note. They have no idea why they're there, but they each get more notes demanding things that will either expose them anyway or get them killed. As Lana obeys the demands, she starts trying to figure out who is behind them and what they want. When she realizes that Zachary is the one sending the notes, and that he's planning to hurt or even kill Miguel and frame her for it, she decides to expose him instead and save her and Miguel. Things get more complicated when she discovers that Zachary was involved in her brother's accident and things there are not what she thought at all. Uncovering Zachary's secrets might be the way to finally rid herself of hers.

▶ Bob wants to divorce his wife Sally and confess his love to Jane, and his fear of standing up to Sally is in his way, but if he doesn't stand up to her, he'll never be happy. He wants to survive the zombie apocalypse, and staying with Sally will also save his life, but staying with her means giving up on Jane and maybe even getting Jane killed. He wants to find a way to trick or convince Sally to go save Jane, but doing so risks her finding out he's in love with another woman, which might make her leave him behind to be eaten. Once they find Jane, Bob wants to take her with them as they flee for safety, but he has no way to explain that to Sally without confessing the truth, so he lies. Sally says the safest place is her lab, and Bob wants to go there, but that will put all three of them in close quarters and he'll probably slip up and say the wrong thing, which could get them both kicked out of a safe place to hide. Once at the lab, things go badly and Bob wants to protect Jane, so he stands up for himself and starts kicking some zombie butt. He's feeling good about things when Jane gets bitten and he has to find a way to save her, but to save her he has to face not only Sally, but a horde of zombies. He does it, saving Jane and finding a way to free himself from Sally. He and Jane live happily ever after.

▶ Adam and Hannah get news of their teacher's death and return home for the funeral. They share a cab and discover their connection to the teacher as well as their mutual attraction. Adam invites Hannah to dinner that night and she accepts. When he picks her up, her family goes nuts because he's from a rival family they've been feuding with for years. To keep the peace, Hannah says maybe dinner isn't such a good idea and cancels the date. Adam is annoyed, and when he mentions it to his family they also go nuts and forbid him from talking to her again. He thinks this is crazy, but doesn't want the hassles and agrees. Except he can't stop thinking about her or what his teacher always told him about taking risks and going for what you want. He calls her again and says screw the family, have dinner with me, and she hesitates, then agrees. They meet in secret and have a good time together. It's clear there's something between them, and reminiscing about the teacher only deepens their bond.

As they two fall in love, the families try to keep them apart. Calls are blocked, events are scheduled to fill up their time, slander campaigns about the other begin, etc. The interference starts out small, but gets bigger and bigger as Adam and Hannah make it clear they're not going to be kept apart. Eventually things get really nasty and one unscrupulous family member crosses a line and makes Hannah look like the most horrible person on the planet. Despite knowing what the family has been doing, this revelation is too bad for Adam to blow off, and it's made worse because there's actually a bit of truth to it. Something Hannah has always hidden in shame. She backs down, gives up, and submits to her family even though she's in love with Adam and wants to tell him what really happened. Adam is equally unhappy, mad at his family, but still thinking about Hannah. He asks why there's a feud and no one will tell him. He figures out no one really knows why anymore and sets out to uncover the reason and make things right. He figures out a lot of clues, and eventually figures out Hannah's secret is what caused the feud. To get Hannah back, he has to end the feud and prove to her that her secret doesn't matter to him and it's all okay.

In Workshop Six, we'll look at determining the type of novel you're writing, and what market and genre it falls into.

# Workshop Six: Determining the Type of Novel You're Writing

**What You Need to Start This Workshop:** An idea of what kind of novel you'd like to write.

**The Goal of This Workshop:** To determine your novel's market and genre (if applicable).

**What We'll Discuss in This Workshop:** How to: identify genre elements in your idea and what market makes the best potential audience for your novel.

**Writing Terms Used in This Workshop:**

**Genre:** The category the novel fits into, such as romance, science fiction, or fantasy.

**Market:** The demographic traits of the target audience for the novel, such as adult or young adult.

**Trope:** A literary device or element commonly found in that category or genre.

# Welcome to Workshop Six: Determining the Type of Novel You're Writing

Some writers know their market and genre before they start writing. Others have ideas that could develop in any number of ways. Still others have multiple genre elements in one novel and aren't sure where the book would fit. And there are always those who have no idea what genre their novel is or what market it might be for.

It's not unusual for ideas to start vague and develop as we write them. It can take time for a genre or market to become clear, and we *can* just start writing and see where it leads us.

However...

Knowing the market and genre can be helpful in developing and planning the novel growing in your imagination. If this is your first novel, I recommend having at least a basic idea of what type of novel you want to write before you start writing it. This will make it a little easier to plan and write overall, because you'll have some parameters to guide you.

When readers pick up a book, they expect and even want certain traits. When those expectations aren't met, they can be disappointed in the novel.

Picture your favorite band. Now imagine going to their concert and hearing them play a totally different type of music—country instead of rock, rap instead of jazz. Even if you like the new sound, odds are you'd be pretty unhappy because it wasn't what you were expecting or looking forward to.

Knowing the market and genre can help you determine certain aspects of the novel that aid you during the planning and drafting stages. The category provides a lot of information, such as general word count range, common tropes, what else has been published in that market and genre that's similar, what's popular, and what's been done to death.

If you think, "Well, I'm just writing a story," that's also fine. You're probably writing mainstream fiction, because not every novel fits a genre. If the novel develops into a genre, great, if not, that's okay too. Stories change. They even turn into novels that cross over boundaries and defy categorization.

Of course, if you're writing to learn or for fun, don't feel pressured to know any of these things beforehand. These market and genre distinctions are more important for novels you hope to one day sell (after they've been revised and polished, of course), since these are marketing tools designed to help readers find the types of novels they're looking for.

But if your end goal is to publish and sell a novel, it helps to remember that books are a product. Like any product, knowing who is going to buy it helps in creating it. Market and genre categories help readers find the types of books they want to read. They also help bookstores know where to shelve books, and what books to suggest to their customers. Ditto for libraries. Knowing what kind of book it will be before you start can go a long way toward creating a product people want to buy, which means readers who want to read that book.

It's not necessary in the planning stage, but it can be extremely helpful.

If you're writing for fun or don't want to worry about markets or genres yet, then feel free to skip ahead to Workshop Seven: Determining the Size and Scope of Your Novel.

## Figuring Out Your Market

Market refers to the broader audience the novel is targeting, determined by age group, gender, or a defining characteristic—adults, young adults, children's fiction, LGBT (lesbian, gay, bi-sexual, transgendered), etc. Sometimes a novel will cross markets (referred to as crossover books), appealing to several different age groups or genders.

Markets also play a role in determining where the novel fits. For example, young adult is a market, not a genre, so a fantasy novel aimed at teens would be a young adult fantasy.

The age of the protagonist is usually a big clue, though it's not the only determining factor, especially in juvenile fiction, where readers tend to read up (reading books with protagonists a few years older than themselves). There are always exceptions, but most of the time the age suggests which market it's for.

*For example:*

▶ If the protagonist is an adult (18+), it's likely an adult novel

▶ If the protagonist is between 18 and 25, it's likely either an adult novel, or a new adult novel (NA)

▶ If the protagonist is between 14 and 18, it's likely a young adult novel (YA)

▶ If the protagonist is between 9 and 13, it's likely a middle grade novel (MG)

The type of problem also plays a role when determining the novel's market. Stephen King has written novels with child protagonists, but they're still classified as adult novels because they deal with issues of interest to adults. Adults have appeared in Carl Hiaasen's novels for middle grade and young adult readers, but they deal with issues of interest to teens, and the adults aren't the ones resolving those plot issues.

An adult novel centers around problems adults can relate to, resolving them in adult fashion through adult life experiences and perspectives. Even if an adult protagonist is being childish or reliving her youth, the novel is still treated with an adult worldview and set of life experiences.

*For example:*

▶ *The Da Vinci Code*

▶ *A Tale of Two Cities*

▶ *The Lord of the Rings*

Teen novels (young adult or middle grade) are about teens solving problems relatable to teens. The teen protagonist is the one who resolves the problem, and she doesn't run off to get help from an adult. But this doesn't mean teen problems are childish. Teen novels deal with very adult and serious topics, but they approach them from a *teen's* perspective, not an adult's.

*For example:*

- ▶ *Harry Potter and the Sorcerer's Stone*
- ▶ *The Hunger Games*
- ▶ *Charlie and the Chocolate Factory*

**Why knowing the market is helpful:** Understanding your potential audience helps you understand what might be of interest to your readers. It can help you later when you sell your novel, because you and your publisher will know who to target and how to market the book. It also makes it easier to know what to write, as a plot for a novel aimed at a 10-year-old reader will be different from one aimed at a 40-year-old reader (even if that older reader reads and enjoys middle grade fiction).

**How market is different from genre:** Market is a broader category that encompasses multiple genres. For example, adults read mystery, fantasy, romance, etc, so any genre can be a book for adult readers.

⚠ **SOMETHING TO THINK ABOUT:** *Write down who you feel is the best audience for your novel. Choose five novels you feel are aimed at that audience.*

## Market Breakdown

### Adult

Novels aimed at readers in the 18+ age group that deal with issues that explore life in an adult world. They focus on those navigating an adult world and include issues and problems that pertain to an adult.

*For example:*

- ▶ *The Hunt for Red October*
- ▶ *The Godfather*
- ▶ *Jaws*

### New Adult (NA)

Novels aimed at readers in the 18 to 25 age bracket that deal with issues that explore what it means to be an adult. They focus on those navigating the transitional world between *being* an adult and understanding *how* to be an adult.

*For example:*

▶ *Easy*

▶ *Beautiful Disaster*

▶ *Losing It*

## Young Adult (YA)

Novels aimed at readers in the 13 to 17 age bracket that deal with issues that explore what it means to be a teen. They focus on those navigating a teen world and trying to figure out who they are and how they fit in, and often include the first steps toward becoming an adult. Those around them often start expecting them to act like adults.

*For example:*

▶ *The Hunger Games*

▶ *The Outsiders*

▶ *Speak*

## Middle Grade (MG)

Novels aimed at readers in the 9 to 12 age bracket that deal with issues that explore what it means to be a pre-teen or 'tween. They focus on those navigating a pre-teen world, and often include the joys and adventures of being a child. The protagonist is still a child at the end of the novel and has not taken steps toward adulthood. They might be tackling adult issues, but they're still kids and expected to be kids. Note that YA and MG readers typically "read up," and look for protagonists a few years older than the target readers. A 13-year-old reader will commonly look for a 14- or 15-year-old protagonist.

*For example:*

▶ *The Lightning Thief*

▶ *The Secret Garden*

▶ *Tales of a Fourth-Grade Nothing*

**BRAINSTORMING QUESTIONS:**
Answer these questions to identify the market you want to write for.

1. What are the ages of your main characters?

2. What type of problem is the core conflict?

3. What age group do you feel this novel would appeal to?

4. In what section of the bookstore do you see this novel?

# EXERCISE:
## Determine the Market for Your Novel

**>>Write down the market you feel your novel will most appeal to.**

Try to pick the market that contains the majority of potential readers. While young adult novels are often read by adults, the market is still young adult, as that's how it would be promoted and that's who the target audience is.

*For example:*

▶ Young Adult: Three teen protagonists dealing with teen issues they will resolve without the aid of adults. (Three teens summoned to a diner in the middle of the night).

▶ Adult: Adult protagonist dealing with an adult problem he will resolve using adult thinking. (Bob, facing the zombie apocalypse while navigating a love triangle).

▶ Adult: Adult protagonists dealing with adult problems in adult ways. (Hannah and Adam falling in love and trying to bring peace between their feuding families).

## Figuring Out Your Genre

Genre is a term that refers to novels that have strong elements defining them as a particular type of book. There are required tropes, and if the novel doesn't have those, it's not that genre. Readers expect to see those tropes and are disappointed if they're not there.

*For example:*

▶ A romance novel has a romance with a happily ever after at the core

▶ A murder mystery has a murder that must be solved driving the plot

▶ A fantasy novel has alternate worlds and magical elements

What makes something genre is when the core conflict of the novel revolves around a trope of the genre. The novel would fall apart if you took that element out.

*For example:*

▶ If you took away the quest for true love and reuniting the lovers, there'd be no plot in *The Princess Bride,* so it's a romance.

▶ If you took away the murder, there'd be nothing to investigate in *Murder on the Orient Express,* so it's a mystery.

▶ If you took away the magic, there'd be no wizards' school in *Harry Potter and the Sorcerer's Stone,* so it's a fantasy.

**Why knowing the genre is helpful:** Knowing who your potential readers are and how your novel might appeal to them gives you an advantage when you start submitting that novel. It also lets you know what tropes to be aware of, what clichés to avoid, and what's already been written in that genre.

**How genre differs from market:** Genre crosses market boundaries. You might have an adult mystery or a middle grade mystery, but they'd be very different novels with very different readers.

Be wary of trying to force your novel into a genre it isn't. Having two people who fall in love doesn't necessarily make it a romance if the point of the novel isn't to get those two people together. Having advanced technology doesn't make it science fiction if that technology doesn't affect the plot. A murder doesn't make it a murder mystery unless solving that mystery is the goal of the novel. Genre novels have those genre tropes at the core. Everything else is mainstream fiction.

Genre is a great tool to help guide your novel as you write, but don't let it become something that bogs you down trying to label it. Plenty of novels have elements of multiple genres. Look at what's at the heart of your novel and then see where it fits. Or, decide where you *want* it to fit, and add those fundamental elements to your novel (if they fit the story you want to tell, of course). Beyond that, do what the story needs you to do and don't worry so much about the label on it.

## How to Pick a Genre

With all the cross-over and combined genres these days (like paranormal romance and urban fantasy), it's ever harder sometimes to know where a novel stands. It's possible to have a science fiction murder mystery, with all the tropes of both genres.

An easy test to determine genre is to think about where that novel would be shelved in the bookstore. If it would go in the mystery aisle, it's mystery. Mainstream fiction, it's fiction. Online bookstores also break down titles, which can be a good overview of the different genres and subgenres available. Another effective way is to find books similar to yours in plot or concept and see where they're shelved.

⚠ **SOMETHING TO THINK ABOUT**: *Consider the defining characteristics of your novel. Does it have elements of a particular genre that place it soundly in that category? Write down any genre aspects and what genre they'd fall into.*

## Determining a Subgenre

Most genres have subgenres that further break down the novel categories. Sometimes those subgenres cross over into others, confusing the genre questions even more. Paranormal romance has romance, yet it also has supernatural elements like a fantasy. Urban fantasy takes place in the real world, but has fantasy elements as well.

The titles themselves give you clues here. The *type* of romance is paranormal, so it falls under the general romance genre. The *type* of fantasy is urban, so it falls under the general fantasy genre. If a major category is used to describe a novel, it's a safe bet that's the overall genre it belongs to.

### Do You *Need* a Subgenre?

Only if the subgenre has specific rules to how the novel is written, or would appeal to different markets. For example, you can't write a Regency romance without setting it in the Regency era (In the United Kingdom between 1811 and 1820). Cozy mysteries treat the mystery part differently than a police procedural mystery (Think *Murder She Wrote*–a cozy, vs. *CSI*–a procedural). If the subgenre has clear rules or guidelines, you'll want to know the specifics for that subgenre before you start writing it.

*For example:*

- ▶ If you want to write a paranormal romance, you need both romance and a paranormal element.
- ▶ If you took want to write a cozy mystery, you'll need an amateur sleuth and a lack of the more gruesome details of murder.
- ▶ If you want to write a steampunk fantasy, you'll need to know steam technology and what it means to be punk.

⚠ **SOMETHING TO THINK ABOUT**: *Look at your novel idea and see if it fits into a subgenre. If so, which one?*

### Genre Breakdown

Here's a general list of traditional genres. Almost all of these have subcategories that differentiate the genres even further. Please note, genres and subgenres are fluid and change as the markets evolve, but this should give you a basic idea of the various genres in the marketplace.

**Fantasy:** Contains a fantastical element of some type that is central to the plot. It often involves made up or alternative worlds. It explores things that could not possibly be, and a reader must suspend disbelief for the book to work. *Subgenres include, but are not limited to:* alternate world fantasy, Arthurian fantasy, contemporary fantasy, dark fantasy, epic or high fantasy, fairy tales and mythology, historical fantasy, magic realism, urban fantasy.

**Historical:** Takes place during a real period of history and deals with or includes real events and details, even though the story is fictional. Subgenres are broken down into historical time periods.

**Horror:** Horrifies or scares the reader. It explores something that makes the flesh crawl, plausible or implausible. *Subgenres include, but are not limited to:* erotic horror, ghost stories, Gothic horror, Lovecraftian, noir horror, psychological horror, splatterpunk, supernatural horror, suspense or dark suspense.

**Literary Fiction:** Focuses more on the quality of the writing, often lyrical, and the plots are more internal than external. Plots also frequently follow the inner journey of a character.

**Mystery:** Revolves around a puzzle that needs to be solved, with the protagonist spending the book trying to figure it out along with the reader. Finding out "whodunnit" is key. *Subgenres include, but are not limited to:* amateur sleuths, cozy mystery, courtroom drama, crime, detectives, espionage, heists and capers, medical, police procedural, private detective, psychological suspense.

**Romance:** The love story is the primary focus of the book and there is usually a happily ever after or happily for now ending. Getting two people together is what the book is all about. *Subgenres include, but are not limited to:* contemporary series romance, contemporary single title romance, erotica, erotic romance, fantasy and futuristic romance, Gothic romance, historical romance, inspirational romance, novels with strong romantic elements, paranormal romance, Regency romance, romantic suspense, time travel romance, western romance.

**Science Fiction (SF):** The science aspect is central to the plot. If you took out the science, the plot or story would fall apart. It's also defined as exploring things that could plausibly be, but aren't yet. *Subgenres include, but are not limited to:* adventure, alternate history, apocalyptic science fiction, cyberpunk, dystopian science fiction, hard science fiction, military science fiction, soft and sociological science fiction, space and exploration, space opera, space western, time travel.

**Thriller:** It thrills. The point of the novel is often to stop something terrible from happening on a large scale, with regular people caught up in events much bigger than themselves. *Subgenres include, but are not limited to:* conspiracies, crime thrillers, espionage and spy thrillers, legal thrillers, medical thrillers, military thrillers, police procedurals, political thrillers, suspense thrillers, techno thrillers.

**Western:** Stories set in the American west, or encompassing the frontier or pioneer resilience and spirit of the Old West. *Subgenres include, but are not limited to:* Buffalo soldiers, bounty hunters, cattle drive westerns, Civil War westerns, contemporary westerns, cowpunk, gold rush, Indian wars, lawmen and outlaws, railroad and land rush, wagon trains and pioneers.

**Women's Fiction:** Stories aimed at women readers, with female characters dealing with women's issues. They're often heavy on relationships, from family dynamics to romance.

**General or Mainstream Fiction:** Everything else. A plain "novel" fits here. If it's a story about people doing normal people things, it's probably mainstream fiction.

**BRAINSTORMING QUESTIONS:**
Answer these questions to further pinpoint the type of novel you want to write.

1. Where do you see this book on the shelves?

2. What is the one defining characteristic of the novel?

3. What is the core conflict of the novel?

4. What other books are similar to it?

5. What genres are *those* books categorized as?

6. What do *you* feel you're writing?

7. What are the key elements you use to describe the novel to people?

8. What genre are *those* elements?

# EXERCISE:
# Determine the Genre of Your Novel

>>**Write down the genre you feel best suits your novel. If it fits a subgenre, write that down as well.**

If your novel is hard to classify, look for the strongest genre element. If there is no genre, remember that "fiction" is applicable.

*For example:*

▶ Mystery or suspense

▶ Science fiction with romantic elements

▶ Romance

# ASSIGNMENT SIX: Finalize the Market and Genre of Your Novel

>>Using all the notes you made in Workshop Six, choose which market your novel is targeting, and why this is the best market for it.

>>Choose which genre best suits it and state why.

>>Pick a subgenre if applicable, and state how this fits your novel.

*For example:*

▶ Young adult suspense, because the protagonist and main characters are teens dealing with teen issues. The goal of the book is to solve the puzzle and the mystery puts the characters' lives in danger. (three teens summoned to a diner in the middle of the night)

▶ Adult science fiction with romantic elements, because the plot focuses on the zombie attacks, but the character arcs focus on the romance between Bob and Jane. The characters and problems are from an adult worldview. (Bob, facing the zombie apocalypse while navigating a love triangle)

▶ Adult romance, because the focus is on the relationship between two adults, Adam and Hannah, with the plot of overcoming their family issues. The end goal is for them to get together and live happily ever after. (Hannah and Adam falling in love and trying to bring peace between their feuding families)

In Workshop Seven, we'll move on to determining the size and scope of your novel.

# Workshop Seven: Determining the Size and Scope of Your Novel

**What You Need to Start This Workshop:** An idea of what kind of novel you'd like to write.

**The Goal of This Workshop:** To determine the size and scope of your novel.

**What We'll Discuss in This Workshop:** How to examine other books in your chosen market and genre to determine how big you want your novel (and story) to be.

**Writing Terms Used in This Workshop:**

**Pacing:** The speed of the novel, or how quickly the story moves.

**Series:** Multiple books using the same characters and/or world.

**Sequel:** A second book that continues where the first book leaves off.

**Single-Title Novel:** A romance novel that isn't part of a publisher's category.

**Stand-Alone Novel:** A novel that contains one complete story in one book.

**Trilogy:** A story that is told over the course of three books.

**Word Count:** The number of words contained in a novel.

# Welcome to Workshop Seven: Determining the Size and Scope of Your Novel

Sometimes we don't know the full scope of our novels until we write them, but plenty of writers envision a novel as a series before they write the first word. Knowing if it's a stand-alone novel or a series helps to plan the best way to handle that novel.

Just like with market and genre, it's not necessary to know the scope of your novel before you write it, but it can be a useful tool.

If you're writing for fun or don't want to worry about word counts yet, then feel free to skip ahead to Workshop Eight: Turning Your Idea Into a Summary Line.

## How Long Should Your Novel Be?

Although e-books are changing how the publishing industry views word counts (if you don't have to spend money to print it, the size of the book isn't as important), they're still a major part in determining the size of the novel. If you try to sell a 55,000-word epic fantasy, odds are the novel will be considered too short. The opposite problem is likely to happen with a 130,000-word cozy mystery, which is about twice the usual size for the genre.

However, like so much of writing, word counts are general guidelines, not hard and fast rules. Strong pacing is more important to how a novel reads than the number of words, but word count *is* a good starting point when planning a novel. Knowing the target size can help you understand how to structure your chapters and major plot points.

**Why the word count is important:** Word count guidelines provide a framework in which to plan a novel, and can actually make it easier for a writer, because you have a structure to work within.

## Word Count Ranges

Word counts for a typical adult novel run between 80,000 and 100,000 words. There *are* genres that lie outside of this range, though. Mysteries can go as low as 60,000 words and historical fiction and epic fantasy can rise as high as 140,000 words. Juvenile fiction runs between 50,000 to 80,000 words for young adult, 25,000 to 50,000 words for middle grade.

These are general ranges and there is wiggle room. A little bit over or under (say 10 percent) if usually fine, but if the average size of the genre and market you're aiming for is 65,000 words, a 110,000-word novel is certainly going to be too long. That's like trying to pitch a movie for a thirty-minute sitcom slot.

Exceptions do exist, and for every person who says you'll never get published with a 145,000-word book, another says Bestseller Bob's book was 145,000 words. Yes, it does happen, but those novels succeeded *in spite of the word count,* not because of it. Novels stand a much better chance at success when they fall within the norms.

If you feel the novel absolutely-without-a-doubt *has* to be that size, then go for it. Because ultimately...

**It's not about how many words you have, but what those words do, that counts.**

*This* is the holy grail of word counts.

The goal of any novel is to grab readers from the start, offer them a story they just can't put down, and hold that attention until the end. The trick is to make sure every word used does exactly that. Seventy-five thousand words that *don't* grab a reader will make the novel fail. 140,000 words that *do* grab a reader and hold tight will make the novel succeed. It's the execution that matters most. A great novel is a great novel. Tell the story to the best of your ability, however many words that is. If a word isn't pulling its weight, cut it. If it's a star performer, let it shine.

**BRAINSTORMING QUESTIONS:**

Pick five novels that best fit your chosen market and genre. Try not to choose mega-bestsellers, as these novels don't always fit the norm and are often outside the average.

1. What is the word count for each novel?

   To determine this, either look it up online (word count is sometimes part of the product details) or estimate it by taking the average of ten lines of text, then counting how many lines per page, and determining a per-page number. Then multiply that number by the page count. You can do this with a physical book or count in the "look inside" feature online.

   *For example:*

   - Pick the first full page of text in the novel
   - Count the number of words in the first 10 lines (say it's 83 words)
   - Divide that number by the number of lines (10) to get the average number of words (8 words per line)
   - Now count the number of lines on the page (say it's 28 lines)
   - Multiply the number of lines per page by the average number of words per line to get the average number of words per page ( 28 x 8 = 224 words per page)
   - Multiply the average number of words per page by the number of pages to get the general word count (224 x 387 = 86,668 words in the novel)

2. What is the word count range for all five novels?

3. Which novels are your favorites?

4. What are the word counts for those novels?

5. What size feels like a good target word count for your novel?

# EXERCISE:
# Determine Your Target Word Count

## >>Write down the target word count for your novel.

This is a rough estimate, not something set in stone. The goal is to find a target size that will help you determine where classic story structure elements fall when you outline and/or write your novel. It will also give you an idea if your novel fits with your chosen market and genre or if it's outside the average.

*For example:*

▶ 60,000 words (a common word count range for a YA novel)

▶ 100,000 words (a common word count range for an adult science fiction novel)

▶ 80,000 words (a common word count range for an adult romance)

# Writing a Trilogy or Series

At this stage, you might know you want to write more than one novel—either a trilogy (where one story takes multiple novels to resolve) or a series (where each novel follows the same character or is set in the same world with a similar plot type). The story you want to tell is larger than can be contained in one novel.

Planning a trilogy or series is a little different than planning a stand-alone novel, though the process is similar. Each novel has a core conflict that has to be resolved, and that core conflict often leads the protagonist to the next book. In the case of a series, that conflict might resolve in each novel and allow the protagonist to take on a new problem in the next book. In a same-world series (where you have different characters each novel, all living in the same world), you might have new core conflicts every novel or the same conflict through multiple characters over several novels.

**REALITY CHECK:** The idea of writing multiple novels has a certain allure, especially if you're a fan of an author who has a series or two out there. Writing multiple novels with the same characters and world takes a lot of time and effort, so before jumping in, it's worth considering if you really want to dedicate the time to it or not. There's no wrong answer here, it's just what *you* want to do. If you're the type of writer who gets lots of different ideas, you might find it constricting to stay in one world with one set of characters for a long time. If you're the type who hates the thought of saying goodbye to your characters and world at the end of a novel, a series might be for you.

When considering a trilogy or series, it's not a bad idea to do a little extra planning on the front end. The following is some basic information to consider before writing a trilogy or series.

## Writing a Trilogy

A trilogy is a complicated thing to plan, because it needs a core conflict for each novel, as well as an overall story conflict that spans all three novels. It's essentially one large novel broken into parts, but just like all the parts must work together in one novel, all the novels must work together in one trilogy. Every novel should have a core conflict and that conflict should be resolved by the end of the novel, even if something bigger is left hanging until the final book.

What's different about a trilogy vs. a stand-alone novel is that "defeat the antagonist and stop the apocalypse" is a good conflict for one book, and it's even a good conflict for a full trilogy, but each novel still has to be about more than just that *one* conflict. Conceptually, the protagonist spends the entire trilogy trying to stop the antagonist, but not every scene can focus on her doing it or the trilogy will feel repetitive and boring.

To keep readers hooked, it's better to work up to that all-important trilogy goal. Think about *how* each novel is a step toward how she defeats the antagonist and saves the day. The individual novels will have their own plot arcs, and each plot arc will fit into the larger trilogy arc.

**A WARNING ABOUT TRILOGIES:** Sometimes the decision to write a trilogy gets made before the idea has been fleshed out enough to determine if the idea can *carry* an entire trilogy, so the trilogy is planned like a stand-alone novel stretched over three books. This almost always results in a Book One that's all setup and doesn't feel like it's going anywhere, a Book Two that drags the plot out and ends with nothing being resolved, and a Book Three that feels like a slow march to the antagonist that takes way too long. There might be a solid plot arc, but it's filled with fluff to make it fit three books when one book is all it needed. Make sure you have enough conflict and story to fill three books before you write them.

Sure you want to write a trilogy? Then let's dive in and look at ways to make planning your trilogy easier.

## Figure Out the Rough Plot in Advance

It helps to think of a trilogy like a stand-alone book broken into acts. In a novel, there's act one, the setup and inciting event; act two, where all the real trouble happens and the stakes escalate; and act three, the final showdown with the antagonist, the climax, and the wrap up. In a trilogy, Book One is like the setup and inciting event, Book Two is like the middle, and Book Three is like the resolution and climax. However, writing it like that often results in the too-stretched-out feeling I just mentioned, so you'd want to tweak it a little to have a trilogy story arc as well as individual story arcs per book.

If we look at the trilogy goals the same way we look at the stand-alone novel goals, we can see the major plot points that need to happen over the course of that (three book) story.

**Book One = Act One:** It's setup, but not in the bad "too much exposition" way. The protagonist learns about a problem, and something major happens that sets her on the path to the larger story goal (the inciting event). Resolving that larger goal resolves the book's core conflict. The difference in a trilogy, is that resolving the first book's conflict also resolves the trilogy's "inciting event" and launches the second act of the story. The events of Book Two happen *because of* the resolution of Book One.

Let's use my fantasy novel, *The Shifter,* as an example:

> ▶ The Book One/Act One inciting event is all about the protagonist, Nya, discovering that her sister is missing. That discovery is what launches the core conflict of the novel. By the time she resolves that problem (the end), she's uncovered the fact that the Duke is up to no good (the antagonist for the entire trilogy, who is only mentioned in Book One). That discovery launches Book Two, same as the discovery that her sister was missing launched the plot in Book One. The trilogy goal of defeating the Duke isn't even a blip on the radar in Book One, but the story *is* heading in that direction. Nya doesn't know there's a larger trilogy problem until the end of the first book, just like she doesn't know there's a book problem at the start of the first book. The structure of the first book mirrors the structure of a stand-alone novel's act one.

**Book Two = Act Two:** In Book Two, there's the middle. The inciting event has created a situation where things get worse and worse and sacrifices must be made. The Book One goal will be carried over since that's usually what's launching Book Two, but now it's time to throw in the next step of the overall series goal. Just like a midpoint reversal, something will likely happen in Book Two that sends the story in a new direction, often toward what the series goal is. Book Twos are often resolved in a darker way with more lost because they represent the dark moment of the story arc.

*For example:*

▶ Nya knows the Duke is bad news by the end of Book One, and her Book Two goal is to prevent him from getting what he wants. She isn't out to defeat him yet, she just wants to throw a wrench in his plans. But her actions cause things to get worse, and then she reaches that tipping point where she realizes she's in way over her head and getting out of this mess won't be easy. In stand-alone book terms, this is act two's dark moment of the soul, the point of no return that often happens right before act three and heads into the climax. For a Book Two, it's often the resolution to the core conflict of that book.

**Book Three = Act Three:** In Book Three, it's the race to the climax, same as an act three. This is where that trilogy goal is most likely going to come center stage and become the core conflict of the final book. The discovery or realization of that trilogy goal is often Book Three's inciting event. The protagonist figures out what has to be done (same as in a stand-alone act three) and then takes steps to do it. The entire Book Three is similar to a stand-alone novel's climax, and can include many of the same traits—such as travel to a new location, a surprise twist, and a major sacrifice.

*For example:*

▶ Nya finds herself in a situation in the beginning of Book Three where she realizes the only way to get what she needs (her book goal) is to defeat the Duke. This realization starts her on the path of the plot of Book Three, and she makes a lot of sacrifices to work her way toward that final showdown with the Duke (same as a typical stand-alone act three). She figures out what to do and resolves this conflict. The resolution is satisfying not only for Book Three, but it resolves the larger trilogy goal that was hinted at in Book One, deepened in Book Two, and put front-and-center in Book Three.

By looking at the three books as three acts, you can see how you might develop the plot using the same story structure. You can treat each step as a goal that must be resolved per book, and plot from there. Instead of leaving things unresolved at the end of an act (each book), resolve it in a way that would satisfy a reader, yet still launch the next book in the trilogy. A few subplots might be unresolved, and that's okay as long as the core conflicts for that book are resolved.

⚠ **SOMETHING TO THINK ABOUT**: *Consider how your idea might span three books. Are there steps from the start of the problem to a bigger conflict? List those steps.*

## Figure Out the Characters in Advance

Characters slip in as trilogies evolve, even when we plan ahead. Adding five or six new characters each book might not seem like a big deal, but then in Book Three, there's a huge, unmanageable cast with dozens and dozens of characters, each with his or her own small subplot. It can be maddening trying to wrap up all those extra subplots.

Consider pre-planning some characters that can be recycled each book to help eliminate character creep. Perhaps some walk-on characters like shopkeepers or neighbors can play dual roles and show up in later books. For example, if an expert on some topic is needed later, why not give a neighbor that skill set in an earlier book? Or a guard that has to be in the right place in Book Three to help, might be someone the protagonist works with in Book One.

It's not critical to know exactly who will be needed at this stage, but just knowing that by Book Three the story will need someone who "is willing to turn against the antagonist" can suggest possible recurring characters to slip into earlier books. Maybe something that happens in Book One or Two is the trigger that *makes* that character decide to turn against her boss in Book Three.

This is also a great way to layer in characters and subplots, so it feels as though you planned it all along.

⚠ **SOMETHING TO THINK ABOUT**: *Consider the characters you might want or need in your trilogy. The main characters, any possible characters or types they might need later, supporting characters or roles that could come in handy. Write down your ideas.*

## Figure Out Any Big Secrets in Advance

Naturally, you won't know everything before you start writing, and secrets are always discovered as the novel develops, but a little planning can save a lot of frustration later. If you know certain secrets or information won't come up until later books, you can consider plot or story options that lead into those—where the right spot to reveal them is, and how they might be positioned for the most impact, where they might do the most damage to the protagonist's plan, etc.

*For example:*

▶ The protagonist's parents are actually still alive (so you can drop hints at various times in the trilogy, and decide where this reveal will happen).

▶ A trusted friend is really a spy for the evil king (so you can decide what clues to drop and when, and figure out how and where the "friend" double-crossed the protagonist without her realizing it).

▶ The *"bon voyage* ceremony" is actually executing the people who participate in it (so you can establish what the characters might think happens and then shock them later when they uncover the truth).

Another handy use for secret reveals is to keep the story moving during slower plot moments. In areas where not a lot is going on, adding a reveal might be enough to keep readers hooked.

⚠ **SOMETHING TO THINK ABOUT:** *Consider what secrets or information you might have in your trilogy. It might be history, or a reason why something is the way it is. Write down any ideas on how you might surprise the reader (and the characters) and when in the trilogy that might occur.*

**BRAINSTORMING QUESTIONS:**
Try breaking your trilogy idea into the three major turning points, and do a rough outline or quick summary of how it might unfold.

1. What is the moment/event where the protagonist first realizes there's a larger trilogy problem? This is likely connected to the resolution and core conflict goal of Book One.

2. What is the moment/event where the protagonist first realizes she's completely in over her head and has only made things worse? This is likely connected to your Book Two core conflict and goal.

3. What is the moment/event where your protagonist realizes the only way to win is to resolve the trilogy goal? This is likely the core conflict and goal of Book Three.

4. How might you escalate the stakes at each of these stages? This is likely connected to your character arc in some way, as your protagonist has to make a sacrifice or face tougher choices.

5. What secrets might be revealed over the course of the trilogy? This is a good way to tie in your conflict arcs with your character arcs.

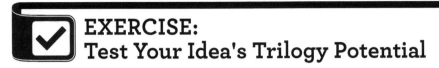

# EXERCISE:
## Test Your Idea's Trilogy Potential

Not every idea will be right for a trilogy, so if you're thinking about writing one, test it to see if it has what it needs to span three novels.

- Does each novel have a core conflict that can be resolved?

- Does each novel have something personal at stake for the protagonist?

- Do the stakes escalate in each book?

- Does each novel trigger the next book?

- Does the final book resolve a problem that has been building for three books and connects the previous core conflicts?

If you answered yes to these questions, then you likely have a workable trilogy idea. If you answered no to one or two of them, you might want to develop your idea more before you start writing. If you answered no to three or more, you probably don't have a big enough idea for a trilogy yet.

## Should You Write the Whole Trilogy at Once?

One common question when planning a trilogy is: Do you write it all at first, or do you write only the first book and see if it sells before writing the rest? There's no right or wrong answer here, it's whatever you want to do, but there are benefits and detriments to both options.

The "write one book first" camp advises writing only the first book of the trilogy and worrying about the rest if/when it sells. This allows you to explore an idea without feeling like you have to stay in that world for a long time if other ideas spark interest.

**Upside:** If the first book doesn't sell, there's no wasted time on a sequel that also won't sell. Though it is a good idea to prepare a synopsis for the next two books so important information doesn't get lost.

**Downside:** Once the book is written and published, you can't make changes to the first book. You're stuck with whatever you wrote. If you come up with a great plot idea in Book Two, you can't go back and add hints or groundwork to Book One.

The "write them all" camp advises working on all three books as if they were one book broken into parts (generally speaking). That way, anything can be adjusted in any book as needed. I suspect this would be especially helpful for pantsers who don't always know where the story is going to take them.

**Upside:** If you write the entire trilogy at once, anything new you come up with or change in Book Three can be included or setup in Book One. The entire trilogy can be fleshed out as one story so all the pieces work together seamlessly.

**Downside:** It'll probably take a lot longer to get a full trilogy written than a single book. This could be problematic if there are contracts to fulfill, or if you're in a hurry to start querying. It can also trap you into writing one story for a long time, where you can't move on to new ideas.

A good compromise can split the difference. A detailed outline or synopsis gets the major points of a trilogy aligned, and still allows for writing one book at a time. Some in-depth character and world building notes can ensure there's a solid understanding of how things work and how people live in that world. If the goal is to write one book and then wait, then the more details you gather about the next book would be a tremendous help in writing it later.

---

 **BRAINSTORMING QUESTIONS:**
Answer the following questions to determine whether or not to write the entire trilogy first.

1. Can the first book stand alone even if you never write the others?

2. Do you need to see how it ends before you'll feel confident submitting or publishing it?

3. Do you know where the story is going or are you still figuring out the major parts?

4. Do you have other novels you'd rather write or feel might be more marketable?

5. Which way do *you* want to go?

6. Will the trilogy be better if you write the whole thing at once? Worse?

7. Do you want agent/editor/reviewer feedback before you write the rest?

---

## Writing a Series

If your story needs more than three novels to tell it, you might have a series brewing. A series is an investment, both on the writer's part, and the reader's. It's designed from the start to span multiple books, and those books are often open-ended. It's a commitment to live in the same world with the same characters for years—or even decades. It can also be rewarding and enjoyable to do, because you have so much time to develop stories and characters in the same world.

A series also makes a promise to readers that you'll continue with this story and characters and keep giving them the books they've come to love. If you promise your protagonist will grow and learn from her mistakes, she'd better grow and learn. If you promise your protagonist will always be the person she is now, then don't change her into something readers won't recognize.

Just like a stand-alone novel or a trilogy, a series follows the same structure as any other novel. Each book will have a core conflict, a protagonist, antagonist, and a resolution at the climax.

What's different about a series vs. a trilogy is that a series doesn't always continue the same story, or even the same characters. It might be a series of stand-alone novels that all explore a common concept, like a romance series set in the same world with a different pair of lovers each book. Or a mystery that has the same detective solving a different case each book. It might have a common element that ties the books together, like characters who all work at the same law firm or who are all part of the same family. Some series can be read out of order; others require reading them in chronological order to fully understand them.

Here are some things to consider when planning a series:

## The Concept or Hook Behind the Series

A successful series is more than just a lot of books about a character or world. There's a concept behind it that ties the books together and gives readers a reason to come back book after book. It could be as simple as a detective doing his job, a unique person dealing with a recurring situation only she can handle, or a fascinating world connecting a group of characters.

*For example:*

▶ A series about a family of assassins as they navigate life, love, and paid hits (The Bombay Series, Leslie Langtry)

▶ A series of novels that start with every letter of the alphabet (The Kinsey Millhone Alphabet Series, Sue Grafton)

▶ A barbecue-themed series that includes recipes (The Memphis BBQ Mystery Series, Riley Adams)

The concept or hook will be at the heart of every book. It will likely be how you describe the series to people, as it will define what the series is about.

⚠ **SOMETHING TO THINK ABOUT**: *If the concept is at the core of your series, how might this concept carry multiple books?*

## The Overarching Series Conflict

If the series is situational, like a mystery with a detective, each book will have its own goal and there might not be a bigger issue hanging over the protagonist's head (though there might be a larger character arc goal to work toward as the series develops). But if the series is designed to feel like an ongoing character in an evolving world trying to resolve a larger problem, the plot of each book will march toward that final conflict. The core conflict of the series is never resolved until the final book of the series, even if readers know what that end goal is all along.

*For example:*

▶ Defeating Voldemort (The Harry Potter Series, J.K. Rowling)

▶ Getting a war-weary fleet home through enemy space (The Lost Fleet Series, Jack Campbell)

▶ Solving a deadly puzzle and uncovering a dark secret (The Maze Runner Series, James Dashner)

The series conflict is more than one problem that never gets solved. An ending that always feels delayed can make readers feel like the story is being artificially dragged out. The world and characters will have a variety of problems and issues that can be tapped at any time in any book so it always feels like things are progressing toward that larger goal. There will be multiple conflicts to drive multiple novels.

⚠ **SOMETHING TO THINK ABOUT**: *If the series has an end point, what conflicts and potential problems might occur between the first and last books of the series?*

## The Characters

If the series will follow one or two characters, knowing who they are and what they have to gain is key to knowing what each book will be about later. If it's a common world with common characters who each take focus in different books, then it'll likely have common secondary and support characters as well.

*For example:*

- ▶ A series that follows a telepath and recovering addict working with a futuristic Atlanta police department (The Mindspace Investigation Series, Alex Hughes)
- ▶ A series that focuses on the romantic lives of different characters in the same paranormal world, each playing a role of protagonist or supporting character in different books (The Blud Series, Delilah S. Dawson)
- ▶ A series that focuses on one character with a clear purpose that has a new plot each book, such as an occult bounty hunter trying to rid the world of monsters (The Deacon Chalk Series, James R. Tuck)

The intended genre can also play a role in character creation and development. Some genres expect character growth while others never have the protagonist change. James Bond is the same in every book, while Stephanie Plum learns and grows from her experiences. If the characters are all part of the same world, they might learn from each other's experiences or have one plot affect another in the series.

*For example:*

- ▶ Cammie Morgan, girl spy, grows from a (mostly) innocent teen to a capable spy over the course of her years at a boarding school for spies (The Gallagher Girls Series, Ally Carter)
- ▶ Nancy Drew stays the same girl detective in every book (The Nancy Drew Series, Carolyn Keene)
- ▶ Jack Ryan grows from CIA analyst to President of the United States over multiple novels (Jack Ryan thrillers by Tom Clancy)

The main characters will also need enough conflict to sustain a series. They'll be connected to the core conflict of the series, and have reasons to solve all the problems that will be encountered over the course of the series.

Consider the difference between various television dramas. Some shows resolve an issue every week and very little changes about the cast. Who they are at the end of the show or even the season is the same as when they started. Character growth isn't the point of the show, it's what the plot problem is every week. There's also little to no character turnover as the cast *is* the cast. In some cases, the characters don't even age.

*For example:*

▶ The medical drama *House*

▶ The police procedural *NCIS*

▶ The comedy *Seinfeld*

Other shows evolve every week, and the characters change in significant ways. Characters come and go and you're never sure who might be on the chopping block. Character growth is clear and characters have changed considerably from when they first came on the show.

*For example:*

▶ The paranormal drama *Buffy the Vampire Slayer*

▶ The medical drama *Grey's Anatomy*

▶ The comedy *How I Met Your Mother*

There are also different kinds of characters in a series: the bulletproof cast, and the fair game cast.

Bulletproof characters are just what they sound like—the ones that won't die. These are your main characters and the ones readers come back to visit every novel. Killing these characters will make for some *extremely* unhappy readers.

Fair game characters are, well, fair game. These are the ones who can die, be horribly injured, and have terrible things happen to them without unduly upsetting your readers. Some of them are even in the series for the purpose of dying to show stakes or trigger something in the protagonist.

Fair game characters are different from throwaway characters—characters who are there just to kill off to make a point. Readers don't usually care about those characters, so their deaths aren't meaningful. But a fair game character means something to a reader, and her death can hit hard.

A mix of character types can work best, as you'll always have options for whatever story you're telling at any stage in your series.

⚠ **SOMETHING TO THINK ABOUT**: *Where do you see the characters in your series? Are they static or will they grow? Are they bulletproof or fair game?*

## The Series Timeline

The series might take place over a few weeks, or it could follow a family for generations. How long the story will take to unfold can affect how it's written and what characters will be part of that world. If it takes place over years, the characters might age (like in the Harry Potter Series). For a timeless feel, characters might appear the same age or ageless (like in the Nancy Drew Series).

Series where the protagonist never changes are often open ended, because the individual book conflict is what draws readers in (like a mystery). They want to see the protagonist solve the problem and they enjoy reading that plot type over and over. Series where the protagonist changes and evolves often have predetermined events that signal the end of the series. They might even be designed from the start to run only a certain number of books.

⚠ **SOMETHING TO THINK ABOUT**: *What time frame might your series happen in? Does each book happen over a short period of time or is it drawn out over years? Is there a difference in individual books vs. the entire series?*

## The Series World

No matter what the setting, the series will take place somewhere, and that world will appear in every book. Rules and common elements might change over the course of the series, especially in genres with special rules (magic, science, history). It's a good idea to establish those rules before writing so they aren't accidentally broken later.

*For example:*

- ▶ Dyslexia is common among half-bloods (demi-gods) (Percy Jackson and the Olympians Series, Rick Riordan)
- ▶ Grave witches' eyesight is affected when they use their magic (The Alex Craft Series, Kalayna Price)
- ▶ Vampires exist in the world and even drink synthetic blood (The Southern Vampire Series, Charlaine Harris)

The more inherent conflict in the world, the more available plot options there will be over the life of the series. It's worth considering the types of conflict as well, and designing a world or setting that provides the deepest pool to drawn from.

⚠ **SOMETHING TO THINK ABOUT**: *What about your world might remain the same every book? What rules might apply? What might you need to establish right away that could cause trouble for your protagonist in later books?*

## The Reader's Investment

A series asks a lot from readers. We want them to invest time and emotion in the characters and world. Think about possible rewards for their commitment, what they can expect from the series, and how it will be worth their time.

Also consider what readers expect from a series in your chosen genre. If readers are accustomed to a happily ever after, they'll likely lose interest and stop reading if they never get one. Conversely, if they prefer the sexual tension of a romance, getting the characters together too early could rob readers of their enjoyment.

Readers might also lose interest if the series drags on and never resolves anything—always having things go wrong so the protagonist never wins and never gets ahead can be tiresome. Try to design a series that dangles the carrot, but offers other treats as well.

⚠ **SOMETHING TO THINK ABOUT**: *Because of the commitment a series requires, it's worth considering if you* really *want to write one or if you just like the idea of writing one (either one is fine; this is about what* *you want). How much time and effort are you willing to spend writing a series? Is this a series you want to spend years with? Will you get bored and want to write something different halfway through? Are you excited enough about this world and these characters to keep writing them for as long as you can?*

## The Series Bible

A series bible is a file or notebook that contains all the common and important details about a series for easy reference. It's a handy way to keep track of information as you write the series. Details about the characters, the setting, how special terms are spelled—whatever is important to keep consistent from book to book. It might seem silly to write down the color of the protagonist's eyes in Book One, but by Book Six you actually might not remember. It happens to even the biggest authors.

 **BRAINSTORMING QUESTIONS:**
Answer the following questions about your potential series.

1. Is your concept big enough to maintain multiple books? List five reasons why this series concept might hook readers.

2. Is there enough conflict in the idea to sustain multiple books? List five potential problems that could be the core conflict for future books.

3. Do you want your protagonist to change over the course of the series or stay the same? If she changes, describe a possible character arc that will take multiple books to resolve.

4. In what time frame does the series take place? Describe the length of time you envision, and if it's open ended or finite.

5. Is your world or setting large enough to maintain interest over a series? Describe your setting or world and list five possible ways each might influence a book idea.

6. Why would a reader return to this series after the first book? List five reasons why readers might invest time in this series.

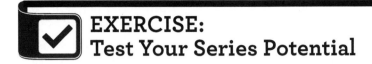

# EXERCISE:
## Test Your Series Potential

>>**Develop five book ideas for your series and craft a one-line summary for each.**

Sometimes an idea feels like it has the legs to become a series, but when you sit down to plot it out, you discover you can think up only a few ideas before it becomes the same plot with different details. Test your idea and see if it has enough depth to become a series.

>>**If your protagonist changes, create a character arc and show the growth over those five books. Write down where you want your protagonist to end up by the end of the series.**

You don't have to be detailed at this stage if you're still unsure. Knowing that your emotionally detached protagonist will eventually form solid commitments and relationships by the last book can be enough to get you started.

## ASSIGNMENT SEVEN: Finalize the Size and Scope of Your Novel

**>>Using all the notes you made in Workshop Seven, summarize:**

- Which market your novel is aimed at
- Which genre best suits it
- The subgenre if applicable
- Its is a series and what kind

If you've decided on more than one idea, answer for all. If this is a trilogy or a series, describe the overall series concept.

In Workshop Eight, we'll move on to writing a summary line of your novel.

# Workshop Eight: Turning Your Idea Into a Summary Line

**What You Need to Start This Workshop:** A fleshed-out idea for your novel.

**The Goal of This Workshop:** To take an idea and develop it into a one-sentence summary line you can build a novel from.

**What We'll Discuss in This Workshop:** What goes into a summary line; identifying the key elements of a summary line.

**Writing Terms Used in This Workshop:**

**Logline:** A one-sentence description of the novel.

**Query Letter:** A one-page letter used to describe a novel when submitting a manuscript to an agent or editor.

# Welcome to Workshop Eight: Turning Your Idea into a Summary Line

It's not uncommon to meet writers who have an idea, but aren't sure what to do with it. It might be a compelling premise they want to play with, a character who speaks to them, a fascinating concept they want to explore, or a plot idea that excites them—whatever it is, that nugget of inspiration is there.

A lack of ideas is not what's keeping these writers from writing their novels. They *have* ideas. Those ideas just aren't developed enough yet to write the novel the writer knows is there. You might have even been one of those writers when you started this book, but by now, you should have a fairly solid sense of the novel you want to write. Now it's time to finalize that idea into a summary line.

A summary line is a one-sentence description that sums up what your idea is about in a way that also captures the key elements needed to turn that idea into a novel.

At this stage, don't feel you have to write a pitch-perfect, one-sentence line. This isn't for agents or editors, it's for *you*. The goal here is to define the key elements of your story and plot so you can further develop them into an entire novel.

Workshop Eight is all about turning your idea (or ideas if you can't decide between a few) into that one sentence that captures the core of your novel.

## Understanding the Summary Line

The summary line has many different names. The hook, the logline, the through line, the premise line, the pitch. Depending on context, each varies a little in meaning, but at the core they all mean the same thing—the one sentence that sums up the novel.

A good summary line provides a clear sense of what the novel will be about. It often contains what first excited you about the idea, but it's more than just a spark of inspiration. It captures the core conflict and essence of the novel in a way that allows you to build a plot from it.

**Why the summary line is important:** During the drafting stage, this line will remind you what the novel is about and what you want to explore or illustrate in the book. Later, this line can develop into your pitch line for agents and editors, and be the answer to the question writers get all the time: What's your book about?

For template fans, a summary line basically contains: [The protagonist] + [what's important about the story] + [the twist or hook].

- **The protagonist:** This is who the novel is about.

- **What's important about the story:** This is usually the conflict or character arc, but it could also include a situation or character detail, or even what's at stake. This is probably why you decided to write this book.

- **The twist or hook:** This is what makes what's important to the story matter. It's the complication, the stakes, the conflict, the goal, or any number of pieces that take the novel and elevate it to "ooooh, that's cool" status.

Believe it or not, two great places to read a lot of summary lines are Netflix and the Internet Movie Database. On those sites you'll find one- or two-line descriptions of movies. Some are pretty good and make you want to see the film. Others are pretty bad and don't grab you at all. These are for finished stories (and thus more polished), but they should give you a sense of the types of elements to capture when crafting your own summary line.

Let's look at a few random ones. While these are for movies, the same principles apply to books:

- ▶ High school student Dave decides to transform himself into a masked crime fighter and becomes an Internet star. (*Kick Ass*)

**Breaks down to:** High school student Dave [the protagonist] decides to transform himself into a masked crime fighter [what's important about the story ] and becomes an Internet star [the twist or hook—the anonymous youth becomes famous].

From this we can guess that the conflict is going to come from his being a crime fighter and becoming an Internet star. Being "masked" suggests hiding his identity, while being a star implies being known, and those two ideas are in conflict. It's not spelled out exactly, but the potential for conflict is there.

Let's look at one that doesn't quite work yet:

▶ An elite assassin learns that someone from his past has put out a contract for his now-tranquil life. (*Killers*)

**Breaks down to:** An elite assassin [the protagonist] learns that someone from his past has put out a contract for his now-tranquil life. [what's important about the story]

See what's missing? There's no twist or hook here. Where's the "and then what?" that would give a sense of where this story might be going? Without a twist, it's often a lot harder to plot because we don't know where the conflict is coming from. Sure, someone is trying to kill him, but there's not a lot of conflict in an elite assassin having to take out someone trying to kill him. There's more to this story, but it's not showing up in the summary line yet.

But let's add the twist this is missing and see what happens:

▶ An elite assassin trying to be a common, middle-class husband learns that someone from his past has put out a contract for his now-tranquil life. (*Killers*)

**Breaks down to:** An elite assassin [the protagonist] trying to be a common middle-class husband [the twist or hook] learns that someone from his past has put out a contract for his now-tranquil life. [what's important about the story]

See the difference? Now we know that he's hiding his past from his wife, and that past is about to cause a lot of trouble in his life and marriage. The twist is the "elite assassin trying to be a normal guy," which is a flip on the "normal guy trying to be special" concept common in a lot of stories.

Let's try one that could be very similar to an early novel idea at this stage of development:

▶ To save 10-year-old Lilith from abusive parents, a social worker brings the girl into her own home, only to learn Lilith isn't what she seems. (*Case 39*)

**Breaks down to:** To save 10-year-old Lilith from abusive parents [what's important to the story], a social worker [the protagonist] brings the girl into her own home, only to learn Lilith isn't what she seems [the twist or hook].

We know nothing about this movie besides this summary, but we can already see the girl is the trouble here, not the parents. Odds are the parents were fighting for their lives in some way. This one has all the right pieces, with conflict and a suggestion of how the story is going to unfold. There are still things to figure out—such as what Lilith really is—but that can be developed more when this summary line is fleshed out into a summary blurb. (More on that in Workshop Nine)

Let's look at a summary line that works fairly well:

▶ A meek bank teller discovers a magical ancient mask that unleashes his deepest desires and gives him superhuman abilities to act on them. (*The Mask*)

**Breaks down to:** A meek bank teller [the protagonist] discovers a magical ancient mask that unleashes his deepest desires [what's important to the story] and gives him superhuman abilities to act on them [the twist or hook].

What I like about this summary line is the word choice. "Meek" conjures up a particular type of person. "Unleashes" suggests setting something free. Unleashing the deepest desires of a meek person has a lot of potential for conflict. Pair that with the twist—superhuman abilities—and you suddenly see where this can go. Meek goes wild. It accomplishes a lot by the words chosen. It doesn't have a specific conflict yet, but we can see where the conflict will come from.

Now that we have a sense of how the summary line might be written, let's take a peek at one for a novel:

▶ To save her sister, a rebellious girl volunteers to fight in her place in a televised game where randomly chosen teens battle to the death in a special arena to earn a year's worth of food for their district. (*The Hunger Games*)

We don't need to read the novel to know that this is a book that will involve sacrifice, family, oppression, fighting, and some pretty radical ideas about kids and violence.

But let's analyze *The Hunger Games* even further and look at how this summary line relates to the elements explored in the previous workshops, and what you can learn about your novel from doing those exercises:

**Is this plot driven or character driven?** This is a plot-driven novel more than a character-driven one. The focus is on the external problem to be solved—survival in the game.

**What type of conflict is this?** The individual contestants work as symbols of the society that forces teens to fight to the death, so this fits the Person vs. Society conflict.

**Who is the protagonist?** The girl who volunteers to fight to save her sister.

**Who is the antagonist?** On one level, the other contestants, on a grander scale, the people (society) forcing them to fight.

**What is the conflict?** The protagonist wants to survive and help her sister (and people). The other contestants want to kill her so they can survive. Everyone in the game wants to live, so everyone is an obstacle to what the protagonist wants. The book will be about surviving the battle, which has the additional stakes of the entire district surviving, since a year of food is part of the prize.

**What is the goal?** The protagonist wants to survive and return to her family and district.

**What are the stakes?** The protagonist's life, the survival of her sister and the district they live in.

**What is the theme?** Survival and sacrifice.

**What is the setting?** A battle arena, and the district in which the protagonist lives.

**What is the hook?** Kids battling to the death for entertainment.

All the pieces are here, even if not everything is fully fleshed out (nor does it need to be at this stage). But see how all the pieces come together to create that one sentence that takes the general idea and pinpoints what's important about it. The key elements that will turn that idea into a novel are all represented and connect back to the core conflict goal of the novel.

Even if the summary line doesn't use all the elements you've developed, simply writing them down and having them on hand can be helpful later. It's an easy reference sheet on what you want from the novel. It's also a useful test for any weak or underdeveloped areas before you start writing.

 **BRAINSTORMING QUESTIONS:**
Think about the things that might go into your summary line.

1.  Identify who your protagonist is and what's unique about him or her. Try listing three or four things you might use. Pick the most critical details or traits readers would need to know about this person (or people if you have an ensemble cast).

2.  Identify the most important elements of your story. Make of list of three or four of these. They can be anything you want, not just plot or world details. Next, if you had only *one* of those details to tell someone, which would it be?

3.  Identify the twist in your novel. You have an interesting person with some interesting trait, something interesting about the world he or she lives in or the situation—now list how these two things are connected. Your conflict will come into play here, and there's a good chance it'll be your inciting event. Inciting events are the setups for a novel, where the character faces a problem and has to decide to act or not. The character acts and the story begins.

# EXERCISE: Identify the Key Elements for Your Summary Line

>>**Using all of your notes and previous exercises, answer the following questions:**

- What is your idea?

- Is this a plot-driven or a character-driven novel?

- Who is your protagonist?

- Who or what is your antagonist?

- What is the conflict type?

- What are the core conflicts?

- What is the protagonist's goal?

- What is the antagonist's goal?

- What are the stakes?

- What is the theme?

- What is the setting?

- What is the hook?

# ASSIGNMENT EIGHT:
# Write Your Summary Line

By now you should have a pretty good idea what your novel is about, what the core conflict is, who your main characters are (both protagonist and antagonist), what their goals are, what the stakes are, the setting, the theme, and the hook. Some of the details might still be vague, but the foundation of the novel is there.

## >>Put it all together and write your summary line.

If you're having trouble getting started, try this template:

[The protagonist] + [what's important about the story] + [the twist or hook].

Don't be afraid to mix it up or move the order around if that works better for your idea.

*For example:*

▶ Three teens with dark secrets meet at a roadside dinner, unaware that one of them plans to reveal those secrets and destroy the others' reputations.

▶ A man in an unhappy marriage must find his inner hero during the zombie apocalypse to save the woman he truly loves.

▶ A workaholic entrepreneur and a risk-averse teacher from feuding families fall in love when the funeral of a beloved teacher draws them home and back into each other's lives.

In Workshop Nine, we'll build on this summary line and flesh it out into a summary blurb that could

# Workshop Nine: Turning Your Summary Line Into a Summary Blurb

**What You Need to Start This Workshop:** A summary line that encompasses who your protagonist is, the core conflict, the stakes, the antagonist, and the hook.

**The Goal of This Workshop:** To take the summary line and craft a summary blurb that captures the core plot elements of your novel.

**What We'll Discuss in This Workshop:** How to: develop the goals, conflicts, and stakes of the protagonist; develop the motives, goals, and stakes of the antagonist; develop the inciting event; develop the resolution of the novel's core conflicts.

**Writing Terms Used in This Workshop:**

**Exposition:** Narrative intended solely to convey information to the reader.

**Inciting Event:** The moment that triggers the core conflict of the novel and draws the protagonist into the plot.

# Welcome to Workshop Nine: Turning the Summary Line Into a Summary Blurb

In Workshop Eight we developed a one-sentence summary of your novel. Now, we're going to develop that summary line into a summary blurb that fleshes out the core elements of the plot. This is where you'll eliminate any vague statements and choose specific details to illustrate your novel idea.

The summary blurb helps you identify the protagonist, antagonist, story goal, conflict, stakes, inciting event, and how the novel's core conflicts are resolved. Because if you can't specify those seven things before you start a novel, you're likely to run into problems at the halfway mark, if not sooner.

Why?

Because something needs to be driving the protagonist, and thus drive the novel. That's the core conflict and goal, the big bad problem the novel is about. Tons of other things happen besides that, but that's the driving force behind everything that occurs in the novel, and resolving that issue is the climax of the novel. It's also where the stakes come from. Failure to solve that problem has consequences.

A strong summary blurb gets to the heart of the novel by pinpointing the core elements. The protagonist, the conflict, the stakes, where it all happens, how it all started, and why it all matters. If a blurb is difficult to write, that can suggest the idea is still missing vital pieces to make the novel work. This is why writing a blurb at the start is a good way to test the idea.

And remember, this blurb is for you, not an agent or editor, so it doesn't have to be polished or even well-written. It only has to contain the information that will help you write your novel.

# Getting to the Heart of Your Story

As writers, we create characters and stories in our minds and put them down on paper. Sometimes we know exactly what happens plot wise; other times we have a character shouting in our heads. We all have different processes and write with different voices.

What I find interesting is that no matter what genre we write in or what age group we write for, one thing stays the same.

The story.

On a basic level, stories are all identical—from novels to movies to television shows. They're about characters resolving problems. The protagonist sets off to accomplish a goal and struggles his way to the resolution. Some stories are huge, high-stakes epic dramas, and others are quiet character journeys, but they all fit that classic story format.

To me, this is comforting because I always know where I stand when I plan a novel. I know what I need to do (even if I'm not yet sure how to do it). The details of each book are all totally different, but the same elements are there no matter what kind of novel I'm planning.

- What does the protagonist want?
- Why does he want it?
- How will his life change if he doesn't get it?

These are the elements of a good summary blurb. Having these elements means if you get stuck during the writing process, you have a solid foundation of what your novel is about to help you move forward.

## What the Protagonist Wants

This is the reason the character decides to act—the goal. This goal works with the external plot and the internal character arc. Sometimes the goal is plot focused (to stop the terrorists before they blow up the Statue of Liberty). Other times it's character based (to be free from personal demons), or even a mix of the two (to find love again with the man she left behind).

The protagonist might not know he wants it when the novel opens, but it won't be long before he's been smacked in the face with the core conflict. Then what he wants will drive him to the end of the novel.

**Why the protagonist's goal is important:** It gives him something to do to help advance the plot. Without a goal, the protagonist would stand around waiting for things to happen to him, instead of causing the novel to happen by his actions.

**How this affects the summary blurb:** This goal is what the blurb will focus on. It's the essence of the novel, whether it's an external goal in a plot-driven novel or an internal goal for a character-driven novel.

*For example:*

> ▶ **What does the protagonist want:** To stop a group of thieves from robbing a building's vault.

⚠ **SOMETHING TO THINK ABOUT**: *What does your protagonist want? Write down some desires, both internal and external, big or small, that could work as goals throughout the novel.*

## Why the Protagonist Wants It

Just having a goal isn't enough. When a co-worker says, "I'm going for a cup of coffee, be right back," we don't worry that he won't get it. The same thing happens with the protagonist if his goal doesn't mean something to him.

This is where character motivations come in.

*For example:*

> ▶ **What does the protagonist want:** To stop a group of thieves from robbing a building's vault.
> ▶ **Why does the protagonist want this:** He's a cop and it's his job.

Does this make you any more intrigued than when a co-worker goes for coffee? Probably not, because it's still missing a vital part of the goal—the personal connection that turns the goal into something the protagonist is highly motivated to achieve, a reason the protagonist is acting that readers can relate to and empathize with.

**Why the protagonist's motivations are important:** Character motivation is key to making readers care about what the protagonist wants. People don't act for no reason. Even if that reason is selfish or dumb, there is a reason and it makes sense to the person doing it. What's more, that reason is personal. It's a reason that applies to this person in this circumstance. Otherwise, anyone in the vicinity of the plot could be the protagonist.

Let's try again:

▶ **What does the protagonist want:** To stop a group of thieves from robbing a building's vault.

▶ **Why does the protagonist want this?** Because his estranged wife is being held hostage by the thieves.

Stakes have been added and now it's *personal*. The price of failure is high. The protagonist is motivated to resolve his problem or something terrible will happen to his wife.

This is why having only a plot reason for the protagonist to act often results in weak, "why should I care?" novels. Any cop could show up at that building and the novel is basically the same. The protagonist should act because it matters to him personally.

The first, non-personal example is any forgettable cop plot. The second, personally motivated example is the movie *Die Hard*.

**How this affects the summary blurb:** The character motivations help make readers care about the character, and thus the book. They add credibility to the protagonist's actions and give him reasons to act that make sense. They help readers relate to the protagonist and the events of the novel.

⚠ **SOMETHING TO THINK ABOUT:** *Why does your protagonist want this goal? Write down some reasons, both personal and general, that could work as motivations.*

## How the Protagonist's Life Will Change if He Doesn't Get It

It's all about the stakes here. The consequences. The protagonist needs a *reason* to act (motivations), so let's give him a price if he fails (the stakes).

In character-driven novels this might be the number-one-most-important question in the entire book. If there are no life-altering consequences to the protagonist not getting what he wants, why spend an entire novel on this part of the character's life?

Even in plot-driven novels, the consequences of failure are driving the protagonist to act. He doesn't want the stadium to blow up, he has to find the missing treasure, he must stop the alien invasion. He might not go through as strong a character arc as in a character-driven plot, but his life will be worse off if he fails.

**Why the protagonist's stakes are important:** If the protagonist goes through this experience and failing doesn't affect him, then what was the point of the novel? Being sad about a bad thing happening isn't enough. We're all sad about bad things that happen every day, but they don't affect us in any lasting way. Stakes are life changing, and not in a good way. They make everything that happens in a novel matter.

Let's go back to the building and the hostages:

> ▶ If the cop doesn't stop the thieves and save his estranged wife, his wife will die.

That's personal *and* life changing. Not only will the cop have failed to save the woman he loves, but he'll know that he was there in the building and failed to protect her. For a cop, that has to be doubly hard because it hits him on a personal *and* a professional level. Professional he could get over, it's part of the job, but add that personal level? Now even the professional is made more personal.

If he fails to save his *wife*, then how good a cop could he really be? This creates professional doubt in him. It's even worse since he and his wife were estranged, because now he might worry that on some subconscious level, he failed on purpose. Did he *want* her to suffer a little for all the pain she'd put him through? Now there's doubt about the kind of person he is in addition to doubts about being a cop, a husband, and even a man. He'd have to explain to his kids why he couldn't save their mother and how he let her die. They'd never look at him the same way again.

That hits *hard*.

If the protagonist can pick himself up, dust himself off, and start all over another day with no repercussions if he fails, then the stakes aren't high enough.

**How this affects the summary blurb:** The stakes give a sense of urgency to the novel. It's the horrible fate if the protagonist fails, and often the reason he must act now instead of later. Readers will wonder, will the protagonist win or will he suffer the terrible consequence? What sacrifices will he make to achieve his goal? Will he make it in time?

⚠ **SOMETHING TO THINK ABOUT**: *What is your protagonist risking to achieve his goal? What consequences might he face? What ways might his life change, both for good and bad? Write down some consequences for both failure and success.*

It's important to add that "life and death" stakes aren't the only kind. You can have high, life-altering stakes over smaller issues and problems. Death can be metaphorical. A loss of confidence, a change in how you see yourself in the world, the death of a belief you always held as truth are all life changing, even if you go on afterward. The key is failing changes the protagonist for the worse.

And since we're talking about life and death . . . Be wary about making the death of the protagonist the main (or only) stake. Having the protagonist die seems like the highest stake you can have, but how often does the protagonist *actually* die in a novel? Readers know the protagonist will survive, and even that he'll succeed in the end, because that's how storytelling typically works. Try looking for fates worse than death that could actually happen.

**BRAINSTORMING QUESTIONS:**
Ask these three questions of your own idea. Use your notes to build the strongest and most compelling goal-motivation-stakes trio you can.

1. What does the protagonist want?

2. Why does the protagonist want this?

3. What about the protagonist's life will change if he or she fails?

# EXERCISE:
# Determine the Goal of Your Novel

>>**Describe what your protagonist wants, why it matters, and how his or her life will change if he or she fails to get it.**

*For example:*

▶ Lana wants redemption and forgiveness for causing her brother's accident, because the guilt is eating her alive, and if she doesn't get it, she'll descend onto a dangerous path of trying to punish herself by acting recklessly.

▶ Bob wants to divorce Sally and be with Jane, because he's miserable, and if he doesn't change his life he'll end up feeding Sally to the zombies just to get away from his misery.

▶ Adam wants to fill the empty void his life has become, because he fears he's turning into the despised person his business reputation says he is. If he doesn't change his ways, he'll be alone and unloved forever. Hannah wants some excitement and meaning in her life, because she's always played it safe and that hasn't brought her happiness. If she doesn't do something to shake up her life and seek out happiness, she'll wind up alone with a safe, predictable, but unhappy life.

# Getting to the Heart of Your Conflict

When writing a summary blurb, the conflict portion tends to focus on the hook, because the hook is the thing that will make the reader (and hopefully the author) think, "ooooh." It's typically where most of the story questions are going to come from—the things readers are going to want to know and will be willing to read the novel to find out.

There are two common hooks that get readers interested in the novel—the intellectual hook, and the emotional hook. While intellectual hooks are often stronger in plot-driven novels, and emotional hooks are stronger in character-driven novels, both are important in *any* novel to hook readers and keep them reading. The more hooks, the richer the reading experience.

## The Intellectual Hook

The intellectual hook is the plot. The things that happen, the overall external problem. Readers want to know how the plot unfolds because an interesting question has been raised right from the start of the novel (usually in the cover blurb). Intellectual hooks typically come from the external core conflict, because those are the puzzles that need solving.

Intellectual hooks can also be a great story question or a fascinating premise. Readers are offered something they haven't seen before (or haven't seen in this way before) and are kept on their toes, always guessing what will happen next. They want to see how this unfolds or what the twist is.

Intellectual hooks can be tougher to craft in character-driven novels, since the focus is on the internal not the external. If there's little happening to advance the plot externally, there's little to capture readers' curiosity on an intellectual level. If you're having trouble, try looking at the plot goals and think about what puzzles or questions might be developed there.

**Why the intellectual hook is important:** It gives you something to write about, and gives readers a reason to pick up the novel. It keeps an idea from being boring or unoriginal. It also crystallizes what's fresh about the idea.

**How this affects the summary blurb:** The intellectual hook is what the novel is about externally. It's the problem driving the novel and what readers are going to be interested in seeing resolved. It's the heart of the plot and a finish line to aim for.

⚠ **SOMETHING TO THINK ABOUT**: *What puzzles or mysteries are in your novel idea? What story questions do you want readers to ask when they pick up your novel? Write down what you want readers to wonder and how you might answer those questions.*

## The Emotional Hook

The emotional hook is what readers want to know on an emotional level—the internal struggles of the characters, the personal mysteries or drama, the things readers become emotionally invested in and want to see how they turn out. Emotional hooks typically come from the internal core conflict, the character journey, and that emotional growth.

Emotional hooks are often found in the character arc, because that's where the character growth occurs. It's the flaw the protagonist has to overcome, the secret holding her back, the personal demon causing her trouble (because perfect people are boring in a novel). It's the element that makes readers care if the protagonist succeeds in her goal or not.

Emotional hooks can be tougher to craft in plot-driven novels, since the focus is on the external not the internal. In order to engage with the emotion the character is feeling, readers need to care about the protagonist. Starting with universal themes can help here—a child in trouble, a lost love, grief, etc.—things that everyone can relate to and empathize with. If you're having trouble, try thinking about the flaws of your protagonist and how she has to overcome them to succeed.

**Why the emotional hook is important:** It's what makes readers care how the plot unfolds. It turns external plot elements into an emotional investment for readers.

**How this affects the summary blurb:** The emotional hook answers the "why should I care?" question, and shows readers (and you) why this novel is more than just a series of scenes where plot stuff happens.

⚠ **SOMETHING TO THINK ABOUT**: *What emotional hooks exist in your idea? What personal struggle is your protagonist going through? What emotional growth do you want readers worrying about and rooting for with your protagonist?*

 **BRAINSTORMING QUESTIONS:**
Explore the potential hooks in your novel.

1. What intellectual problem does your protagonist need to resolve?

   This is likely the external core conflict, or a larger problem the novel will spend time resolving. For example, finding the chef's killer, stopping the alien invasion, uncovering how Clara knows Matthew's secret and what she's up to. You might also want to write down any other major or interesting problems the protagonist faces as well, as there could be a theme developing you could use as an intellectual hook.

2. What are some story questions you want readers to wonder?

   Posing story questions to readers is a great way to keep them hooked. For example, who killed the milkmaid? What's in the black box? How will Harold get past the defense grid? They can be smaller, scene-driving questions that get answered quickly, or larger, novel-length questions. The biggest one is most likely the one you'll want for your summary blurb.

3. How are these questions going to be answered?

   The biggest question is typically the climax of the novel and how the core conflict is resolved. For example, the killer turns out to be Larry, the aliens are defeated by a brilliant tactical move, Clara is tricked into revealing her secret plan. For the smaller answers, the step-by-step questions can draw readers through the novel. If these smaller answers can lead to more questions, even better.

**4.** What emotional problem is your protagonist facing?

This is likely your internal core conflict. For example, personal self doubt, uncertainty about what she's doing, or a flaw the protagonist has to overcome. It can also be the smaller emotional conflicts as the novel unfolds, such as someone being arrogant and never listening to show a character who must learn to value the opinions of others.

**5.** What emotions do you want readers to feel as they read your novel?

If you want readers to worry, odds are your protagonist or other characters will be worrying. They'll feel and express the emotions you want to trigger in your readers. If your protagonist never fears for her life, then why should readers? It's also fun to plan the rise and fall of emotions to put readers on an emotional roller coaster over the course of the novel.

# EXERCISE:
## Determine the Hooks of Your Novel

## >>Describe the intellectual and emotional hooks.

The hooks can be phrased as questions readers might ask, or things you want to create in the story.

*For example:*

▶ **Intellectual Hook:** Who called the teens to the diner? What's the plan? Will their secrets be exposed?

**Emotional Hook:** Will Lana find redemption before she's exposed and loses her chance? Why does the bad guy want to hurt these people?

▶ **Intellectual Hook:** How did the zombie apocalypse happen? Is there a cure and will they find it?

**Emotional Hook:** Will Bob find the strength to tell Sally and Jane the truth, and if so, will it really make him happy?

▶ **Intellectual Hook:** What caused these two families to hate each other so much for so long?

**Emotional Hook:** Will Adam and Hannah be able to overcome their history, end the feud, and find love with each other?

# Getting to the Heart of Your Setting

Setting is a vital part of both a novel and a summary blurb. What happens in a novel is important, and where it happens can have a profound effect on the characters and their worldviews. If the setting doesn't add something to the mix, you might be wasting a great opportunity to deepen the novel or layer in more conflicts.

**Why the setting is important:** Location affects how people act and how they think. It's part of their culture and their history. Someone from 4th-century France has a very different outlook on life than a gal from modern New York City.

**How this affects the summary blurb:** The setting can be another tool in how to plot the novel. You can develop conflicts from how life works in that location, city, or time, and obstacles for plot events can come from common troubles of everyday life. Even internal arcs can be affected by setting.

While you can flesh out your setting more as you write the novel, knowing the general setting beforehand can help make future decisions easier.

For example, it's hard to describe *Gone With the Wind* without mentioning the South or the American Civil War. Racism, political divides, and family dynamics all play a role in the novel, and it wouldn't be the same without them. These details set a tone and an expectation about what the novel (and the characters) will be like. Aspects of the setting influence or define the novel so intimately that taking them out affects how the story unfolds.

A core element of the plot is Scarlet O'Hara trying to keep her family land and home, but if you took away the war, the major obstacle of the plot vanishes. Sure, you could give her other reasons to fight for her home, but you'd also lose the thematic elements the Civil War setting brings to the novel. If you can change the setting of the novel and nothing else changes but the background, that's a red flag you might not be taking advantage of all the opportunities a great setting has to offer.

The setting can also be used to deepen the theme. A novel with a love conquers all theme might work well in a location where love affected the history of that place in a positive way. If you're trying to show sexism is wrong and bad for everyone, setting the novel in a world where sexism is rampant, and has very clear effects on the people, lets you get that idea across without ever having to say "sexism is bad." You might also use different settings to show different ideas, such as, a town that follows one belief runs smoother than one that follows the opposite—though beware of anything that might come across as preachy.

Setting can even offer challenges to the protagonist that go beyond plot. If you want to show the protagonist learning to be self-reliant, putting her in a setting where she must do everything herself could be a great way to show her finally learning that valuable lesson. You might even use the setting to show that transformation, by starting her out in a setting where everything is done for her, then gradually taking things away as the novel progresses.

Setting is more than just what the environment looks like. It can convey a tone, a mood, a sense of history or culture. If you're writing a fantasy world, the type of magic or governmental structure might be important to the conflict. A murder mystery can be made all the more chilling if it's set on an island cut off from the mainland by a storm.

What something looks like is rarely as interesting as why it's there or how it affects things, so take advantage of all the meaning the right setting can bring to your novel.

For a summary blurb, you want to be able to describe the setting in a few words or sentences, otherwise it can risk bogging the idea down. It's also a red flag that there's too much world building if you spend more time on the setting than the conflicts or characters.

**BRAINSTORMING QUESTIONS:**
Think about where your novel is set and answer the following questions.

1. What are the critical elements of the setting?

2. If you changed your setting, what else would change?

3. What type of inherent conflicts occur in this setting?

4. Is there a history that creates a deeper thematic meaning?

5. Does the setting allow you to make a point you couldn't otherwise make?

6. Does the setting provide a challenge for your characters you couldn't otherwise have?

# EXERCISE:
# Embed the Setting Into Your Novel

**>>Describe your setting as it pertains to your novel and the conflict of that novel.**

*For example:*

► A roadside diner just outside of town, where few locals go but lots of traffic passes through. People are constantly coming and going, and any one of them could be the person who asked the trio there or could have something to do with why they're there.

► Cleveland during the zombie apocalypse, showing the world falling apart as Bob's life falls apart. The city is overrun, all of Bob's favorite places are destroyed or abandoned, his world is gone and just as lost as he feels.

► The small, southern town of Henderson, with quaint shops and streets, where everything *looks* perfect and wonderful. But in reality, it's all a lie, a facade used to hide the long-time family feud and decay of the town, suffering because the two sides can't make amends. Adam and Hannah are the key to fixing that and bringing new life and vitality back to the town (and the families).

**>>Next, boil your setting down to one or two sentences (if your first description was longer).**

*For example:*

► A rundown, roadside diner on the outskirts of town, perfect for a clandestine meeting

► Cleveland during the zombie apocalypse

► The small, southern town of Henderson, where everything looks perfect on the outside

# The Inciting Event

The inciting event is the moment early on in a novel when things irrevocably change for the protagonist. It's the event that sets her on the plot path of the novel, which is likely the whole reason someone picked up the book in the first place.

**Why the inciting event is important:** This is the point at which the protagonist leaves her normal life and enters the plot of the novel. It's the moment when her life changes and she's forced to face a problem that is either the core conflict of the novel, or—more commonly—the first step on the path to that core conflict.

It's important to note here that just because the inciting event can appear later in the novel, that doesn't mean the beginning of the novel is all setup and exposition. A solid goal, stakes, and conflict of some sort should be established right on page one. There's a catalyst that gets the protagonist to the inciting event (if the opening isn't the inciting event).

The inciting event can work as a bridge between the opening scene of the novel and the core conflict of that novel. It helps ease readers into the novel while still keeping them hooked and entertained.

How this affects the summary blurb: It states what triggers the plot and suggests what has to be done to resolve that plot. This is Point A, and understanding where the protagonist starts makes it a lot easier to get to Point Z at the end of the novel.

The inciting event can be small, or it can be something the protagonist doesn't even know connects to it yet, but there's a moment where if she turned left instead of right, she never would have had this experience. It's the moment when she made a choice or acted in a way that sets her on the plot path.

This moment will sometimes seem innocuous, but it has far-reaching consequences. Novels typically start in the normal world of the protagonist's life, so odds are the protagonist will be doing something normal that somehow doesn't go as it usually does. She has no idea that turning left instead of right will change her life forever, but that's exactly what happens.

Inciting events are not random, no matter how much they may seem so to the protagonist at first. There's a reason this moment puts the protagonist on that plot path.

**BRAINSTORMING QUESTIONS:**
Think about the moment in which your protagonist first discovers there's a problem, or the first step taken that will become that problem.

1. When is the first moment where something happens to bring your protagonist into your core conflict?

2. What's happening when the protagonist triggers that moment?

3. How does this event connect to your core conflict?

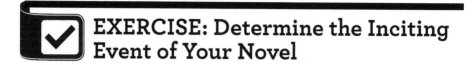

## EXERCISE: Determine the Inciting Event of Your Novel

### >>Describe your inciting event.

*For example:*

▶ Lana finds a note stuck in her locker at school, claiming someone knows what she did to her brother and that she'd better come to the diner tonight at 9:00 p.m. or everyone will find out.

▶ Bob is working up the nerve to ask his wife for a divorce when he hears groaning and shuffling outside. He goes to check, thinking it's some kind of wild animal going through his trash. But it's a zombie, and it tries to eat him. He starts screaming and Sally rushes in and saves him, then totally takes charge of everything.

▶ Adam and Hannah are both notified that their favorite teacher has passed away, and each decides to attend her funeral despite being estranged from their families and not wanting to face home again.

# Your Novel's Ending

Novels end when the core conflict of the plot is resolved in a satisfying conclusion. "Satisfying" can mean anything, and it might have a happy ending—tying up every loose end and leaving readers joyful and bubbly—or a sad, poignant ending—leaving certain things unresolved and having the protagonist fail, yet perhaps learn a valuable lesson. Either can work, as long as readers are satisfied by how the novel resolved its conflict.

Although it's not critical to know the ending of a novel before it's written, having a general idea can make it easier to develop and plot that novel. You'll have a clear moment to write toward.

**For pantsers:** If your process is to write to discover how a novel turns out, then you don't have to worry about how it ends at this stage. However, if the story question that first intrigued you about the idea gives you a general sense of the type of ending you *might* have, feel free to explore that.

**Why the ending is important:** Everything in the novel has been building to this moment. For many readers, the ending is what they'll remember and this will determine how much they liked the book. From a writing standpoint, this is the finish line that will guide the development of the novel.

**How this affects the summary blurb:** This often works as the goal for the protagonist and the reason why she's acting in the novel. It might be to achieve this goal or to avoid it. It's also a good indicator of where the stakes might come from, as knowing how the book ends also suggests how it could all go wrong.

The ending satisfies the promise you make at the start of the novel. Readers pick up a book because it sounds like a story they want to read for X reason. Somewhere in the cover copy (the polished form of your summary blurb) is that reason. It poses a question readers want an answer to, or describes a situation readers want to explore. They want to see the murder solved, the star-crossed lovers united, join the adventure to find the Holy Grail, hang out with the kooky ladies that share life wisdom. Whatever it is, readers care about the characters and the problem enough to want to see how it all ends. They want to see if the protagonist "wins."

⚠ **SOMETHING TO THINK ABOUT**: *What does "winning" mean to the protagonist? Some event or action means the novel is over and the problem has been resolved. It's the last step of the journey that started with the inciting event.*

Depending on what your story question is, the novel's ending might be obvious and inevitable and won't be a surprise. That ending is *why* readers picked up the book. To see the hero win, the couple united, the child saved. Some things will be inevitable. If you're thinking about an ending that isn't how readers will likely want it to go, make sure it's clear that that's how it *needed* to go for these characters and this story.

You don't have to tie up *all* the loose ends, but there are probably a few major questions or problems in the novel readers will want to know the answers to.

One way to test your ending is to pose it as a question: Will Frodo get the ring to Mt. Doom? (*The Lord of the Rings*)

This is the plot goal of the novel, and it will be a yes or no question. This is the story question readers expect to have answered by the end of the novel. There won't be a surprise if this happens, but readers *want* this to happen. The surprises come in how the plot unfolds and what happens between points A and Z. How the protagonist solves that problem, how it affects her, and what price she pays to do it. The journey to answering that question.

Even if the point of the book is character growth, it's still about something happening, and thus will pose a story question. Will that person change? Will she realize something? She might discover "love conquers all" but she does that by an external plot that changes her. She doesn't just decide to change and then change. Something external triggers that internal change.

But don't forget your stakes. They give the ending events meaning and make readers more invested in how it all turns out. Have you ever been to a sporting event where you didn't care for the sport or either team? Did you care who won, no matter how good the game was? Same thing. Readers need to care about the outcome, and if the protagonist fails and loses nothing, then the problem is meaningless. Even if failure means something horrible happens, if it doesn't affect the protagonist or characters readers are emotionally invested in, they won't care.

Tastes will vary of course, but generally, readers want to see the problem or story question the novel has been exploring all along resolved in a satisfying way at the end. They want to be surprised by something they didn't see coming, but that surprise should still fit with the novel's plot. Readers also want to see the protagonist grow or change in some fashion that made everything she went through in the book matter in a personal and meaningful way.

The ending is the big "this is what my novel is about" question that your protagonist has spent the entire book trying to achieve.

 **BRAINSTORMING QUESTIONS:**
Explore how your novel might end.

1. What constitutes a win for your protagonist?

2. What constitutes a win for your readers?

3. How does your protagonist solve the core conflict problem of the novel?

4. How does this affect your protagonist?

5. What price does your protagonist pay for this resolution?

6. How do *you* want it to end?

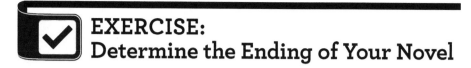

# EXERCISE:
# Determine the Ending of Your Novel

## >>Describe the ending of your novel.

At this stage, you don't have to describe the ending in detail. Just try to figure out what the overall goal is, or what success means for the protagonist. If you're not sure, write down some options.

*For example:*

▶ Lana realizes saving Miguel from Zachary's plan will help her redeem herself for her role in her brother's accident—either by giving her the strength to confess or by making her realize she was never truly the cause.

▶ Bob finds his inner hero, proves he's a good man after all, and is finally able to ask Sally for a divorce and profess his love to Jane.

▶ Adam and Hannah fall in love, heal the wounded families, and live happily ever after.

# Understanding the Summary Blurb

A good summary blurb captures the important elements of the idea in a way that allows you to craft a novel. It introduces the protagonist and any other critical characters to the plot, states or hints at the antagonist, shows where the novel is set, and what the core conflict is.

Let's explore those elements and how to capture the essence of what matters to the plot and story. After the previous exercises, these questions should all be easier to answer and boil down to a single sentence.

## Who the Novel is About

This describes the protagonist. It can be a single person, or a group of people if it's an ensemble cast. It says a little about them, something that is important to the overall novel. This detail is probably the reason you chose her (or them) to be the protagonist.

*For example:*

▶ Lana, a girl trying to keep a dark secret

▶ Bob, a man caught in a love triangle during the zombie apocalypse

▶ Adam and Hannah, a couple from feuding families who fall in love

## The Main Problems to Be Faced

This describes the core conflict of the novel. What the book is *about.* In most novels, this will be an external problem. Literary novels often use internal growth instead of external conflict.

*For example:*

▶ Lana is trying to discover who is threatening her and how she can stop him and keep her secret

▶ Bob is trying to survive a zombie apocalypse and win the heart of the woman he loves

▶ Adam and Hannah are trying to honor their favorite teacher and deal with family interference as they fall in love

## Where the Novel Takes Place

This describes the setting. It gives a sense of place that often shows some inherent conflict or problem in the setting itself or the life of the protagonist.

*For example:*

- ▶ A roadside diner
- ▶ Cleveland during the zombie apocalypse
- ▶ The small town of Henderson

## What Triggers the Novel Problem

This describes the inciting event and what happens to set the protagonist on the path of the novel's core conflict.

*For example:*

- ▶ Lana gets a note to come to a diner late at night or someone will expose her secret
- ▶ Zombies attack before Bob can ask Sally for a divorce
- ▶ A beloved teacher dies, causing two former students to return home for her funeral

## Why it Matters

This describes the stakes. It explains what will happen if the protagonist fails and what's motivating her to act.

*For example:*

- ▶ If Lana doesn't find out who wants to expose her, she'll never find peace or redemption over what happened with her brother.
- ▶ If Bob can't find the strength to stand up for himself and ask his wife for a divorce, he'll never survive the zombies or be with the woman he loves.
- ▶ If Adam and Hannah can't end the feud between their families, they'll never find happiness with each other.

## How the Novel Ends

This describes the resolution, and often it's the biggest obstacle standing in the way of the protagonist. Overcoming that obstacle constitutes a win for the protagonist.

*For example:*

▶ Lana saves Miguel from Zachary, and discovers the truth about her brother's accident.

▶ Bob must enter a zombie-infested lab by himself to retrieve the cure for zombification and save Jane.

▶ Adam and Hannah uncover the reason for the feud and bring peace to the two families, allowing them to be happy together.

These details combine to craft your summary blurb and capture the critical elements of your novel.

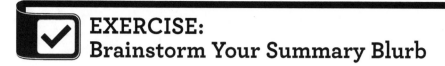

## EXERCISE:
## Brainstorm Your Summary Blurb

**>>Answer the following questions about your novel:**

- Who is the novel about?

- What is the main problem to be faced?

- Where does the novel take place?

- What triggers the novel's core problem?

- Why does it matter that this problem is resolved?

- How does the novel end?

# ASSIGNMENT NINE: Write Your Summary Blurb

>>Put it all together and craft your summary blurb.

A summary blurb can be basic information, or contain the voice or style of the novel. Sometimes it helps to use this exercise to get a feel for how a character might sound or what the novel's tone might be.

If you need a little help in crafting the blurb, try this general template. Feel free to move parts around as they pertain to your novel. This template is a guide to help you think, not something you have to follow exactly as written. You can even cut some of the parts out if they don't work.

[introduce the protagonist] is [tell a little about her] who [why she's in the right place to have something happen to her]. She [what leads her to the inciting event] where [the inciting event happens].

She [reacts to what's happened] and finds herself [how the inciting event has made a mess of the protagonist's life]. To [fix this problem] she must [the main thing that needs to be accomplished to win] before [the antagonist does what she needs to do]. If she doesn't, [why it's bad, and what she has to lose if she fails].

*For example:*

▶ [Lana] is [struggling to maintain her "everything is fine" facade at school after her brother is paralyzed in an accident]. She [receives a menacing note in her locker, threatening to expose her unless she agrees to meet at a roadside diner]. She goes, and [encounters two boys who also received similar notes].

She's [unsure who is behind this or how the other two boys are connected] and finds herself [fighting to uncover who is threatening them and why, before her secret is revealed to the entire town]. But to [uncover the person behind the threats] she must [reveal her secret to the two others boys] before [they're all exposed]. If she doesn't, [everyone will know she caused her brother's accident and she'll never get the forgiveness she craves].

▶ [Bob] [hates his life almost as much as his marriage]. He's [stuck washing dishes and trying to work up the nerve to ask his wife for a divorce], but before he can gather his courage, [zombies crash through the back door, intent on devouring what's left of his brains].

[Ending his life is a tempting escape of his misery, but his pathetic survival skills kick in.] His [fighting—and screaming— alerts his wife, Sally, who barges in, takes control, and saves the day. She then proceeds to lecture him about his ineptitude—just like always]. [Fed up with her abuse and disrespect], he vows [to ditch the harpy, learn to fend for himself, and tell Jane, the woman he truly loves, how he feels]. Of course, [the zombies have other ideas, and Bob isn't exactly a survivalist]. He needs Sally to survive, [and worse, he needs her help to save Jane] before [they all become zombie food].

▶ [Hannah] is [a risk-averse teacher] who [fears she'll never find love while playing it safe]. She's [debating taking an adventurous singles' cruise] when [she receives a call from her mother—her favorite childhood teacher back home has passed away. The funeral is on Saturday. Will she come home to say goodbye?]

[Adam] is [sitting alone at an airport bar] when [he gets the same news]. He [owes his escape from Henderson to this teacher, and despite his misgivings] he [changes his flight and returns home for the funeral].

[On this busy, holiday weekend, Adam and Hannah end up sharing a cab to their small town and find themselves exchanging memories of the teacher and reflecting on how their lives have turned out—each thinking how they wish for something more]. [Their mutual attraction is strong], but when they [get home, they discover they're from feuding families who promptly yank them away from each other]. To [be together] they realize they must [uncover the reasons for the feud and set things right between the families] before [the feud tears them apart for good].

If you want to take the planning stage beyond a summary blurb, move on to Workshop Ten, where we'll develop a working synopsis

# Workshop Ten:
# Turning Your Summary Blurb
# Into a Working Synopsis

**What You Need to Start This Workshop:** A general idea of how you want your novel to unfold.

**The Goal of This Workshop:** To craft a working synopsis you can write a novel from.

**What We'll Discuss in This Workshop:** Basic novel structure, including scenes and sequels, and how you can use structure to plan a novel and write your working synopsis.

**Writing Terms Used in This Workshop:**

**Antagonist:** The person or thing in the protagonist's path of success.

**Backstory:** The history and past of a character that affects his or her actions in a novel.

**Conflict:** Two sides in opposition, either externally or internally.

**Core Conflict:** The major problem or issue at the center of the novel.

**Goal:** What the point-of-view character wants.

**Hook:** An element that grabs readers and makes them want to read on.

**Inciting Event:** The moment that triggers the core conflict of the novel and draws the protagonist into the plot.

**Narrative Drive:** The sense that the plot is moving forward.

**Pacing:** The speed of the novel, or how quickly the story moves.

**Protagonist:** The character driving the novel.

**Scene:** An individual moment in a novel that dramatizes one goal or situation.

**Set Pieces:** The key moments or events in a novel.

**Sequel (2):** The period after a scene goal is resolved where the character reflects on events and makes a decision to act.

**Stakes:** What consequence will befall the protagonist if she fails to get her goal.

**Tension:** The sense of something about to happen.

**Theme:** A recurring idea or concept explored in the novel.

# Welcome to Workshop Ten: Turning Your Summary Blurb Into a Working Synopsis

If you're ready to move on, the next step is writing a working synopsis. This is designed to help organize your thoughts and see how the novel might flow.

A working synopsis captures the basic structural elements of a novel and provides an idea of how that novel will unfold. Some writers prefer to plan every scene and craft a detailed synopsis; others would rather know a few key points and discover the rest as they write. Still others work best with a little information on major turning points or a character's goal and not much else.

How you choose to write your working synopsis is up to you.

- If you're a planner, flesh out your novel as much as you need to to feel comfortable writing the first draft.
- If you're a pantser, do the bare minimum of planning (if any at all) and jump right in.
- If you're somewhere in the middle, plan just enough to know your general course and discover the rest as you write.

This workshop will examine a novel's basic structure:—the beginning, the middle, and the end—and explore the elements typically found in those sections. The goal is to help you understand these elements and turning points, and provide structural tools for writing the first draft.

As always, it's important to remember that this synopsis is to help you write your novel, not something polished you'd show an agent or editor. A working synopsis is often messy, and that's okay. As long as *you* can follow and understand it, that's all that matters.

## Scenes and Structure Basics

Since novels are made up of scenes that build off one another to form a compelling story, understanding basic scene structure makes it a lot easier to write that novel. It's also a valuable tool for planning and writing the individual scenes.

Let's take a look at basic scene and sequel structure:

### Scene Structure

Scenes follow the same beginning-middle-end format as a novel, through the goal-conflict-resolution structure:

▶ Scene opens (the beginning). Protagonist has a goal. He'll act in ways to achieve that goal while something or someone tries to stop him (the middle). The goal will be resolved in some way. Scene ends (the end).

The conflict (tries to stop him) could be a person trying to prevent him from acting, a difficult situation that makes his goal harder to achieve, nature itself, a personal belief that's holding him back—anything that creates conflict for the scene. "Tries to stop him" simply means an obstacle in the way of his goal. It doesn't have to be an actual person trying to physically stop him.

This format works for every scene in a novel, from quiet, character-driven stories to fast-paced action thrillers. It provides structure without forcing the novel into a one-size-fits-all template. It's a person trying to solve a problem and running into difficulty doing it.

Scenes are linked by how they end, like a relay handoff to the next scene. There are four traditional ways a scene can end:

**The protagonist gets the goal:** This usually stops the plot because there's nowhere for the plot to go and nothing for the protagonist to do next.

**The protagonist doesn't get the goal:** This also stops the plot, but the protagonist still has to get the same goal, so there's room to move forward.

**The protagonist gets the goal, but there's a problem:** This gives the protagonist a new goal (often unexpected) and a place for the plot to go to move the novel forward.

**The protagonist doesn't get the goal, and failing makes the problem worse:** This gives the protagonist a new goal, and raises the stakes on the old problem.

Let's check in with Bob and the zombies for an example:

Bob is being chased by zombies. The scene starts with him running, and we could say the scene goal is "Bob wants to escape the zombies." However, just escaping is more of an overall story goal for Bob, as he's been doing this all throughout novel. It also doesn't provide a lot of information to help us write the scene since there's nothing specific for Bob to do. Escaping is really more of a desire than a scene-driving goal. He *wants* to escape the zombies. How he *decides to do that* is the goal of the scene.

The specific goal to defeat these particular zombies might be: "Bob is trying to get to the motel where his extra shotgun is, so he can escape the zombies by shooting them." Bob can't achieve the bigger goal resolution (escape) until he achieves these smaller goals (reach the motel and then kill these particular zombies).

This scene will end when Bob gets to his shotgun and one of these four things happens:

1. Bob gets the shotgun and kills the zombies. (He gets his goal, but now what does he do? This resolution doesn't hand off the scene to the next one.)

2. Bob doesn't get the shotgun and the zombies eat him. (He doesn't get his goal, and the book ends.)

3. Bob gets the shotgun, but he has no shells and has to find some. (He gets his goal, but there's a problem. This leads to a new goal of finding shells for the shotgun, and it raises the stakes because the zombies are getting closer and he doesn't have a weapon.)

4. Bob gets the shotgun, but shoots himself in the foot as he aims for the zombies. (He gets his goal, but makes things worse, because now he can't even run away. He has to kill the zombies or they'll kill him.)

Options one and two stop the novel or make it difficult to know where to go next. There's nothing driving it forward anymore, because no new goal is set. Option three gives Bob something to do that puts him in more danger and moves the plot forward with more risk. Option four makes things worse, raises the stakes, and gives Bob something to do to move the plot forward.

Let's choose option four. He shoots himself in the foot, but he does take out one zombie in the process.

So what's Bob going to do next? Have a sequel.

## Sequel Structure

Sequels are important in directing the plot because this is where the protagonist does the decision making. What he decides to do next is the goal for the next scene (which links the scenes), and it starts all over again. Reaction-reflection-decision.

A sequel unfolds like this:

▶ Protagonist reacts emotionally to event, thinks about or reflects on it, makes a decision and creates a new goal

Sequels aren't actual scenes, as they have no goals to move the plot forward. One common mistake new writers make is to treat sequels like scenes, which usually leads to long, boring scenes where nothing happens.

Scene goals are the steps that lead to the climax of the novel. Sequels are the glue that hold it all together and remind readers why this is all important in the first place. Sequels don't have to be long to be effective. In fact, they're often better when they're shorter since there's nothing driving a sequel, and they can bog down the pacing if left alone too long.

Bob's sequel could be as short as: "Ow! I'm such a moron. Where's the dang first aid kit? I gotta stop this bleeding."

He has a reaction (ow). He reflects and thinks about his situation (I'm such a moron. Where's the dang first aid kit?) and then he makes a decision (I gotta stop this bleeding). There's even a sense of raised stakes (the bleeding). The scene continues with Bob's new goal of trying to make it to the first aid kit before he bleeds to death or gets eaten by the remaining zombies.

If Bob had shot himself at the same time he shot the last zombie, he could have a longer sequel. He might take a few paragraphs and reflect on his situation. How he got into this mess, what he needs to do to get out of it, what's still in his way. With longer sequels, it helps to add a sense of tension or impending doom to keep the plot moving while the protagonist has a reflective moment. Longer sequels are also common after fast-paced action scenes so readers can take a moment to reflect and catch their breath.

## Scene Length

Just because a chapter ends doesn't mean a scene has to end. There can be multiple scenes in one chapter, one scene per chapter, or one scene that spans multiple chapters. Don't be afraid to mix and match scene length, as this is a great way to keep readers guessing and control the novel's pacing.

## Plot Tips

A way to test the scenes is to describe them and look at the words used in that description. If there are a lot of "and then this happens, and then that happens," that's a red flag that there's something missing from the scene (usually goals and/or conflict). "And then" is a scene killer. It describes what happens, but doesn't provide any sense of goals, motivations, or conflict.

There are also words that embody the concept of goals, conflicts, stakes, and motivations, which are all vital components of a scene: Trying to, but, therefore, when, and so. These words force us to think about vital elements necessary for a strong scene.

**Trying to:** The protagonist is trying to do something. His goal.

**When:** Something happens to create conflict.

**But:** Something happens the protagonist doesn't want to have happen.

**Therefore:** Something triggers another event to occur, or the protagonist changes tactics.

**So:** The protagonist changes tactics/ideas/plans and a new goal is created.

If the protagonist isn't "trying to" do anything, and no "whens" get in the way, and no "buts" occur to raise the stakes, there's a good chance there's a problem with the plot.

## Some Key Things to Remember When Plotting

**The goal of plot is to illustrate the story:** If the novel is about a soldier trying to save his king, then the plot is going to be the steps that soldier takes to save his king. Subplots will naturally arise, but even they will illustrate some aspect that ties back to that core conflict.

When creating a scene, look at the core conflict (internal or external) and ask how the scene connects to that. It can be subtle, or it can be an intermediate step to a bigger goal, but it'll be something that has to happen in order for the core conflict to be resolved. If there's no connection to the main goal (and if you took it out, nothing changes), odds are the scene isn't going to advance the story or the plot.

It doesn't have to be a direct line connection, though. If the core conflict is to break the king out of prison, all kinds of things can go wrong while trying to break him out. Those smaller obstacles create plot, because they make it harder for the protagonist to achieve his goal. The end goal is still the same and *that* end goal (freeing the king) is what's critical to the plot.

**Never let the plot dictate the story:** It can guide it, influence it, enhance it, but it's easy to write a scene that's really cool, but not right for the story. And if we love that scene, we bend over backward to try to make it fit. If we're forcing it, it's not working, no matter how cool or how well-written the scene may be. Cut it, save it in another file, but don't let it waylay the story.

For example, while trying to free the king from prison, say the protagonist discovers the warden is corrupt and planning to kill a bunch of wrongly imprisoned political prisoners captured when the king was captured. This is a bad thing, but it has nothing to do with the core conflict goal of saving the king. It might work as a nice inner conflict (the protagonist has to choose between abandoning the prisoners and saving his king), but to go and actually save those prisoners is very likely going to waylay the story and send the plot off on a tangent. Will that scene be cool? Probably. Will it have stakes and goals and everything a good scene needs? Sure. Does it advance the story or the plot? Probably not.

Because the *stakes* don't escalate, and it's basically the same goal with *smaller* stakes. Saving prisoners he doesn't know or care about is a lot less important than saving the king he adores who is needed by the people.

And that's the tricky part of plotting, because it seems like it should be a great subplot, right? But those prisoners aren't keeping the protagonist from anything (no conflict). They're in a sad situation to be sure, but leaving them there isn't going to affect the goal of saving the king at all. The protagonist doesn't have to free them to free the king. He might want to, might be haunted by it because he didn't, but it's not a plot-advancing goal. It's a *delaying* goal instead of something designed to make it harder and raise the stakes of the original goal.

However, if we write something unexpected that looks cool, we *can* start thinking about ways in which saving those prisoners *does* directly affect saving the king or a bigger core conflict goal. Maybe the king needs to be the one to save them to gain supporters. Maybe one of those prisoners is important to the cause or the king in some way. Maybe instead of sending the protagonist right at it, it could be a nifty seed to plant that will be a problem for a later plot twist. Maybe the king refuses to leave until they save those prisoners as well.

**Characters create the plot:** Stories are about characters, and characters create plot, which in turn illustrates a story. So, characters are where the plot is going to come from. What they do drives the plot. They're going to want things (goals), want to avoid things (stakes), want to avoid hassles (conflict). They're not going to just sit there and do nothing. They're going to act in some way.

The soldier trying to save his king is going to do that in his own way, using his world experiences and beliefs. He'll decide the first step to take, and as conflicts arise, he'll decide how to deal with those conflicts. If anyone else could fill the same role and have nothing change, then the characters probably aren't driving the plot, they're acting it out. And that can lead to flat, unexciting novels.

**Plots need stakes:** It's probably more accurate to say characters need stakes, but if there's nothing to lose, the plot won't matter. Something to lose is probably more important than something to gain, crazy as that sounds. It's the struggle that makes a novel compelling, the risk that things might go wrong and the protagonist will fail and face terrible consequences. Why someone acts is a huge driving force behind plot.

The solider will have the king's life at stake, but he'll have personal things at stake as well—maybe his own life, his family's, his reputation, his own self-worth as a soldier. Individual scenes will also have stakes on top of the larger story stakes, with maybe the life of someone under his command, or a random innocent who stands in his way, or something critical *not* happening that's needed to free the king in the end.

**Plots need conflict:** Novels are about interesting people solving interesting problems in interesting ways. Without the problem part, there is no novel and thus no plot. In every scene, consider what's in the way of the protagonist's goal. It might be a person, a difficult obstacle, an emotional quandary, a lack of information, a puzzle, or anything else that creates conflict in the scene.

Plotting can be challenging because there really is no limit to what can happen. But keeping the basic structure rules in mind makes it a lot easier to identify what advances the story and what's just empty plot.

# Writing a Working Synopsis

A novel traditionally has a handful of major moments that make up the turning points of the story's plot (the set pieces). Where they fall in the novel varies, but they usually fit within the classic, three- act story structure: beginning, middle, and ending. Within each of these three sections are common plot points that get the protagonist from Point A to Point Z.

**The Beginning**

- Opening Scene
- Inciting Event
- Act One Problem

**The Middle**

- Act Two Choice
- Midpoint Reversal
- Act Two Disaster

**The Ending**

- Act Three Plan
- Climax
- Wrap Up

When writing a working synopsis, these turning points provide starting and ending points for the plot. They can change as the novel develops, but they're useful guides in the planning stage to get you started. Use them as tools, but don't feel confined by them.

**How the summary blurb works with a working synopsis:** The summary blurb is a condensed version of the novel, and it provides a foundation on which to expand the scenes and flesh out the plot. It's easier to figure out how to get from the opening scene to the end, because you've already figured out the moments that connect those two points.

Let's take another look at the summary blurb template from Assignment Nine:

▶ [introduce the protagonist] is [tell a little about him] who [why he's in the right place to have something happen to him]. He [what leads him to the inciting event] where [the inciting event happens].

In a working synopsis, this describes the opening and the basic setup of the novel. It covers the important details about character and creates a situation that can lead to the inciting event of the novel.

▶ He [reacts to what's happened] and finds himself [how the inciting event has made a mess of the protagonist's life].

This shows the direction the plot will go, and possibly even the act one problem.

▶ To [fix this problem] he must [the main thing that needs to be accomplished to win] before [the antagonist does what he needs to do].

This describes the core conflict of the novel, and what the plot will be working toward resolving. This is where the middle of the novel's plot will come from. It also shows the stakes.

▶ If he doesn't, [why it's bad, and what he has to lose if he fails].

This shows the consequences of failure, and likely hints at the climax.

The steps might be general at this stage, but the summary blurb has all the pieces needed to flesh out the major turning points of a plot, and thus write a working synopsis.

## Try a Rough Outline First

Before you write the final synopsis, it can be quite helpful to outline just the key turning points of the plot. This mini-outline will work as a guide as you develop what scenes you need, how to connect those scene, and where the plot is going.

*For example:*

**The Beginning**

- **Opening Scene:** Bob is in his kitchen thinking about asking Sally for a divorce.
- **Inciting Event:** Zombies crash through the front door.
- **Act One Problem:** Bob has to decide if he wants to go with Sally or go after Jane alone.

**The Middle**

- **Act Two Choice:** Bob decides staying with Sally is his best chance at staying alive and saving Jane.
- **Midpoint Reversal:** Sally gets bitten by a zombie, but doesn't change due to the vaccine she got from her secret government pals.
- **Act Two Disaster:** Jane is bitten.

**The Ending**

- **Act Three Plan:** Break into the government lab and get the cure for Jane.
- **Climax:** Bob fights his way through zombie hordes and retrieves the cure, saving Jane.
- **Wrap Up:** Bob earns Sally's respect finally, and he asks her for a divorce so he can be with Jane.

## Reminder: It Doesn't Have to be Perfect

The working synopsis is a way to brainstorm on paper. It's likely some plot points will be clear in your mind, but the scenes that connect them will still be unformed. This is normal, so don't worry if there are still holes in how the plot gets from Point A to Point B. Also don't worry if you find yourself changing things as you write the synopsis and the story develops more.

When you get stuck, try writing general descriptions of the types of situations you might have. For example, you might know you'll have a chase scene, but not know any details yet. It's okay to write, "The bad guys chase Kelly through the city for hours until she evades them." You can figure out exactly how she does that after more planning, or even during the first draft if you're more of a pantser. Or you might know a series of chapters will focus on the struggles and failures as the protagonist attempts to solve a problem, but only have a vague idea of what those will be. Write down whatever details will guide you when you get to that section.

If notes on what you want to accomplish conceptually come to mind, write those down as well. This synopsis isn't about creating a polished version of your plot. It's getting enough information down to write the first draft. Notes on what you want a scene to do are helpful reminders during the writing process.

You might also find it helpful to jump around as you write the working synopsis. If you know the ending, perhaps summarize that first so you know where the plot it headed. If you get stuck on one section, try jumping to the next turning point you know and working backward to connect the two. Not every plot will unfold chronologically and fleshed out, so fill in the turning points as best you can and develop from there.

## Defining Story Arcs

To help flesh out the working synopsis, look at the various story arcs of the novel. Plot arcs, character arcs, theme arcs, and timeline arcs. Arcs make up the novel and how you braid those arcs together determines how the story unfolds. While you certainly don't have to know all these arcs before you start writing, identifying key events and moments can aid you in plotting and novel development.

## Plot Arcs

Plot arcs are how the plot unfolds. They cover the events that happen between the opening scene and the resolution. Depending on how much outlining you like to do, you might have the whole plot mapped out or just a few key moments—or you might not know *any* plot elements at all if you're more character based or a panster.

## Subplot Arcs

Subplot arcs show the various aspects of the story and support the other arcs. They affect the internal and external conflict, illustrate the theme, and create deeper character growth. They can be tricky because there are probably overlaps where something affects both the plot and a subplot. In multiple points of view, each point-of-view character will have her own arc that ties into both the core plot and various subplots.

## Character Arcs

Character arcs show the emotional growth of the character. They start with examples of the protagonist's flaws and then provide opportunities for that character to grow and change. This arc typically conflicts in some way with the external core conflict, and by going through the external experience, internal growth is achieved. A protagonist in a recurring series might not change much, but a character in a literary novel about inner growth might change a lot.

## Theme Arcs

Theme arcs can help tie the other arcs together. They can track how the theme is conveyed and when and where theme-related moments might occur. If the theme is linked to the character growth, it can be very helpful to see the turning points spelled out in the plot.

## Timeline Arcs

Timeline arcs focus on when things happen, especially if the novel unfolds over a specific time frame. Not every novel will unfold on a tight schedule, but for some (like mysteries or thrillers) it can be vital to know when events occur.

**BRAINSTORMING QUESTIONS:**
List the steps for potential arcs in your novel.

1. **The plot arc:** Look carefully at what steps move the core plot from opening scene to resolution. Make a list of those steps, focusing on the moments that have to happen for the plot to work. Also list the steps the antagonist is taking to make events happen. If the antagonist is off screen, but still strongly influencing the protagonist, sometimes it's helpful to list what he's doing, even if readers never see it happen in the book. It's a good way to keep track of what's going on overall and can help prevent implausible plots and mistakes of time and place.

   Don't forget to list the why on these steps as well. Character motives are critical to tying these events together. Same with the stakes. Each event should have a goal that needs to be accomplished, a reason why it has to be accomplished, and why that particular character needs to do it (internal and external goals), and what will happen if it isn't accomplished.

2. **The subplot arcs:** Consider potential subplots, especially any that connect strongly to the core conflict or character arc. Make another list for any ideas that could deepen various aspects of the novel.

3. **The character arcs:** Start with the protagonist and list all the events/revelations/failures that happen to cause his character to grow or change. Next, look at the antagonist (if he plays an active role) and secondary characters. How might your characters change over the course of the novel? What path could those arcs take?

4. **The theme arcs:** Look for situations where the theme might appear, especially if it causes a change or influences a character. Make a list of all the areas where theme could be used. How might it develop over the course of the novel? What moments or characters could be part of a theme arc?

5. **Timeline arcs:** List when major events happen to make sure there's enough time for things to occur, and things aren't happening out of order.

# The Beginning

From a structure perspective, the beginning of a novel takes up roughly the first 25 percent of the book, so it's helpful to aim for that in the working synopsis as well to maintain a balance. Of course, it's not uncommon for the beginning to be more fleshed out than the ending at the start, so don't worry too much if the beginning is the largest part of the working synopsis at first. If you focus on the key turning points, it should work itself out as you write.

The beginning introduces readers to the characters and world, and sets up the novel to come. However, there's a difference between setting up the novel and dumping a lot of information and backstory into the setup—good setup and bad setup, if you will.

Good setup is laying the groundwork for the plot and creating interesting characters that hook readers. It gives them the information they'll need to understand the novel, but in a way that feels like the story unfolding. It offers something intriguing and compelling right from the first line, and sweeps readers away.

Bad setup explains a lot of history and backstory, and dumps information on readers they don't yet care about. It tells things in a static way that doesn't offer readers a reason to read on, and makes them feel like they're slogging through notes before the actual book can start. It can also confuse readers or create expectations that won't be met, putting the focus on history or world building and not on what the novel will actually be about.

Obviously, you want to avoid bad setup.

Instead, draw readers into the novel and make them want to be there. Give them the critical information they'll need to enjoy and understand the characters, but let them discover the world, not have a metaphorical travel brochure shoved in their faces.

## Common Elements of the Beginning

Here are some common elements found in a typical beginning. Not all of these have to be there, though they frequently are.

- A likable, interesting, or compelling protagonist
- What normal life is like for that protagonist
- An interesting initial problem to solve
- An inciting event
- The introduction of other major characters in the novel
- The introduction of subplots
- The introduction of any potential love interests
- Statements or examples of the theme
- The beginning of the protagonist's character arc
- The beginning's crisis that triggers the protagonist to act toward solving the core conflict of the novel (the story question)

In very general terms, the beginning traditionally unfolds like this:

Opening scene (introduces protagonist – introduces world and setting – introduces initial problem) **which leads to** ▶ the protagonist attempts to solve initial problem **which leads to** ▶ something going wrong, so the protagonist reacts and makes a decision or is dragged into trouble **which leads to** ▶ the inciting event where the protagonist steps or is shoved onto the path of the core conflict **which leads to** ▶ the protagonist involves or meets other characters while trying to solve or deal with the inciting event and subsequent issues **which leads to** ▶ the protagonist discovers the problem is much bigger than expected and/or learns a huge secret that will determine his actions in resolving the core conflict **which leads to** ▶ the protagonist faces a choice to resolve this issue (end of the beginning).

Let's look a little closer at that overview:

**Opening scene:** This is the first thing readers will discover about the novel, the protagonist, and the world.

**Introduction of protagonist:** Odds are the opening scene will introduce the protagonist, but if not, then the introduction scene will come early in the novel. If there's something critical to his character readers need to know, this is the place to show it (unless it's supposed to be a secret).

**Introduction of world and setting:** The opening chapters are where the setting is defined for readers. The critical elements are often found within the first few pages to help ground readers in the world.

**Introduction of initial problem:** When the novel opens, something is happening. It doesn't have to be high drama or fast-paced action, but there should be a sense that *something* is going on or about to happen. This is the hook to get readers to read on.

**Protagonist attempts to solve initial problem:** This is going to be the first goal the protagonist tries to achieve. This problem will either lead to the inciting event or be the inciting event.

**Something goes wrong:** While trying to resolve the initial problem, something goes wrong that adds to the conflict and stakes and raises the tension. It also gives the protagonist something else to do to move the plot forward.

**Protagonist reacts and makes a decision or is dragged into the problem:** The protagonist is affected by this problem and he does something about it. He makes a decision, which creates the next goal and moves the plot to the next scene, or forces greater than him drag him into the problem and he's forced to go along with it against his will. However it happens, the protagonist is now part of the problem in some way.

**Inciting event occurs:** The protagonist steps onto the path or is shoved onto the path of the core conflict plot and his life is changed forever. Stakes are raised at this time, and a ticking clock is often introduced.

**Protagonist involves or meets other characters while trying to solve or deal with the inciting event and subsequent issues:** This is the section where the bulk of the beginning's scenes will come from. The major secondary characters will show up in the beginning, and the antagonist will typically at least be mentioned, even if readers don't see him yet. Subplots will appear during this time that cause additional conflict between what the protagonist needs to do and what he wants to do.

**Protagonist discovers problem is much bigger than expected and/or learns a huge secret that will determine his actions in resolving the core conflict (the act one problem):** This is the start of the beginning's end, likely the final chapter or two before the plot closes in on the first major core conflict crisis. Even if the protagonist doesn't know for sure what that is yet, he'll take the first step toward knowing there is a problem—and a bad one. The stakes often go up here as well.

**Protagonist faces a choice to resolve this issue (transitions into the book's middle):** This choice will become the goal that puts the protagonist on the path to the core conflict. It will pose a question of some type for readers (not always a literal question, but a story question, such as, "Will he get the girl back?" or "Can he build that spaceship in time?" or "Will he find love again?") This choice will be an important part of the middle's beginning.

These steps can take as many (or as few) scenes as needed to get from one to the other, and they can be developed however best fits the story. Remember, they're not rules, just guides for basic novel structure. There's plenty of flexibility here to craft the novel however it needs to be written.

Let's look at the three major turning points in even greater detail.

## The Opening Scene

The opening scene is, of course, the way the novel opens. It usually introduces the protagonist, though sometimes an opening scene starts with the antagonist, or a bit of history instead. It shows the world and gives a taste of why the protagonist is different or special enough to ask someone to read about him. It also sums up the key points readers need to know to understand the character.

**Why the opening scene is important:** It sets the tone and gives readers an idea of what they can expect from the novel. It also provides the all-important hook to grab readers and make them want to read this novel.

The primary goal of an opening scene is to make readers want to read the next scene. You'd be surprised how often this is forgotten, because the focus is on establishing the setting, introducing the protagonist, and telling readers all about the cool story waiting for them. These are all important, but on their own they're not going to do what an opening scene needs to do—grab readers and keep them reading.

The best way to grab readers is to give them a question they'll want to know the answer to—an intriguing first line that poses a question (literal or metaphorical), an unusual situation, a mystery, a contradiction that doesn't quite make sense. Another way to hook readers is with a great voice and character they want to get to know better. Almost anything can work as a hook as long as it's something or someone that makes readers think, "I want to know more about X."

### Key Elements of an Opening Scene

- Shows the protagonist exhibiting some likable or compelling trait
- Shows the world and setting and what life is like for the protagonist
- Shows the protagonist just before the moment where he needs to act. Acting is critical here, as the protagonist needs to drive the plot, not just have things happen to him

## Start With a Problem

The opening scene problem doesn't have to be part of the core conflict. It can be something inherent to the world the protagonist lives in. Maybe he's being chased by monsters, or dodging a nasty boss, or even arguing with his ex-spouse. Whatever a typical issue is for the protagonist can work in an opening scene. Of course, it's also fine if the opening problem is part of the core conflict and gets readers into the main plot right away.

Whatever the problem may be, look for ways to set the protagonist on the plot path, using the opening scene problem as a bridge to get to the rest of the plot.

⚠ **SOMETHING TO THINK ABOUT**: *What problem might your novel open with?*

## Start With Action

The old "start with the action" advice has frustrated many a writer due to its ambiguity. "Action" suggests opening with someone in dire straits or in peril, but those scenes rarely grab readers. A random character in peril doesn't make readers care yet because they don't know anything about this person or why he's in danger.

What "start with action" actually means is to open with something happening, or a question left hanging in the air to entice readers in. The protagonist isn't just sitting around thinking or musing to herself (though that can be part of it), he's doing something important to him that also has a consequence. He has a goal with something at stake, and a conflict to complicate that goal. It doesn't have to be life threatening, it just needs to be interesting.

⚠ **SOMETHING TO THINK ABOUT**: *What might happen as your novel opens?*

## Start With Setting

Providing a sense of place is important to ground readers, but you also want to show how the protagonist fits *into* that setting or world. If nothing is going on but a description of the setting or a history lesson about how the world got this way, there's little to encourage readers to keep reading.

Setting can often be paired with conflict to great effect—something about the setting or world is causing a problem (conflict) with the protagonist's goal. This allows for setting description to occur in ways relevant to the scene, while at the same time creating the conflict necessary to drive that scene.

⚠ **SOMETHING TO THINK ABOUT**: *What setting details best introduce the world to the readers?*

## Don't Forget the Conflict!

If the problem is solved without hassle, it's probably not the right problem to open the novel with, as there won't be enough conflict. Goals, conflicts, and stakes are what drive a plot forward, so look at every scene as a stepping stone to the next part of the plot. Why does this goal and scene matter? And remember, conflict doesn't have to be fighting. It can be quiet if the story calls for it. One person refusing to tell another a secret he's dying to know is a scene with conflict, same as someone trying to fight off a serial killer.

⚠ **SOMETHING TO THINK ABOUT**: *What conflicts might occur in the opening scene?*

## If the Opening Scene Doesn't Include the Protagonist

On a basic level, all opening scenes need to accomplish the same thing—hook readers and make them want to read on. If the opening scene focuses on someone other than the protagonist, there should be a good reason, such as:

▶ It needs to show a moment from the past or something happening outside the protagonist's knowledge

▶ It centers on the antagonist triggering what will be the core conflict of the plot

▶ It's creating a puzzle or mystery

However, be wary of scenes that open to "set the scene" in the bad way. Prologues that explain the world, or a moment from the protagonist's past that explains why he's the way he is, are often just backstory and infodumps readers don't need to know right away—and they rarely care about it at this point. "Start with action" holds true no matter who the focus of the opening scene is.

This also applies to flash forwards, where a scene from later in the novel is shown first as a teaser. Often, this happens because the writer's instincts are saying "the opening is weak," but he's not sure what to do to fix it. A more exciting scene is pulled up front to create "mystery," hoping readers will be hooked and want to know how that scene came to pass. This rarely works, as readers have no context for the scene and haven't connected to the characters yet. Instead of being hooked, they're confused. Trust your instincts if this happens to you, but try strengthening the weak opening you have instead.

Remember, the opening is the first thing readers are going to see. They'll decide if they want to keep reading based on this scene. Give them a reason to turn the page.

**BRAINSTORMING QUESTIONS:**
Find your opening scene.

1. **What is a typical day like for your protagonist?**

   Your protagonist has a life, and that life is going on before the problems of the novel appear. How would you describe a normal day in that life?

2. **What problems might occur in that typical day?**

   These are the possible things that could go wrong and send your protagonist toward the core conflict of the novel. Any problem might work, but try to think of things that could connect in some way to that larger core conflict or the protagonist's character arc. You can also try looking at what a bad day for him is like, as opening-scene problems are often found there.

3. **What is the core conflict of your novel?**

   This may seem like a strange question to ask about a beginning, but the beginning is all about sending your protagonist toward this core conflict. If you don't know where he's going, it's harder to know where he starts that journey. It's good to remind yourself what the end goal of the novel is as you develop your beginning. Look at both the internal and external conflicts as well.

4. **What critical setting or world-building details are needed to understand the world?**

   If you're writing genre or have characters with special powers, it's good to get those details in right away (unless hiding them is part of the plot). While you don't want to bog the story down with explanation, there might be vital details about the setting or world you want readers to know in the opening scene. How might you add those elements? Could they be part of the opening scene problem?

**5.** What is likable or compelling about your protagonist?

What are the vital details readers have to know to connect with this character? What will make them like him? Feel for him? Be intrigued by him if he isn't likable? You don't want to tell the whole history in the opening, but a few things that illustrate who this character is as it relates to the opening scene can help draw readers in. If the character *isn't* likable, then show what makes him compelling enough to read about.

**6.** What is the first image you want readers to see?

An opening scene sets the tone and mood of a novel. How do you want readers to feel as they start your novel? What expectations do you want to set? What event or situation might get those images, emotions, or ideas across?

**7.** Is the opening scene the inciting event or a problem that leads to the inciting event?

This can determine how connected to the core conflict the scene problem is. If the inciting event is still to come, this scene might focus on another aspect of the protagonist's life or the inherent conflict of the world.

**8.** How does the opening scene end?

The scene will end with something that transitions into the next scene or chapter. An "oh no" or "oh cool" moment that will keep the character moving ahead in the plot. When designing an opening scene, think about how it will hand off the plot to the next scene.

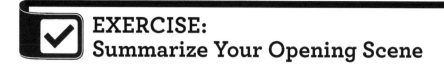

# EXERCISE:
# Summarize Your Opening Scene

## >>Describe how your novel opens.

Be as detailed or as vague as you'd like. Try to end the scene with something happening that will create a goal that leads to the next scene.

It's not uncommon for this scene to change as you learn more about your novel and plot. As ideas hit you, come back and flesh out this summary.

If you're not sure how much to write, aim for one or two paragraphs that describe how the novel opens, what the protagonist is doing, why he's doing it, what goes wrong, what's at stake, and what the protagonist decides to do next. Writing more is also acceptable if you want to continue with how the plot would unfold to the next major turning point.

Feel free to add in any notes about what the scene is trying to do if you know conceptually what you want, but prefer to figure out the details during the writing process.

*For example:*

▶ Bob and Sally are arguing about what they plan to do that day. Sally has the day all scheduled doing things Bob doesn't want to do, and as much as he protests, she won't compromise. He says he has to work today and go into the office and she doesn't buy it. She starts belittling him as always, making him feel worthless. [Show how bad Bob's marriage is and why he wants to divorce his wife and get away.]

Bob heads into the kitchen to wash the breakfast dishes while Sally goes upstairs to get dressed. He's feeling less than manly, still bristling from the fight, thinking of all the things he should have said. One thing stands out above the others—he should have asked her for a divorce. No, he should have *told* her he wanted a divorce. He imagines the scene in his head, using it to build up his courage to actually do it. His fantasy shifts to what he'll do after he's free of Sally. [Show Bob's dreams and goals and what he really wants from his life that he doesn't have now.] He thinks about Jane working at the office on a Saturday, and wishes he'd been able to convince Sally he really did have to work.

## The Inciting Event

As discussed in Workshop Nine, the inciting event is the trigger that sets the rest of the plot in motion. Sometimes the inciting event is in the opening scene or chapter; other times it's farther along in the novel. It traditionally falls somewhere between page one and thirty, or page one and fifty for longer novels.

Wherever it falls, it doesn't have to be a huge action-packed deal if that doesn't fit the novel. It can be subtle, or it can be in-your-face obvious. It just needs to *lead* somewhere and cause something that's much bigger, even it if takes a few chapters to get there.

**Why the inciting event is important:** This is the moment that sets the protagonist on the path to the rest of the plot. It's also a major turning point in the plot, and a vital component of the working synopsis. This scene typically connects the opening scene to the act one problem scene, working as a bridge between the beginning of the novel and the middle of the novel.

## Key Elements of an Inciting Event

- The protagonist is presented with a problem and an opportunity to act.
- The protagonist chooses to act and steps onto the path to the core conflict, or is dragged onto the path by greater forces.
- This action triggers the rest of the novel.

The trigger is an important distinction with an inciting event. The action has consequences that ripple throughout the novel. If this moment did not occur, the novel would have turned out differently, or the plot would not have happened at all.

**BRAINSTORMING QUESTIONS:**
Using what you created in Workshop Nine, further develop your inciting event.

1. Write down the inciting event from Workshop Nine.

2. How does the protagonist get to this moment from the opening scene?

3. What's the protagonist trying to do when this moment occurs? (the scene goal)

4. What is the conflict of the scene?

5. What's at stake in the scene?

6. How is this problem resolved?

7. Does this event also affect the protagonist's character arc? How?

8. How does the resolution trigger the next step of the plot?

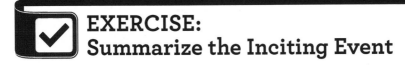

# EXERCISE:
## Summarize the Inciting Event

>>**Describe the moment where the protagonist's life changes and he starts on the path to the novel's core conflict.**

Be as detailed or as vague as you'd like. Consider how this scene builds off your opening scene and how it might lead to the next scene. Include any notes that might help later.

If you're not sure how much to write, aim for one to three paragraphs that describe how the protagonist went from the opening scene to the moment the inciting event happens, what he's trying to do, his reasons why, what goes wrong, what's at stake, and the decision that will transition to the next scene. Writing more is also acceptable if you want to continue with how the plot would unfold to the next major turning point.

*For example:*

▶ Bob has just about gathered enough courage to confront Sally about the divorce when he hears a weird moaning coming from outside. At first he ignores it, thinking it's an animal. But when the noises get louder and it sounds like things are getting knocked over, his built-up righteous anger sends him outside to investigate and give the trespasser a good lecture.

The last thing he expects to find is one of his neighbors, chewing on something. It takes him a minute to realize that "something" is one of the other neighbors. He screams, which alerts the zombie and it charges him. He slams the door shut and backpedals into the house, freaking out and not quite understanding what he saw. He's pretty sure it was a zombie, but knows that's impossible. The door crashes open and the zombie gets inside. Bob grabs something to fight it off, but his choice is poor (a pan? a chair? something that symbolizes his weakness at this point in his life?) and the zombie gets the upper hand. Bob is more upset about not telling Jane how he feels than he is about possibly dying. For just a second, he debates letting the thing get him.

Just as Bob thinks he's breakfast, Sally rushes in with her gun and shoots the zombie. It has little effect, but does distract it long enough for Bob to get a few inches out of biting range. He yells to go for the head and Sally does, killing the zombie. Bob is surprised he's happy to be alive, and then panics that Jane is all alone at the office with these things on the loose. He has to get to her. Sally takes in the scene and starts yelling at Bob for his poor choice in weaponry and what was he thinking? He's just about to lay into her when they hear more moaning from outside. A lot more.

## The Act One Problem

After the novel opens, the protagonist encounters the inciting event, and he steps firmly on the path of the plot and eventually comes to the act one problem. The act one problem is the start of the beginning's end. It's when the protagonist discovers he has a big problem and needs to solve it or else. Typically, this is the result of what happened when he tried to deal with whatever problem he encountered in the inciting event.

**Why the act one problem is important:** It's the transition to the middle of the novel and gives the protagonist something to do (a goal), and a choice to make. It's the first major step once the protagonist is on the path to the core conflict. It's also where the stakes are significantly raised for the first time.

### Key Elements of the Act One Problem

■ The protagonist is presented with a problem that asks him to leave his comfort zone.

■ The stakes are raised and become more personal.

■ The protagonist is presented with a choice.

The act one problem ends with the protagonist facing a decision and having to make a choice on how to proceed. The choice is the key moment here, and the protagonist must *choose* to act. Greater forces might have gotten him here, but he must decide to move forward on his own. Agreeing to act will force him out of his comfort zone and into an unfamiliar (and often emotionally scary) situation. But this step into the unknown is vital for his goals, both the external plot goal and his internal character arc goal. This choice is what officially launches the middle of the novel (more on that in the next section).

⚠ **SOMETHING TO THINK ABOUT**: *What problem or situation might occur to get your protagonist involved with the core conflict of the novel?*

How many scenes fall between the inciting event and the act one problem vary. A very general guide is the opening scene and the act one problem scene are roughly the same size, starting and ending the beginning (or act one). Somewhere between those two points lies the inciting event. The scenes will lead to and ramp up to the act one problem like a wave, raising the stakes and increasing the conflicts at the key points (inciting event and act one problem). Adjust the sizes as needed.

Subplots will play a role and help raise the stakes and deepen the conflicts. They'll also help flesh out the beginning's scenes and will likely be instrumental in causing the internal conflict at the act one problem, as well as trigger additional external conflicts. Aim for a good balance between core plots and subplots, and don't let subplots take over the novel.

---

 **BRAINSTORMING QUESTIONS:**
Further develop your act one problem.

1. What is the protagonist's goal and how does that lead to the core conflict?

2. What is motivating him to act?

3. What's at stake if he fails or refuses to act?

4. Where does this scene take place?

5. Who else is in the scene?

6. Who else might be at risk?

7. How does this scene build off the inciting event?

8. What subplots might lead to this or cause additional trouble at this moment, both internal and external?

9. What choice does this problem present to the protagonist?

10. What conflicts affect this choice, both internally and externally?

11. How does this choice lead to the next goal?

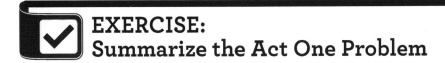

# EXERCISE:
# Summarize the Act One Problem

## >>Describe the problem that ends with a choice, and how the protagonist got to that problem.

Be as detailed or as vague as you'd like. Consider how this scene builds off your beginning and how it might transition to the middle part of the novel. Include any helpful notes that come to you.

If you're not sure how much to write, aim for one to three paragraphs that describe what the problem is, how the protagonist ended up here, what choice he has to make, and how the stakes escalate. He had X problem, but now he has Y problem and has to decide what to do, which leads to the next scene. Writing more is also acceptable if you want to continue with how the plot would unfold to the next major turning point.

*For example:*

▶ Bob and Sally flee upstairs, zombies close behind them. They barricade themselves in the extra room and Sally breaks out the guns and camping gear (she keeps her adventure survival stuff in the spare room), and starts packing. She seems oddly prepared for this, though Bob doesn't really notice [lay groundwork for later reveal about her work at the lab]. He's still having a hard time coming to grips with what just happened, worrying about Jane and having no clue how to get to her. Sally snaps at him to suck it up and be useful, which angers him again. But he does what she orders and they figure out a quick plan to get out of the house and down to the fire station a few blocks away. They think they'll be safe there. It's on the way to the office, so he agrees, hoping the firemen can help with Jane's rescue. A small part of him wishes he could rescue her like Sally did him. Wouldn't he be the hero then?

They climb out the window and onto the roof, using the height to get their bearings. Sally is very competent and Bob feels lost [show how unprepared he is for this type of emergency]. Whatever has happened is clearly citywide, and there is smoke and fire in pockets as far as they can see. People are in chaos and running around. The number of zombies is still small, but growing before their eyes. [Show the world building and how zombification works, how long between someone getting bitten vs. becoming a zombie, etc.] His panic over Jane grows. Sally sees a route to get to the fire station—even though she has little faith they'll be safe there—and starts off. Before they get too far, Bob sees a neighbor in trouble (a child maybe? someone who needs saving and will allow Bob to show his heroic and likable side to make readers care about him). Bob wants to stop and help; Sally doesn't. He stands his ground and they try to help, only to fail. They watch in horror as the person gets eaten.

Sally blames Bob and says now they're in danger because of him, and they have a tough time getting away. Things escalate on all levels as they make their way to the fire station. They get there, only to discover a slew of people who had the same idea, and a lot of zombies taking advantage of frightened, defenseless people. Sally doesn't hesitate, grabs a hose and uses it to blast back some zombies and save some people. They get away as a group and reach a place to catch their breath and regroup. Sally is clearly in charge and blows him off when he tries to help or make suggestions on what to do next. He tries to tell her the office would be safe (need plausible reasons why) but she continues to ignore him. He's really fed up now, and wants to tell her to take a hike, and he'll go for Jane all by himself. Then he notices how calm and dangerous Sally looks, how much everyone else is looking to her for help, and realizes that his only chance at surviving this is staying with her. But does that mean leaving Jane behind?

# The Middle

Just like a good beginning sets up the expectations and a good ending resolves the core conflict, the middle is where it all gets explored. Middles make up roughly 50 percent of a novel, so aim for 50 percent in the working synopsis.

Good middles show the struggle the protagonist goes through to win, and the growth he undergoes while doing that. It braids together the plot and subplots, smacks the conflicts against each other and poses enough questions that readers aren't sure what's going to happen next—which makes them *want* to know what happens next. Without the middle to add depth and show what it all means, the novel can feel like characters acting out plot with little to no tension to keep readers interested. The events in the middle also give the ending meaning.

By the end of the beginning (act one), the protagonist is on the path to the core conflict. He won't immediately know what to do to resolve the problems and bring about the ending, and he'll need to figure things out piece by piece. Each clue, discovery, and action brings him closer to the act two disaster that sends him hurtling toward the climax and resolution of the novel. He'll often start off with some level of confidence and belief in himself, sure of his plans, but as things spiral out of control he'll become more and more uncertain and filled with self-doubt until he's forced to consider giving up entirely.

**A PLOT WARNING:** The middle isn't just a series of problems one right after the other for the sake of creating conflict. This is a common snag for many new writers, because they know they're supposed to have conflict, but don't plot enough turning points to sustain real narrative drive. They fill the middle with "stuff" that doesn't actually advance the story.

When plotting, look for things that will keep the story moving and raise the stakes at the same time. Have the protagonist face choices that matter and make those choices tougher and tougher. Reveal secrets so the puzzles begin to make sense. This is where the subplots and character arcs really kick in and all those connections start to form a bigger picture. Set up a lot of events in the beginning, then let them play out and cause trouble in the middle, forcing your protagonist to make impossible choices.

## The Key to a Good Middle is Escalation

- Escalation of stakes
- Escalation of problems
- Escalation of knowledge

The middle is when things get bigger as more and more of the story is uncovered. It also tends to get more personal, because the protagonist is becoming embroiled in the plot and the problems presented. Things also tend to get out of control, either literally or metaphorically. The protagonist has left his comfort zone and is in new territory he's not sure how to navigate—and nothing is easy.

Since the middle is half the novel, it helps to break it into two sections— the ramp up to the midpoint and the ramp down from the midpoint.

## The First Half of the Middle

The first half of the middle typically unfolds like this:

The protagonist makes a decision about the problem presented at the end of beginning **which leads to ▶** another problem (often subplot related) and forces the protagonist to make another choice **which leads to ▶** the protagonist realizing the problem is bigger and he needs some help (often shows a weakness the protagonist needs to overcome), or help appears in a problematic way to cause even more conflict (possibly another subplot or character arc) **which leads to ▶** the protagonist discovering a secret or gathering information regarding the problem or antagonist and deciding to do something, but there's a risk (raises stakes) **which leads to ▶** the protagonist acting on that information, thinking he's going to be victorious **which leads to ▶** something unexpected happening and the plot goes sideways, leaving the protagonist in serious trouble (either physically or emotionally) or changing his view on everything that's happened so far.

After totally shaking the protagonist's world, it's time to move on to the second half of the middle.

## The Second Half of the Middle

The second half of the middle is different from the first half, because the characters are often feeling pretty dejected or confused. Things have not gone well and they're scrambling to regroup, retreat, and deal with the major curveball that just hit them. Often, there's a ticking clock that's making everything even harder now, requiring them to succeed before something horrible happens. By the end of the middle, the protagonist is positioned so he has to face the antagonist if he wants to win.

The second half of the middle typically unfolds like this:

The protagonist scrambles to deal with the events (or discovery) that just happened at the midpoint reversal (any advantages achieved are gone and the antagonist is on the offensive–friends desert or die, those believed to be trustworthy turn out not to be, betrayals might occur here) **which leads to ▶** the protagonist gets more and more determined to win at any cost, setting up a possible major sacrifice later (a ticking clock is introduced if applicable, raising the stakes again–subplots cause extra trouble and put the protagonist under tremendous emotional pressure) **which leads to ▶** the protagonist feels that all is lost and there's no way he can win which leads to the protagonist goes through some deep soul searching (often accompanied by an event to trigger this) **which leads to ▶** a major step of the protagonist's character arc is achieved **which leads to ▶** the protagonist realizes the only way to succeed is to risk it all **which leads to ▶** the protagonist decides to take the fight to the antagonist in some spectacular way (or go on the offensive if the antagonist has already brought the fight to him).

The middle doesn't end with the climax, but the beginning of what *leads* to the climax. Everything is set up so the protagonist is ready to march toward the ending and that final showdown with the antagonist.

Let's look a little closer at those overviews:

**The protagonist makes a decision about the problem presented at end of beginning:** This will be the choice that launches the middle (act two), and the main focus of the plot until it gets to the midpoint reversal.

**New problem (often subplot related) forces the protagonist to make another choice:** While trying to solve the act two problem, something often occurs to complicate that. This is frequently a subplot, and it could be part of the character arc as well. This problem must be resolved before the original plan can continue.

**The protagonist realizes the problem is bigger and needs some help (often shows a weakness the protagonist needs to overcome), or help appears in a problematic way to cause even more conflict (possibly another subplot or character arc):** Things get complicated and often the protagonist will go to friends for help. More subplots come into play, more impossible choices with no easy answers are faced, and often there are several examples that show the protagonist struggling or failing because he hasn't learned the valuable lesson he needs to learn for his character arc yet. These are the early stages of the protagonist realizing how unprepared he is to live in this new reality.

**The protagonist discovers a secret or gathers information regarding the problem or antagonist and decides to do something, but there's a risk (raises stakes):** Despite the problems and self doubts, the protagonist decides to act. There's a risk involved, often a big one, but the payoff is worth it.

**The protagonist acts on that information, thinking he's going to be victorious:** He thinks he's figured out how to deal with things now, and believes he's going to win (or lose if you prefer).

**Something unexpected happens and the plot goes sideways, leaving the protagonist in serious trouble (either physically or emotionally or both):** The midpoint reversal. The unexpected appears to knock the protagonist for a loop. This is usually something readers never saw coming, but might have been lurking in the background the entire time. Things change for the protagonist, either physically, emotionally, or both here.

**The protagonist scrambles to deal with the events (or discovery) that just happened in the midpoint reversal (any advantages achieved are gone and the antagonist is on the offensive—friends desert or die, those believed to be trustworthy turn out not to be, betrayals might occur here):** The old plan or worldview is useless now, and the protagonist is often in jeopardy—either physically or emotionally, maybe both. Everything has changed and not for the better. The antagonist appears to be winning and causing even more trouble for the protagonist. A new plan must be created based on whatever new information or realization the protagonist has discovered.

**The protagonist gets more and more determined to win at any cost, setting up a possible major sacrifice later (a ticking clock is introduced if applicable, raising the stakes again—subplots cause extra trouble and put the protagonist under tremendous emotional pressure):** The metaphorical noose tightens around the protagonist's neck and he often starts getting a little reckless. The need to win overcomes the need for safety or even decency, and he might be willing to abandon his beliefs if it gets him what he wants. Everything he's learned so far (from a character arc perspective) is put to the test and he often fails. Additional problems will occur that test him and further complicate his plan (and his character growth). He might win or lose externally, but emotionally, it's a loss and a setback to the character arc. Or vice versa.

**The protagonist feels that all is lost and there's no way he can win:** The protagonist hits rock bottom, feeling he will never succeed and that he's lost more than he could ever win. He wants to give up, but someone or something triggers a realization that causes him to do some soul searching.

**The protagonist goes through some deep soul searching (often accompanied by an event to trigger this):** The soul searching leads to the realization that the goal can still be achieved, but the cost is either much higher, or different from what he first thought.

**A major step of the protagonist's character arc is achieved:** The lesson the protagonist needed to learn for his character arc finally sinks in and he starts acting the way he should have been acting all along. He sees the truth now instead of the lie.

**The protagonist realizes that the only way to succeed is to risk it all:** The protagonist has learned the lessons of the character arc, and this enables him to get back up and devise a plan to win. But the plan is risky, the stakes go up yet again, and it's an all or nothing battle.

**The protagonist decides to take the fight to the antagonist in some spectacular way (or go on the offensive if the antagonist has already brought the fight to him):** The first step to the climax of the novel, where the protagonist faces off against the antagonist and resolves the core conflict of the novel (but not the actual climax yet).

These moments are the skeleton of the middle's plot, and mixed throughout them are minor problems that deepen the inner conflicts of the protagonist. They present the protagonist with impossible choices that go against his internal goals or beliefs, so when he does have to solve that core conflict, it means more or costs more and is more satisfying for readers.

## Quick Overview of the Middle

Middles can be plotted in any number of ways, but here is a basic guideline that works well in developing a working synopsis:

**Act two choice:** This leads to the problem or goal that drives the plot into the middle (act two).

**Minor problem one:** The plan to solve the act two problem has run into a snag, and obstacles must be overcome before the plan can get back on track. This often creates a subplot.

**Midpoint problem:** A major problem is discovered, possibly sending the plot in a new direction or really shaking things up. Stakes increase.

**Minor problem two:** A snag occurs in the plan to fix whatever problem occurred at the midpoint, and more obstacles must be overcome before the plan can get back on track. This either continues the subplot or creates a new one.

**End of act two disaster:** The discovery of a major problem will shatter the protagonist and be the focus of the ending (act three). It will lead the protagonist directly to the climax of the novel.

The number of subplots and character arcs will be determined by how large the novel is. Having the subplots conflict with the core conflict and main goal works very well to keep a tight plot and the story moving. A subplot might get the protagonist what he needs (internal goal), but not what he wants (external goal) and vice versa. All the various story arcs (plot, character, theme, etc.) will unfold further in the middle as well, setting up both victories and failures for the protagonist to experience in the end (act three).

This also allows areas to deepen the characters and make readers care more about what the protagonist is going thorough, and it provides places for the theme to shine through. These moments can be woven throughout the main plot to add additional layers to the novel.

Which basically is what the middle is all about. Deepening the story. It's not about adding more, it's about fleshing out what's there so the beginning and the ending come together in a way that satisfies the reader.

The middle is the real heart of the story.

Let's look at the three major turning points in even greater detail.

## The Act Two Choice

The act two choice is a transitional moment, linking the beginning of the novel and the middle of the novel. The protagonist embraces whatever problem he's confronted with, and accepts the opportunity it offers to resolve that problem. How he decides to deal with that problem establishes how the plot is going to unfold until the next step on the plot path. The act two choice launches the goal for the middle of the novel and drives the plot forward.

**Why the act two choice is important:** This shows the protagonist isn't just reacting to what's happening, but being a proactive character and making the novel happen. It's his *choice* to move forward. And that choice creates the goal for the book's middle.

## Key Elements of the Act Two Choice

- Shows the protagonist choosing to embrace the problem of the novel
- Creates a goal and direction for the plot to follow
- Has consequences for the choice not taken, or the choice made (or both)
- Leads to the midpoint reversal

The act two choice frequently launches the protagonist's character arc as well, because his flaw will be his weakness during the middle of the novel. He'll struggle and fail, not seeing what he needs to do to become the person he wants to be.

 **BRAINSTORMING QUESTIONS:**
Further develop your act two choice.

1. What opportunity is offered at the end of act one?

2. Who is involved in this opportunity?

3. What are the choices offered?

4. How do these choices lead to the core conflict?

5. What consequences are there for making a choice?

6. How will this lead to the midpoint reversal?

7. What possible subplots might result from these choices?

8. What about the protagonist's old world is he leaving behind?

9. What new opportunities or discoveries will the protagonist make going forward?

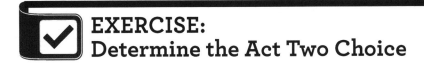

# EXERCISE:
# Determine the Act Two Choice

>>**Describe what your protagonist decides to do and how this set him on the plot path to the midpoint.**

Be as detailed or as vague as you'd like. Consider how this scene might lead to the next turning point of the novel. Add notes as you see fit.

If you're not sure how much to write, aim for one to two paragraphs that describe what the choice is, why it's important, how it changes things for the protagonist, how the stakes escalate, and where the protagonist will go from here. Writing more is also acceptable if you want to continue with how the plot would unfold to the next major turning point.

*For example:*

▶ Bob decides to stay with Sally and figure out a way to convince her the office is the safest place and they need to go there (and save Jane in the process). He actually manages to get her to listen [find a clever way to show Bob does indeed have some skills] and they head off with several of the other survivors. (Is there a possible subplot to be had from one of the survivors? Maybe connected to Sally and the lab?) Bob is surprised Sally isn't leaving them behind, and wonders if she thinks they'll work as human shields. He feels guilty for thinking it since she did save most of them when she didn't have to. They make their way to the office building where Jane is. [Show various obstacles that illustrate Bob's weakness, him trying to step up and failing, Sally's disapproval, hints at her ulterior motive for agreeing to his plan—involves her job at the lab, maybe there's something in the same building she's after. Medical related?] Several close calls and a few deaths to show the stakes.

Eventually they get to the office building and it looks bad. There's no easy way inside, and Sally wants to abandon the idea. But Bob sees movement in the upper floors, signs for help stuck to the windows. He knows Jane is alive up there and that proves it's at least defensible against the zombies. Sally is only half convinced, not seeing any clear way to get inside without losing more people. Bob spots a way, but it's risky (a construction crane? something that requires climbing?). Sally hesitates, not wanting to leave the group defenseless to get inside. Bob volunteers to go, and has a strange determination about him. Sally finds this odd, but likes the glimpse of the old him and finally relents. She has no idea it's another woman suddenly making him brave [play with subtext].

Bob has a few mishaps, but manages to do what he needs to do and gets everyone access to the building without danger from the zombies. The survivors enter the building several floors up. Sally is impressed by Bob and actually says something nice to him. [Show him starting to find his inner strength.] Sally lingers at the floor directory and seems overly interested. When Bob asks her why, she says she thought there was a medical supply company in the building, and it would be a good idea to get some supplies. Bob agrees, not wanting to delay getting to Jane, but knowing Sally is right. He knows the floor and takes them there.

They break into the office and Sally starts looking around. It becomes clear pretty fast that she's there for more than just first aid kits. Bob wants to know what she's doing, and she gives him a half answer. He's feeling good after his heroics, and pushes her for a real answer. Sally starts to swat him down, but she likes how he's behaving and decides to answer him as a reward [show in subtext]. She says she's looking for something that might deter the zombies from biting them. Bob doesn't find this likely, but Sally is the biologist, so he doesn't argue. They gather supplies and head upstairs.

## The Midpoint Reversal

The midpoint reversal occurs in the middle of the novel. Something unexpected happens and changes how the protagonist (and the reader) sees the story. The plan or worldview the protagonist had all along no longer works or is no longer viable, and things have to change. This choice and new plan is what sends the plot into the second half of the middle.

**Why the midpoint reversal is important:** It shakes up the plot and causes the protagonist's world to be turned upside down—things he thought he knew won't be true. He'll start looking for help as this problem gets bigger and bigger, and the stakes get higher and higher. Dealing with this problem creates the goal for the second half of the middle and eventually transitions to the ending (act three).

### Key Elements of the Midpoint Reversal

- Shows the protagonist didn't have it all figured out
- Reveals new information that changes how the protagonist views his world and problem
- Surprises with something unexpected
- Makes the ending less predictable
- Raises the stakes

A good midpoint reversal is something that throws the entire plot sideways and leaves readers open-mouthed in shock, because they never saw this coming (or they worried it might happen and were desperate to find out if they were right). It changes the plot and suddenly the ending is unpredictable. Readers are flipping pages fast, amazed by the unexpected turn of events, and dying to see where this new predicament goes.

A good midpoint reversal will also raise the stakes, even if they were high to begin with. It often adds a level of personal consequence that wasn't there before, or reveals a secret (or problem) that was hidden. Sometimes it requires a sacrifice, be it a personal belief or an ally. Sometimes it's all of these things at the same time.

Once readers are shocked, there's new momentum driving the plot toward the ending. The midpoint reversal makes the protagonist's goal harder to accomplish, costs him more to win, and has serious consequences if he fails (sometimes even if he wins).

**BRAINSTORMING QUESTIONS:**
Discover your midpoint reversal.

1. What is the absolute worst thing that can happen to your protagonist at that moment?

2. How can you make that happen and force him to work overtime to get out of it?

3. Is there a way to make your protagonist's inner goal clash with his outer goal in a disastrous way?

4. What's the one thing that could happen that would make your protagonist give up?

5. If this happens, what would keep him trying anyway?

6. Are there any deep dark secrets that could be revealed and ruin everything?

7. How might the result *not* be the one the protagonist was worried about—it's *worse*?

8. Can you mirror the climax in any way or foreshadow the ending or choice that is to be made later?

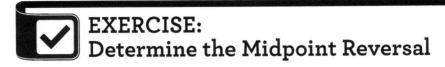

# EXERCISE:
## Determine the Midpoint Reversal

>>**Describe the midpoint reversal of your novel, and how it changes the life, goal, expectations, and/or beliefs of the protagonist.**

Be as detailed or as vague as you'd like. Consider how this scene might lead to the next turning point of the novel.

If you're not sure how much to write, aim for one to three paragraphs that describe how the protagonist reaches this moment, what happens, how it affects him, and where he has to go from here. Writing more is also acceptable if you want to continue with how the plot would unfold to the next major turning point.

*For example:*

▶ The gang makes their way to Jane's office and Bob is relieved to see her alive and well. She's also thrilled to see him, but not for the reason he'd have hoped. She's just glad to find someone else alive. Sally wants to know if she's heard any information about what's happening, and Jane updates them. She also shows them a radio/CB she stole from another office (who might have one of these? PI with a police scanner?) and says she's heard people calling for help and offering it, but those have been getting fewer and fewer. Bob is impressed with her resourcefulness and says so. Jane is pleased by the flattery. Sally is too distracted to notice. She pulls binoculars out of her survival bag and stares off into the distance toward her office building. She tries the radio and says some odd things, almost like a code. Bob has no clue what she's doing but figures it's something she learned from all her work retreats [set up that her office did survival retreats as team-building exercises]. When done, she pulls Bob aside and says they need to get to her building, but they can't bring the rest of these people.

Bob wants to know why, only half shocked that she'd leave them behind. She dodges the question, but he won't let it go this time. She says that her office is the safest place for them, but there's not room for the whole crew. Bob glances at Jane, and says he won't leave her. Sally wants to know why not, then gets suspicious the more Bob tries to gloss over the reasons. She asks if he's having an affair. He blurts no, a true answer, terrified she might realize that he wishes he could. His shock makes her think he's telling the truth, but she still wants a reason to keep Jane along. Bob realizes that he has to stay in Sally's good graces to save him and Jane, and makes up a plausible excuse (perhaps Jane has some skill Sally might find valuable). Sally eventually agrees. She says they need to convince everyone to stay here. She comes up with a story about checking out the roof and setting up a sign for anyone flying overhead to alert the authorities they're there. She orders Bob and Jane to go with her, since it's Jane's building and she knows the way. They don't tell Jane they're really leaving everyone behind.

They reach the roof and Sally acts like she's expecting someone. Jane asks about the sign, and gets more and more agitated when no one will tell her what's going on. Bob tries to explain, but Sally cuts him off and says someone is coming for them. Jane is confused, asks about the others, and no one answers her. She gets it, is horrified, backs away and asks how can they be so cruel. A helicopter appears, clearly headed for them. It's not very large. Sally points to it and says, "That's why. How many do you think that thing holds?" Jane struggles, but accepts it. Bob consoles her by saying she survived okay in her office, so the others will be fine. They'll send back help. Sally doesn't say anything and he hopes that's true.

The helicopter lands and Sally knows the pilot. But something is off, both in the landing and him as he leaves the copter. He seems injured and Sally goes over to help. The pilot shrieks just as Bob notices the blood and bite marks on him. He turns into a zombie and lunges at Sally, digging his teeth into her shoulder.

It's chaos. Bob wavers between terror and the sick hope that she dies, feeling bad for even thinking it, but unable not to. He dives in and kills the zombie, and then expects the worst. They have a general idea of how fast people change and they know Sally doesn't have much time. (He tries to be heroic for Jane, though he does feel bad about Sally after their years together. He's very conflicted.)

Oddly, Sally is more pissed than upset. She digs into her bag for the first aid kit, has trouble and starts ordering Bob around. He doesn't get it, tries to tell her there's no hope and little time. Thinks about the things he always should have said, but they quickly turn into angry things and he shoves them aside. Sally gets more and more frustrated and eventually blurts out that she's not going to change, she's been vaccinated for this.

# The Act Two Disaster

This act two disaster is the moment when it all goes wrong for the protagonist. The big plan to save the day fails miserably and he's worse off now than he's been the entire novel. The stakes are raised yet again, and it all becomes too much to handle.

Often, whatever lie the protagonist has been telling himself (or what he believed was true) is stripped away, forcing him to see the truth, however harsh. If the antagonist has been a secret or a mystery, this is often where her identity is discovered (often with devastating effects). Even if the antagonist has been known all along, new information is revealed about her to make solving the problem seem insurmountable now.

In cliché speak, it's the darkness before the dawn.

**Why the act two disaster is important:** This is where the character arc kicks in. The fatal flaw of the protagonist causes things to turn out worse than expected, and now he has to overcome that flaw to succeed. It's where characters frequently face their inner demons and emerge victorious, the moment when all is lost and they must dig deep down and examine who they really are.

## Key Elements of the Act Two Disaster

- Is often created by the protagonist not learning the lessons he needed to for his character arc
- Drops the protagonist into the all-is-lost moment where he abandons all hope
- Forces him to dig down and examine who he is and what he wants

All through the middle, the protagonist has been trying and failing, feeling the pressure, ignoring his flaw and the lessons the plot is trying to teach him. Just when things are the most dire, he acts in a way that causes catastrophic failure. (Adjust this to fit the scale or scope of your story. What's catastrophic in a science fiction epic is usually different from catastrophic in a romance.)

This disaster triggers two classic storytelling moments—the all is lost moment and the dark night of the soul. These are critical turning points for both the protagonist's character arc and the external plot, and it's frequently where the two arcs merge into one.

## The All-is-Lost Moment

Everything the protagonist has tried so far has failed. He fully believes the worst things about himself and sees no way to win or get out of his problem. He's lost all hope and wants to abandon everything and slink away in failure and despair.

## The Dark-Night-of-the-Soul Moment

This moment occurs at the very bottom of the protagonist's despair. It doesn't have to be an actual night, just a moment (whatever length you choose) where the protagonist is forced to examine his life and his choices and accept how he got to this point. He then manages to dig deep down, gather himself up, and realize what he has to do after all. It isn't truly hopeless, but he'll have to sacrifice something. (This can be any number of things, from a literal sacrifice to abandoning a belief or self doubt.) He's learned his lesson and he now knows what to do.

 **BRAINSTORMING QUESTIONS:**
Discover your act two disaster.

1. What is the thing that would make the protagonist want to give up?

2. How might that happen in the story?

3. How might the protagonist get to this point? What events need to happen before this occurs?

4. What is the protagonist's flaw?

5. How might this flaw cause the protagonist to fail, or lead the protagonist toward failure?

6. What realization might the protagonist have that pulls him out of the dark night of the soul?

7. How might the protagonist put this realization into practice? How might it change him?

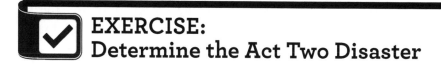

# EXERCISE:
# Determine the Act Two Disaster

## >>Describe what goes wrong or how the protagonist fails, and how this sets him up for the march to the novel's climax.

Be as detailed or as vague as you'd like. Consider how this scene might lead to the climax of the novel.

If you're not sure how much to write, aim for one to three paragraphs that describe how the protagonist's flaw led him to this moment and what goes wrong, how this sends him to the all-is-lost moment—what he feels and how he reacts, what depths he sinks to during the dark night of the soul, and what realization comes to him that makes him pull himself up and devise a new plan. Writing more is also acceptable if you want to continue with how the plot would unfold to the next major turning point.

*For example:*

▶ Bob and Jane are both floored. How did she get vaccinated? Sally confesses that her lab has been working on a bio-weapon for years, and everyone on the project was vaccinated as a precaution. (Issues over her lying to him all these years about what she did.) Bob asks if she created the zombification virus. She says no, it was supposed to be something else, but it obviously had unforeseen side effects. There was a test on it a few days ago, and clearly something went very wrong. Jane wants to know if the vaccine will work for the survivors, and Sally says yes, as long as they haven't been exposed yet. After that, they'd need the cure, and there are only a few vials of that deep in the lab's vault.

Bob wants to go get as much of the vaccine as possible and help the survivors. Jane agrees. Sally isn't so sure, saying it only works for bites, not if you get torn apart, and most of those people downstairs wouldn't survive long enough for the vaccine to help. Bob asks if she can make more of the cure. She says no, that wasn't her department. Even though things are clearly not right at the lab, they decide to head there anyway to get the vaccine for Bob and Jane. Bob suggests they use the radio first to call in help for the survivors and Sally relents and does it.

Getting across town isn't easy. The first challenge is getting off and out of the building, and they barely squeak by. Sally's blood is drawing the zombies, and her injury slows her down. Bob keeps having thoughts about "accidentally" letting the zombies get her, but talks himself out of it every time. Jane seems to be more impressed with him than ever before, clinging to him as they make their way through the streets. Sally notices and isn't happy about it.

After close calls and difficult challenges [use to show Bob taking charge now that Sally is injured and how he's stepping up], they reach the lab. It's a zombie madhouse, with zombies and bodies everywhere. A lot of them have lab coats or identification from the lab and building Sally works in. This is where it all started.

Sally outlines a plan and they make their way inside. They half sneak, half fight to the right floor and lab. It's crawling with zombies. Bob has an idea to lure some away so Sally can get to the vaccine. She has the least risk from being bitten (but not eaten). Jane is to stay put in what they think is a safe place. Bob sets off, drawing the zombies' attention. It works and Sally darts for the lab. Bob continues to race around, following the pre-ordained path that will lead him somewhere that he can lose the zombies and make his way back without them. As he gets there, Sally is coming out of the lab with the vaccine. They hear a scream. It's Jane.

They run over and she's fighting off a zombie. Bob goes crazy and kills it, but not before it bites Jane. He gives her the vaccine anyway, and it does nothing. She's going to turn. Bob demands to know where the cure is. Sally says there's no way they'll get it, she's sorry, but there's nothing they can do to help Jane.

Bob is inconsolable. Jane is trying to deal with it, but not very well. Sally just wants them all to get away before more zombies come. (Does Sally have an ulterior motive for coming here as well? Feels like she'd not do it just to save Bob) Bob sees a way to get rid of Sally for a little while so he can at least tell Jane how he feels. He says he'll leave with Sally and she should scout ahead and find the best way out. He'll tell Jane they're going to go for help and get her somewhere where she can die in peace. Sally doesn't like it but agrees, and sets off. Bob goes into a small office with Jane and struggles over his feelings. He blames himself for what happened, wishing he'd gotten back sooner, or found a safer place for her to wait. She says it's not his fault, that she probably lasted longer than most. He blurts out that he loves her, how he wishes he'd have found the courage to tell her sooner. She smiles, says me too, then the change hits her.

She almost bites him, but he gets away before she can. He manages to get her locked in the closet. His mind is whirling, trying to figure out if she meant she wishes he'd said something or that she loved him too. It's too much for him, and the grief and stress is taking its toll. He has to know, has to cure her no matter what he has to do. He got this far, he can do it.

When Sally returns, Jane is locked up and clearly a zombie. Sally says sorry, but her heart isn't in it. She tells Bob she found a way out. He says he's not going, he's going after the cure for Jane. Sally wants to know what it is with this woman. Why is he so determined to protect her? What's the deal between them? He says he loves her and can't let her die.

Sally is less than thrilled to hear this. She starts yelling. They get into a fight, and draw more zombies. They call a truce to escape, but don't get very far. They take shelter and continue the fight, trying to be as quiet as possible. Bob lets loose on her, saying all the things he never could before. It feels great, cathartic, even though he knows he's hurting Sally. He feels bad about that, which surprises him. Eventually Sally gets quiet. Bob thinks she's about to really explode, when she says she never knew he felt this way. She wished he'd told her sooner, before they spent so many years making each other miserable. It's awkward, but also good to talk this way. Bob begs for her help, even though he knows she has every reason to say no. Shockingly, she agrees.

# The Ending

Getting to "The End" is pretty satisfying, but there's also a lot of pressure. There are many things that need to happen by that point—plots and subplots to wrap up, pesky character arcs to fulfill, loose ends to tie—and then there's the whole "satisfying resolution" to worry about.

The ending is the last 25 percent of the novel and the working synopsis. There's a good chance you won't know all the specifics about the ending in the planning stage, so don't worry if it's still vague. Ideas and situations will develop over the course of writing the novel that will help you flesh out the ending. Even if you *do* know exactly how the ending will unfold, you might find deeper meanings or ways to make it resonate more once the first draft is written.

Structurally, the protagonist has just gone through a deep, dark moment and has made the choice to stand and fight. He's taking the problem to the antagonist. He'll use all the things he's learned over the course of the novel to outwit and defeat that antagonist. They battle it out, and he'll win (usually), then the plot wraps up and readers see the new world the protagonist lives in, and the new person he's become.

This pretty much sums up the ending. The final march by the protagonist to get to the final battle with the antagonist. It doesn't have to be an *actual* battle, just two conflicted sides trying to win.

## Common Elements of the Ending

- The journey to face the antagonist, either a literal trek or metaphorical
- A twist or surprise that changes the outcome
- A gathering of allies to aid in the battle (however that conflict unfolds)
- A realization of the final piece of the character arc

## What Makes a Good Ending

Endings start long before the actual climax, because that's when we start laying the groundwork for them. Everything in the novel has been building to this moment.

Pacing is also critical, because speeding things up helps build that breathless on-the-edge-of-your-seat feeling. Let the characters worry a bit more, think a bit less, allowing things to go wrong and cascade into more and more trouble—perhaps everything they try fails or makes things worse. Put the protagonist on that slippery slope, and don't give him a lot of time to catch his breath. Make him struggle, make things get worse and worse but let him still manage to squeak by. Then hit him with the climax.

And make him lose.

Okay, not "lose" lose, but force him into a position where he really has to think outside the box, find something unexpected and crazy that no one will see coming. For this to work, he has to be pushed beyond anything you've done to him so far. He needs to feel like it's all or nothing, do or die, and that puts him right where he needs to be—thinking up an over-the-top, last-ditch effort to succeed.

Whatever the ending, remember that it's only as good as what's come before it. The entire novel builds to this moment, and everything the protagonist has done will be put to the test in some way to resolve this final problem. Look back in the early sections of the novel and find things to pull forward: stakes to raise again, failures to revisit, problems to exacerbate. The climax is the resolution of the whole novel, so it makes sense that everything that came before can provide the fodder for the protagonist to save the day. Or not, if that's the kind of ending you want.

The ending breaks down roughly like this:

The protagonist starts the journey toward the antagonist **which leads to ▶** obstacles are thrown in the protagonist's way that will have to be overcome (results or conclusions of subplots often come into play here) **which leads to ▶** examples of how the protagonist has changed, showing what he's learned and how he's grown through his experiences in the novel (the character arc) and is now able to handle the issues he failed at before **which leads to ▶** the resolution of minor subplots and secondary character arcs **which leads to ▶** one last surprising twist that raises the stakes and/or pulls together a variety of clues (this can be helpful or detrimental to the protagonist, though it's usually bad) **which leads to ▶** the protagonist reaching the antagonist, facing a do or die moment **which leads to ▶** the protagonist doing or dying **which leads to ▶** the protagonist wins (or loses) **which leads to ▶** the core conflict is resolved **which leads to ▶** the novel wraps up.

Let's look a little closer at those overviews:

**The protagonist starts the journey toward the antagonist:** This is the goal created at the end of the dark night of the soul. The new plan to solve the problem or win the day.

**Obstacles are thrown in the protagonist's way by the antagonist that will have to be overcome (results or conclusions of subplots often come into play here):** Getting to the antagonist won't be easy, and challenges will have to be overcome. It's not uncommon to see a setting or location change at this point. The protagonist literally has to go to the antagonist.

**Examples of how the protagonist has changed, showing what he's learned and how he's grown through his experiences in the novel (the character arc) and is now able to handle these issues he failed at before:** Many of these challenges are likely things the protagonist would have failed at had he faced them earlier in the novel. They show how he's grown and what he's learned.

**Resolution of minor subplots and secondary character arcs:** Many (if not all) of the smaller conflicts and arcs of the novel are resolved, and doing so might even be steps to the final battle.

**One last surprising twist that raises the stakes and/or pulls together a variety of clues (this can be helpful or detrimental to the protagonist, though it's usually bad):** Typically, there's a surprise twist to add unpredictability at the climax—a secret revealed, a betrayal, a revelation, an unexpected attack, etc. It's usually bad for the protagonist, but it can also be a surprise by the protagonist to defeat the antagonist right at the moment where the antagonist thinks she's won.

**The protagonist reaches the antagonist, faces a do-or-die moment:** The showdown between protagonist and antagonist. This is the official climax of the novel.

**The protagonist does or dies:** How the climax unfolds.

**The protagonist wins (or loses) and the core conflict is resolved:** No matter what form it takes, the core conflict of the novel is resolved, and the protagonist needs to resolve it on his own. A little help from friends is fine, but he needs to do all the real work, because it's his problem, he's the hero, and readers want to see *him* win. Convenient or contrived actions here will kill the ending and leave readers unsatisfied. They want to feel that the protagonist *earned* this victory.

**Novel wraps up:** After the final battle is the wrap up. This is usually a chapter, maybe two if there's a lot to resolve (say with a series). Loose ends are tied up (though sometimes not all or it can feel too pat), readers get to see the fates of the various characters they've come to love (or hate), and the new life of the protagonist is revealed. We see the change this experience has brought him, good and bad.

## Some Things to Consider When Planning Your Ending

**Pacing:** The pace will pick up as the plot closes in on the ending, keeping readers hooked and pages turning. Tensions are raised, emotions are tweaked, and readers are fully invested in what happens to these characters. They're desperate to know how this all turns out.

**Call Backs:** At some point, there's a good chance the protagonist will face something he failed against before. His biggest flaw or greatest weakness comes back to haunt him. It might be in the actual battle with the antagonist, or be part of the final piece of the plot to get there. It's the moment when readers get to see, yes, the protagonist *has* learned from his mistakes and will prevail.

**Subplots and Character Arcs:** The ending is also where many of the subplots and secondary characters arcs are resolved. This is important, because if too many threads are left hanging, it might muck up the climax, or make the wrap up feel long and anticlimactic because the plot keeps going long after the story is technically over.

**Stakes:** One common pitfall with endings is that the stakes don't get any higher after the act two disaster. Body counts might go up, but thousands dying vs. the main characters dying isn't actually an increase in stakes, even though it feels like it should be. Stakes go up when the consequence requires a more personal cost and will force the protagonist to make a huge sacrifice. When planning the ending, make sure the personal stakes of the protagonist are raised.

Endings need to be satisfying, though they don't need to be happy, as long as whatever story problem posed at the start of the novel has been resolved. It can be a bittersweet ending if the goal was to teach the protagonist something and not so much about the event itself. He can "lose" and still win if that loss gets him what he really needed deep down. However the resolution is set up, fulfill that promise to readers. Give them the ending they want to see.

Let's look at the three major turning points in even greater detail.

## The Act Three Plan

After digging deep down and finding the emotional strength to continue, the protagonist puts a new plan into action, using everything he's learned over the course of the novel. Like the act two choice, this is a conscious decision by the protagonist that will pit him against the antagonist in the climax.

**Why the act three plan is important:** This sets the protagonist on the path to face the antagonist and resolve the core conflict of the novel. It's when he uses his experiences in the book to achieve his goal.

### Key Elements of the Act Three Plan

- Merging old ideas and beliefs with new ideas and beliefs learned in the novel
- Gathering allies to help defeat the antagonist
- Overcoming past fears and embracing the protagonist's new self
- A "do-or-die" mentality

The act three plan is the moment when everything falls into place for the protagonist. He finally knows who he is and what he's supposed to do, and he sets off to accomplish that. There can still be plenty of uncertainty and even fear on the protagonist's part, but most of that personal self doubt is typically gone by now. The remaining fear is for the antagonist and the ability to win, not the fear of not being good enough to even try.

The plan is usually ambitious, clever, and unexpected, even though it also feels inevitable. This is what the protagonist and the supporting characters were meant to do all along. The plan may or may not be revealed to readers at this point, and often the actual details are kept secret, even though the general idea is mentioned to help drive the plot forward. It's up to you how much to reveal.

One thing to remember is that the plan doesn't have to be something that will actually work if you want to surprise the protagonist in the climax and force him to think on the run. What's important is that the protagonist thinks it will work. Once the climax starts, plans can fail and the protagonist must revise in a hurry to win.

 **BRAINSTORMING QUESTIONS:**
Discover your act three plan.

1. What weaknesses might the protagonist have discovered about the antagonist that could be exploited?

2. What was the protagonist afraid to do before, but now has the courage to try?

3. How have the protagonist's old and new beliefs merged?

4. What insight has this new outlook given the protagonist?

5. What has to be done to reach the antagonist?

6. What skills might the protagonist use to defeat the antagonist?

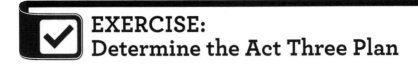

# EXERCISE:
# Determine the Act Three Plan

## >>Describe what your protagonist plans to do to reach and defeat the antagonist.

Be as detailed or as vague as you'd like. Consider how this plan will lead to the climax of the novel.

If you're not sure how much to write, aim for one to two paragraphs that describe how the protagonist's dark night has given him new insights into what has to be done to win, how to go about reaching the antagonist, and what might be required to defeat her. Writing more is also acceptable if you want to continue with how the plot would unfold to the next major turning point.

*For example:*

> ▶ Sally finds a floor plan of the lab (fire escape route?) and sketches out a plan. She has no idea if the vault can even be opened, if there's any power to it, etc. (research vaults and security measures). The more she talks the weaker she gets, and Bob realizes she was hurt a lot worse than he thought. He even hopes she's going to be okay. [Show how maybe they'll be okay after all and part as friends, maybe even work it out if they can't save Jane.] She gives him some of the gear (ammo, guns, etc) and wishes him luck.
>
> Bob sets off for the vault, encountering zombies and other obstacles along the way [These will all be similar tests to what he failed in the first half of the book. Succeeding here shows how he's grown.] He gets to the vault, manages to bypass the security, and gets inside. He finds the cure, a single vial inside a case. He grabs it and heads back to Sally and Jane.

## The Climax

The climax is the final showdown with the antagonist. The protagonist faces whomever or whatever has been making his life miserable for four hundred or so pages, and because he's learned XYZ over the course of the novel, he wins (or loses spectacularly if that's the type of book you're writing). Whatever happens, the core conflict problem is resolved.

**Why the climax is important:** This is how the novel ends and how the story questions are answered. This often determines how much readers like the book. Everything in the novel has been building toward this moment.

## Some Things to Consider About the Climax

**What constitutes a win for the protagonist?** If you're not sure, look at your beginning. What major thing happened that set your protagonist on his journey? What has he been trying to accomplish all along?

**What constitutes a win for the reader?** Expectations will be setup throughout the novel and readers are going to want to see those expectations satisfied. What promises did the story make? What problems were dangled? What risks were taken that hinted at greater consequences?

**Does it resolve the core conflict of the novel?** This is the big question that the protagonist has spent the entire novel trying to answer, so make sure that the climax resolves the core conflict.

**Does it satisfy the major questions posed in the novel?** Not all the loose ends have to be tied up, but there are probably a few major things in the novel readers will want to know the answers to. Too many left answered can leave readers feeling unsatisfied.

**Is this the ending most readers are hoping for?** Readers are going to root for X to happen, because you've likely written the novel for just that event and have led them to expect a certain outcome. Part of a satisfying ending is getting the ending you hoped for all along, even though we've all read books where we wanted one ending, but the book ended another way.

## Key Elements of the Climax

- The protagonist faces the antagonist directly
- The protagonist proves he's changed and fully embraces who he is now
- A surprise twist
- A final increase in stakes
- A sacrifice

The climax often has one last increase in stakes, making this final battle matter on a bigger scale. Look at what the protagonist has at stake on a personal level and how that ties into the story from a thematic aspect, so the ending has more poignancy. It's not uncommon for this rise in stakes to happen after a twist or surprise.

A surprise at the end isn't mandatory, but endings we can see coming a mile away usually bore us. However, readers expect the protagonist to win in any book they pick up. There is only so much mystery we can squeeze out of "will he win or not?" The tension and wonder comes from *how* the protagonist wins and what it costs him. This is why personal stakes are so critical. But we also want the protagonist to act in a way that is unexpected, so the way he resolves his problem is a surprise.

Try looking at the moral beliefs of the protagonist and having him do something he'd never consider doing otherwise. But the trick is, he still has to be true to himself. He can't just throw out all he believes in. He has to make that *choice*, hard as it is, for reasons that fit who he is *now* (the final piece of the character arc). Maybe it was a line he refused to cross before, or a risk he was never willing to take, or something that might even have been suggested earlier in the novel and rejected. But the stakes are higher now, and not doing it will result in something far worse than doing it. It's a sacrifice he's willing to make, even though it's going to cost him a lot.

**BRAINSTORMING QUESTIONS:**
Discover your novel's climax.

1. What inner conflict has the protagonist been struggling with all along?

2. How can the inner conflict butt heads with the outer problem in the climax?

3. How might the inner conflict influence what the protagonist needs to do to solve the final problem?

4. How might the theme be used to make the ending more powerful, and thus raise the stakes?

5. How might the risk be more personal for the protagonist?

6. What surprise might happen to throw either the protagonist or the antagonist off?

7. How does the act three plan compare to the climax? Does it work? Where does it fail?

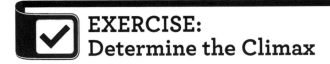

# EXERCISE:
# Determine the Climax

## >>Describe how the climax unfolds.

Be as detailed or as vague as you'd like. Consider how the climax resolves the core conflict of the novel.

If you're not sure how much to write, aim for one to three paragraphs that describe how the climax unfolds, where it takes place, what (if any) surprise occurs, and how the protagonist deals with that surprise to resolve the core conflict. Writing more is also acceptable if you want to continue with how the plot would unfold.

*For example:*

► When Bob returns to Sally, she's pale and in bad shape. He's concerned, but as he gets closer he notices something's not right. Sally asks if he got it. He doesn't want to tell her. She comes closer, aggressive though trying not to be. She demands he give it to her. She'll inject Jane with it. He says no. She says she's better suited to it, give her the vial. Bob is freaking out. Sally is changing, even though she was vaccinated. He says as much and she laughs. Says she guesses it wasn't as useful as they all hoped it would be, and no wonder the whole lab changed into zombies. She lunges for him and he barely avoids it. She's right on the verge of becoming a zombie, fast, strong, dangerous, and he doesn't know if he'll be able to beat her. He's not sure if he even should. Does she deserve the cure? Does he owe it to her? But he also thinks about how she was part of those responsible for this whole mess. He's still trying to decide when she goes full zombie. [Show how Sally has always been the antagonist, but here she becomes the symbol of everything bad that has happened.]

Bob's in a lot of trouble, barely staying ahead of Sally, fighting her off and unsure what to do. The fight takes him close to the closet Jane is locked in, and he hears moaning and crying, even speaking, with a weird mix of not-quite-zombie. His heart leaps and he thinks maybe the vaccine helped enough to keep her from totally turning. If the vaccine only half worked, then the odds of the cure curing Sally now that's she fully turned are slim. Jane stands a much better chance of surviving.

It's not much comfort, but it's enough to help him separate Sally from the thing she's now become. He digs into the fight with renewed courage, and manages to kill her. He feels really bad, but it had to be done. He rushes to Jane's closet, wary and ready to defend himself. Jane is struggling to stay Jane, but she's not going to win. He gives her the cure. It doesn't seem like it's working at first, but then Jane's color starts returning and her eyes clear up some. She's still in trouble, but better than she was.

He can hear more zombies coming, so he doesn't wait around for her to fully cure. He grabs her hand and they head out using Sally's plan. The whole time he's worried it's a trap, that she set it up so they'd never get out as revenge. He sees a way out that isn't on Sally's plan, and decides to trust himself, not her.

## The Wrap-Up

The wrap-up is the happily ever after, or the burning apocalypse—what the protagonist is going to do now that he's resolved his problem. If there's a moral or lesson the protagonist was supposed to learn in the story, this is a good spot to sum it up.

**Why the wrap-up is important:** It allows a sense of closure for characters and readers, and allows the resolution of any important details or subplots that weren't critical in the climax.

### Key Elements of the Wrap-Up

▶ The protagonist is happy or satisfied in his new life

▶ A sense of things resolved

▶ A hint at where the characters will go from here

It's not uncommon for the closing scene to mirror the opening scene as a way to show how the character has changed. If the protagonist was a selfish person, the final scene shows him being generous. If the opening shows him being scared of commitment, the wrap-up might have him getting married or making a commitment. It might even be a darker, more disturbing scene if the novel was about a fall from grace or the descent into darkness.

**For series writers:** If you're writing a series, there might be plot elements or questions left hanging, and things might *not* wrap up quite so neatly. This type of wrap-up is often tricky, as you want to leave readers with a satisfying ending, yet still entice them to pick up the next book.

It might sound like a good idea to craft a cliffhanger ending with the protagonist in dire straits, but if the book just stops, you risk annoying readers. They spent an entire book waiting to see how a problem you posed to them is going to turn out, then you cheat by having the book end before that happens. That's like turning off a movie fifteen minutes before it's over.

There's nothing wrong with a series ending that has loose ends, but try to resolve whatever promises you made to readers.

In essence, the final scene says, "Yes, there was a point to this novel and here it is." It gives readers a sense of closure and reassurance that the novel was worth their time.

**BRAINSTORMING QUESTIONS:**
Discover your novel's wrap-up.

1. What events might come after the climax?

2. What final image might mirror the opening image?

3. Where do you want your protagonist to be at the end of the novel?

4. What mood or emotion do you want to leave readers with?

5. What do you want readers thinking about after they've finished the book?

6. If it's a series, what hints or questions do you want to dangle for the next book?

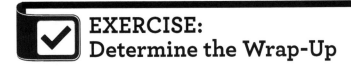

# EXERCISE:
# Determine the Wrap-Up

## >>Describe how and where the protagonist ends the novel.

Be as detailed or as vague as you'd like. Consider what image you want to leave readers with at the end of your novel.

If you're not sure how much to write, aim for one to two paragraphs that show the change and where the protagonist is (physically and emotionally) at the end of the novel. Think about where he started out and how this final image works with that opening image.

*For example:*

▶ They make it out (at some point finding themselves in a kitchen so Bob can redeem himself where he failed in the opening scene) and manage to grab a truck. As they drive away, Jane is looking much better. They crash through obstacles and zombies and get to the open road. They're not sure where they're going, but at least they're together.

Jane refocuses and is more like herself. She thanks Bob for saving her. He says he loves her again, and she says she loves him too. Bob grabs the radio and starts calling for other survivors. He wonders if one of them can create a cure from Jane's blood. Despite the world in shambles around him, for the first time in a long time, Bob's happy and thinks there's hope for the future.

# ASSIGNMENT TEN: Write Your Working Synopsis

>>**Put it all together and write your working synopsis.**

If you need a little guidance, try using these reminder questions to guide you through:

- How does the novel open?

- What is the first problem the protagonist faces?

- How does this problem lead to the inciting event?

- How does this lead to the core conflict and the larger act one problem?

- How does this result in the protagonist facing a major choice?

- How does this choice lead to a series of struggles and tests in the middle of the book?

- What is the midpoint reversal?

- How does this lead to an increase of problems and attacks by the antagonist?

- What is the act two disaster?

- How does this disaster lead to the all is lost moment and the dark night of the soul?

- What results from that soul searching?

- How does this create the new plan to act?

- How does this plan lead to the final showdown with the antagonist?

- How does that showdown unfold?

- What happens afterward?

# Time to Write!

Congratulations! You made it.

You've done a lot of work in this book, and now you should have a solid plan to write your novel. Since developing a novel is a complicated process, it's not uncommon to discover you still have a few holes to fill in. If so, return to the exercises you need to and strengthen the weak spots in your plan.

Another option is to go through the exercises one more time and see what's changed since your first pass. Odds are you came up with some great ideas while writing your summary blurb or working synopsis that can help you deepen the novel as a whole. Elements that were vague when you first brainstormed them have direction now, and you'll find layers and connections you originally didn't see.

If your goal is to dive in and start writing, then consider coming back after your first draft is done and doing some of the exercises again. They're excellent guides during the revision process as well.

I hope you've enjoyed the workshops and feel confident about writing (or revising) your novel. If you've found this book helpful, please share with friends or leave reviews on your favorite sites.

Most of all, best of luck and good writing!

Janice Hardy
January 2014

# Glossary

**Antagonist:** The person or thing in the protagonist's path of success.

**Backstory:** The history and past of a character that affects his or her actions in a novel.

**Conflict:** Two sides in opposition, either externally or internally.

**Core Conflict:** The major problem or issue at the center of a novel.

**Exposition:** Narrative intended solely to convey information to the reader.

**Filter Words:** The specific words used to create narrative distance in the point-of-view character.

**Freestylers:** Writers who write out of chronological order and arrange the book afterward.

**Genre:** A category or novel type, such as mystery, fantasy, or romance.

**Goal:** What a character wants.

**Hook:** An element that grabs readers and makes them want to read on.

**Inciting Event:** The moment that triggers the core conflict of the novel and draws the protagonist into the plot.

**Logline:** A one-sentence description of the novel.

**Market:** The demographic traits of the target audience for the novel, such as adult or young adult.

**Narrative Distance:** The distance between the reader and the point-of-view character.

**Narrative Drive:** The sense that the plot is moving forward.

**Outline:** The structured overview of how a novel will unfold, typically written as a guide before the novel is written.

**Outliners:** Writers who write with a predetermined outline or guide. They know how the book will end and how the plot will unfold before they start writing it.

**Pacing:** The speed of the novel, or how quickly the story moves.

**Pantsers:** Writers who write "by the seat of their pants," without outlines. They often don't know how the book will end or what will happen before they start writing it.

**Plot:** The series of scenes that illustrate a novel. What happens in the novel.

**Point of View:** The perspective used to tell the story.

**Premise:** The general description of the story.

**Protagonist:** The character driving the novel.

**Query Letter:** A one-page letter used to describe a novel when submitting a manuscript to an agent or editor.

**Scene:** An individual moment in a novel that dramatizes a goal or situation.

**Series:** Multiple books using the same characters and/or world.

**Set** Pieces: The key moments or events in a novel.

**Setting:** Where the novel takes place.

**Sequel (1):** A second book that continues where the first book leaves off.

**Sequel (2):** The period after a scene goal is resolved where the character reflects on events and makes a decision to act.

**Single-Title Novel:** A romance novel that isn't part of a publisher's category.

**Stakes:** What consequence will befall the protagonist if she fails to get her goal.

**Stand-Alone Novel:** A novel that contains one complete story in one book.

**Structure:** The framework a novel is written in, typically based on established turning points at specific moments in the novel.